WHAT'S AWAKENING REALLY LIKE?

Marianne Broug

What's Awakening Really Like?
Twenty ordinary people talk about life beyond the spiritual search

First published in Australia by Marianne Broug 2021

Copyright © Marianne Broug 2021
All Rights Reserved

 A catalogue record for this book is available from the National Library of Australia

ISBN: 978-0-6480787-2-2 (pbk)
ISBN: 978-0-6480787-3-9 (ebk)

Cover image by Michaela Marie: A dead flower in the light of the always-present Sun

Typesetting and design by Publicious Book Publishing
Published in collaboration with Publicious Book Publishing
www.publicious.com.au

No part of this book may be reproduced in any form, by photocopying or by any electronic or mechanical means, including information storage or retrieval systems, without permission in writing from both the copyright owner and the publisher of this book.

Dedication

To Life.
To our original nature.
To that which we all are.

***

This book is also dedicated to those who
are new to the terrain of post-awakening life,
and find the world as they know it, to be upended.
Awakening, in one sense, is the end of the journey,
but in another it is just the beginning.
Additionally it is terrain that is rarely discussed or understood.
We hope our words meet you,
and provide support, understanding,
insight, reassurance and inspiration.

***

Contents

Gratitude .... *i*
Preface .... *iii*
Disclaimer .... *xii*
Chapter 1 – What is 'awakening'? 1
Chapter 2 – Stories of awakening 9
Chapter 3 – What advice would you give your newly
    awakened self? 35
Chapter 4 – Identity 43
Chapter 5 – Myths and misconceptions about awakening
    and enlightenment 52
Chapter 6 – What has been awakening's greatest gift or surprise? 61
Chapter 7 – What has been awakening's greatest challenge? 69
Chapter 8 – Languaging, communication and words 78
Chapter 9 – An ordinary day. An ordinary life 88
Chapter 10 – The stabilization of awakening 100
Chapter 11 – Teachers 112
Chapter 12 – Meditation 130
Chapter 13 – Religion, spirituality and God 141
Chapter 14 – Relationships 150
Chapter 15 – Mind, cognition and memory 167
Chapter 16 – Emotions 180

Chapter 17 – Motivation 191
Chapter 18 – Body and health 197
Chapter 19 – Sleep 206
Chapter 20 – Humor 213
Chapter 21 - Creativity 221
Chapter 22 – Work and money 232
Chapter 23 – Global challenges 240
Chapter 24 – Death 254
Chapter 25 – Ego and suffering 266
Chapter 26 – How to awaken 278
Chapter 27 – Recommended reading 292
Glossary *301*
Biographies *304*

Gratitude

Gratitude always to the magnificent thrust of Life.

Gratitude to the nineteen people who joined me in putting together this book. Thank you for hearing its call to be written and understanding its power and its necessity. Thank you for giving of your time and sharing your lives and your wisdom. Thank you for your openness, sincerity, vulnerability and courage. Thank you for your support and encouragement. Particular thanks to Maureen Bush whose advice and suggestions on editing matters and also general support was invaluable and very much appreciated.

Gratitude to the other 40 people of our wonderful group who chose not to take part in the book. Thank you for putting up with us this last year. Thank you for your suggestions, moral support, discussion and all-round good humor. Thank you for suggesting such titles as *The real sh*t-storm they don't tell you about awakening* and *If you are on this path it's too late to turn back: a survival guide*. We'll consider those options next time.

Gratitude to my beautiful partner, Sharon. Thank you for believing steadfastly in another one of my projects. Thank you for standing by me through so many years. Thank you for your love.

Many thanks to both Sharon and to Mark Harding for reading through our tome and giving it the thumbs up.

Thanks to Michaela Marie for the use of her photo on the cover of the book.

Marianne Broug

***

Preface

It was early 2008.

I was lying in a hot bath, my head resting back on the rim and looking up at the stark white of the ceiling. There was an ache of queasiness in my stomach, in my bones.

Countless times in my life I had come to a point of desperation, when my only thought was of suicide. But now, this was different.

I was thoroughly sick and tired of myself.

I had tried so valiantly to live a good and meaningful life, I had sought tirelessly for the Truth from the time I was very young, I had undergone two lengthy therapies to release the legacies of the past, I had gained so much insight and understanding, and yet it seemed that on a very basic level nothing had ever changed.

The same words, the same stories, the same problems, the same search, the same suffering. There may have been different contexts over the years, but in their essence they were same. Always the same. I was living an endless loop. And I was fed up. It was boring, mind-numbing, tedious repetition. I didn't want to rehash the same issues over and over and over for another 40 years. I wanted it all to stop. I'd had enough. Completely and utterly enough. Enough of myself.

But where could I go? What could I do that I hadn't already done? It seemed there was no solution. No way out. Was I doomed to spend my life like this? I felt utter exasperation. Even a hot bath was no longer soothing.

Then, without any warning, from the depths of my defeat, words gushed out. I was pleading to a God I did not believe in: "How do I stop this? Please God, how do I stop this? Please God, tell me! I am so tired of it! Please God, give me a break! Give me a break!"

All of a sudden, it was as though God really did give me a break. God broke me open.

Parading in a line in front of me, I saw all the identities I had ever been: the fearful child, the seeker, the nature lover, the musician, the young woman in desperate pain, the woman who wanted to kill herself.

Preface

I saw all my patterns of behavior through the years: the words, the tears, the defences, the dissociations, the contractions, even the most subtle hand or eye movements were included. And I felt how each of them was held in my body with its own particular bearing and its own unique awareness. And in that instant I knew without a doubt that I was none of them and never had been.

It was a profound experience and its resonances were deep, but I didn't yet fully grasp its significance; I didn't understand what it was showing me.

Then, one morning a few days later, I spontaneously 'awoke'. One moment I was sitting at the computer checking my emails and then the next moment it was as though the tightly held contraction of thoughts, feelings, beliefs, identity and history that I had always assumed was 'me', somehow let go and I awoke into the vastness of the reality that I am: my true nature. My first word was "sh*t"! Then there was laughter. *I* was what I had been seeking and it was closer than close, more obvious than obvious.

The sense was one of relief, surprise and of coming Home. All the teachings I had ever heard or read about spirituality now made sense. This was where they had all been pointing.

For a time I lived from a vast peace, presence and stillness that seemed perfect and unshakable. Later I would come to know this time as the 'honeymoon period'.

***

Although I had come across the words 'awakening' and 'enlightenment' many times before, I had assumed they were solely the preserve of sages and mystics or Western spiritual big-noters with large followings. I had never considered that awakening might be a possibility for a very ordinary woman living a very ordinary life in suburbia. Nor did I ever consider that my lifelong spiritual quest to know what was true, was synonymous with the pursuit of 'enlightenment'. Awakening. Enlightenment. A fairy story. Nothing to do with me.

Now that had all changed.

Awakening was my reality.

I had also assumed that intrinsic to awakening or enlightenment was an all-knowing, all-seeing omniscience and a life of endless bliss, ease and beatific joy. I imagined perfect human beings walking lightly upon the earth, unencumbered by the everyday problems that occupied the rest of us mere mortals. During the 'honeymoon' period this did indeed seem not so far from the truth.

But as the newness waned and the awakened perspective became my norm, the blinkers of bliss came off and I realized that what had actually happened was destruction: everything I had thought or believed about the world and existence had essentially collapsed. I was in uncharted and unfamiliar territory. In addition, it was becoming increasingly clear that the old lenses and layers of egoic conditioning hadn't magically burnt up in the fires of realization; crisis or difficulty brought them quickly to the surface.

The metaphor of a 'baby Buddha' is a good one; I knew my true nature, but I had to start all over again, learning how to function from a completely new perspective.

Questions pressed in: How do I live in a world in which duality and separation are the norm? How do I embody the enormity of this? How do I have relationships when I only see One? Is it unusual for conditioning to arise? Why do I feel such a lack of motivation? How do I talk to people? Why is it so hard to find words to describe this shift? What happens now?

And underneath all those questions was a persistent and needling belief that I shouldn't actually have any questions. I assumed that because I had awoken I should automatically know everything. And I didn't. I had no clue about anything.

I longed to meet others who had experienced awakening.

***

My first thought was of a woman I had known for many years. She worked as a therapist and spiritual counsellor, and carried a wise depth I had always admired; I was sure she must be awakened. I contacted her. We sat in a coffee shop and after exchanging small talk, I told her what had happened. Her words to me were short and cutting: "Well that's quite a claim to make, isn't it!" I may have mumbled something in response, but I can't remember what it was. I was dumbfounded; I had no words to bridge the gap. In actuality I had never felt more ordinary.

Next I contacted an assistant to a well-known non-dual teacher. I described the awakening to him and was heartened that his response was of immediate recognition. He knew what I was describing; he had experienced it himself. We had a lively conversation. I asked him, "But what do I do now?" He said, "Put up a website and become a spiritual teacher." Once again, I was dumbfounded. I had nothing to teach. Awakening hadn't brought me to a state of specialness or guruhood; rather I was a rank beginner who had not yet learnt to walk or talk.

I then found an enlightened teacher who also confirmed the awakening. He taught meditation and suggested I meditate. There were times I asked him why I was meditating when I was already awake and his response was always, "Just meditate". Any talk other than inquiry was frowned on as 'of the ego' so I kept silent. In any case, amidst everyone else's inquiry into ultimate reality, my questions about how to live awakening seemed misplaced. I hoped that by simple observation of my teacher I would eventually find the answers I was looking for, but after two years I was no clearer. Additionally I found his embodiment of 'enlightenment' to be stark and unappealing. Was that how I would end up living my life? I hoped not.

My longing to find others intensified. I wanted to speak about awakening in a simple and open way.

***

Eventually I moved onto the Internet and its online non-dual communities.

Many teachers and groups pointed only to the portals of awakening and not beyond. Others pointed only to the rarified, transcendent perspective without ever mentioning a life lived in supermarkets and messy families. The only spiritual teacher I found at that time who addressed the post-awakening terrain in a balanced way was Adyashanti. His books and the clarity of his teaching were a godsend. He described the profound implications and deepening process, but also the disorientation, pitfalls, lack of sleep, lack of motivation, energetic movements, difficulties of relationship … and so I chose to start my online journey in a group that focused on his work (although it was not affiliated with him personally). I thought it would be a good place to make mistakes and find my feet.

… and in some respects it was. I met people there I now regard as friends. But in many ways, although the subject matter was spirituality, the interactions were no different to any other online group. At times it was a minefield. And it deeply distressed me.

Previously I had experienced no issues with putting myself in the public arena. With the publication of books and also articles it had been a profound stance of solidity in my life to be openly vulnerable. But in the online community it seemed that whichever way I moved, there was someone there to take issue. Simply by using the word 'awakening' the explosions of derision and vitriol took my breath away. I tried to tread more carefully, choosing my language slowly and deliberately, solely communicating from my own perspective and never laying claim to anything, including 'how awake' I was, but it made no difference.

Over time I was harangued mercilessly by a number of people: my language it seemed betrayed my unawake-ness; my inability to cite ancient texts to substantiate my point of view was seen as laughable; if I referred to 'myself' or 'I', I was relentlessly pointed to the Absolute; if I dared to claim awakening to those who weren't awake I was seen as arrogant and posturing.

I started to search for a place where people who had awakened could find their feet. Where they could be vulnerable, learn how to language this terrain, allow doubt to arise, make mistakes, speak of residual conditioning, express themselves freely, ask any questions whatsoever, request guidance or discussion if it was needed, share the movements of deepening and insight and life, find companionship, sit in silence, dance … a place with no hierarchy, no presumption of teaching, no proselytizing, no pretensions of attainment or perfection, no intellectual meandering. A place of authenticity, respect, intimacy, maturity, gentleness … A place where all perspectives and all depths of this terrain were welcome …

***

Then one day it came to me that I would start exactly that group. It was an unshakeable knowing; it was quite simply what I was going to do. Or more correctly, quite simply what would be done through me.

When I looked a little closer at the logistics of such an undertaking – the time involved, my lack of experience, the responsibility, the fact that I'd never been a 'group' person – I tried to back out, but it felt so unequivocally wrong to do so, that I knew I had to proceed.

And so in November 2017 a Facebook group called *A group of 'baby Buddhas'* was born.

***

The first few weeks of the group were difficult and I slept little. There was a core of members who understood exactly why I was starting the group but there were also others who joined who did not fit and were removed. A couple were troublemakers. One was clearly not awake and was offended by our claim that we were.

However, in those first days and weeks (and also occasionally through the years) it was those who wished to 'teach' or could not tolerate others' perspectives, that were most problematic and also the most determined, self-righteous and lacking in the requisite emotional maturity. The identity of a spiritual teacher and the assumption that others need to be 'taught' or told that they are 'wrong' is very compelling to some. My injunction that it was not a 'teaching group', that it was non-hierarchical, and that there was in fact tremendous potency and invitation in always speaking from one's own experience, rarely made any difference. In any case, I learnt how to be more assertive, and we framed more detailed membership questions and group norms. At all times I was aware that one of the foundational aims of the group was that those who were recently awakened would find a safe space in which their newfound perspective and depth could truly land … and so we made our way.

What was immediately and palpably obvious (and also surprising considering the online setting) was the group's deep and all-encompassing Presence and Silence. This was felt by all. It was described by one of the members as being "deeper than depth". Participating in the group and opening oneself to that Presence is extraordinarily powerful. It cuts through lenses and identifications without the need of scissors or knives, and always allows expansion evermore into the infinite Mystery that we are.

The words of members echo my own reflections of the group:

> Awakening can be like stepping into another world and there is benefit from mirroring, sharing and guidance. This group has been especially valuable to me because it is a group of equal peers without a teacher or a guru.

> We are walking each other home.

> A collective co-created field of unconditional love can help stabilize and integrate Awakening. This group is the only place I can go that isn't on some level about fixing, healing or attainment.

> It's a community of other humans dropping layers of conditioning and other influences, who see through phenomena to the silence. It is SO refreshing.

Not many teachings point to what life is like post-awakening. I was looking for others with whom to deepen this understanding. While no validation is needed there is power in walking together on uncharted territory.

Our seeing doesn't usually come all at once. Most of us have some big chunks of awakening followed by the clean-up of places we haven't yet questioned … intimate relationships, work, money, health …

It is precious to have others to 'connect' with in this visceral felt sense of One.

Awakening can result in a gravitation towards isolation. Sitting alone in a cave staring into the Infinite is only one option among limitless options.

I've found, that like tuning forks, realization stabilizes and deepens when in the company of other awake folks! It is a delight!

It's a tremendous help to connect with others who are called to live their lives referenced in a very different way to 99.9% of humanity. It's one thing to know yourself as That Absolute Reality. It's another thing entirely to learn to live that Truth in Relative experience. It can mean major life changes and questioning all you've taken for granted your entire life. This shift can also bring release of conditioning, beliefs and trauma. Why would anyone go through this adjustment period alone?

There is more here in this group than I have ever seen elsewhere. There is no confusion, no ego porn and no gibberish of the mind used to conceal a lack of depth.

It's a bit like a recursive mirror … Love recognizing Love recognizing Love, on and on … what joy!

***

Preface

Approximately two years after starting the group there again came an unshakeable knowing. This time, rather than starting a group, it was that the group would now put together a book. In my sensing, it was as though the book in its entirety already existed in the 'ether' and my task (and that of the group) was to take the necessary steps to bring it into form.

There had been extraordinary discussions and interactions in the group over the years and my sense was that the book was a natural outcome. It was a movement of responsibility, necessity and Love that the wealth which we had been gifted was now also shared.

I put the idea of the book to the group and it was embraced unreservedly. Group member Stacy wrote, "Whether or not this book is 'needed' is not up to any of us to say. Not to diminish the work that has gone into it, but this book just happened. It wanted to be born and Marianne both birthed and midwifed it into existence."

I was clear from the outset that there was no obligation to take part and that the normal group interactions would continue alongside the book writing. Approximately one third of the group chose to write. I was pleased that contributors came from a wide age range (30s to 60s), wide range of backgrounds and also from around the globe. Five men contributed and 15 women. Some wrote for each chapter, some for fewer. There was no requirement whatsoever as to what to write, when to write or how much to write.

I made it clear that I would edit all contributions. This was of major concern for me. Reworking or even 'improving' members' offerings was a very different role to that which I normally have in the group. Although I didn't want in any way to alter the flavor, meaning or message of the material, its readability was a priority. I encouraged communication and discussion on this at all times. Additionally for five contributors, English is a second or third language, and so some editing was necessary.

Another concern for me was that contributors remain aware at all times that they were writing for a public audience and not for a closed group. Over the years a deep level of trust, friendship and love had developed between members; many intimate details of life and its living had been shared that would have been inappropriate for broader consumption.

I also made clear, that if so desired, the contributors could remain completely or partially anonymous.

I then set about organizing the writing of a book within the Facebook medium (although some correspondence was done through messaging and email). I added various book-related headings to the "Topics for Posts" section (Book Info, Book Chapters Questions, Book Chapters Complete) so that all material could be easily accessed. I kept the group informed at all times of my next step.

As with the book as a whole, I could 'feel' each chapter topic in the 'ether' prior to putting it up. I then posted the chapter heading on the group to which participating members were free to respond. Once posted, a response was open for discussion to all group members and much further discussion took place over time. Only the specific initial response was included in the book. The subject matter of the chapters was very much in line with the subjects of group discussions over the years. The chapters were not written in the order in which they appear in the book.

Once all material for a specific chapter was written, I copied the material from Facebook, pasted it into a Word file, organized and edited it, and then posted the file on the group for further addition, modification or comment. The file was then revised and uploaded again for any further comment.

In my initial 'sensing' of the book as a whole, I had 'seen' the various chapters interspersed with creative material. For some of us, poetry and photography had arisen as a dynamic part of the new terrain and as such were often shared in the group. It was therefore more than fitting that they also be included in the book.

Over time we formed a glossary, wrote biographies, debated a title, re-ordered the chapters, carried out some final editing … and so we put together a book.

Over and over, of greatest surprise and also greatest power when reading through our material, is the vast diversity in how we got here and the similarity of what we found.

Erick's words and sentiments to those reading this book sum up my own:

> My words in the chapters of this book are simply descriptions, cross sections of my perspective when they were written. They are not prescriptions and they are not the only way to describe awakening. Awakening is indescribable, unquantifiable and ever an enigma, yet it is more real than anything in this world, even more real than my own self.

Preface

> I hope that these words can resonate with the awakening that is within everyone, that it might add a little more power to the glow within you until, like a star being born from a ball of cosmic dust, you burst into self-radiant effulgence. May you ever radiate Love, Light and Truth, and, above all, be your own natural Self.

... above all, be your own natural Self.

Marianne Broug

***

Disclaimer

Each contribution contained in this book is solely the perspective of its contributor, and does not reflect the opinions or perspectives of any other contributor.

Paying heed to the fact that life and its circumstances can change quite dramatically, each contribution represents the contributor's perspective at only one particular point in time.

This book is not a prescription of any kind, nor is it intended as spiritual teaching, professional advice, treatment, therapeutic guidance or service. No liability will be accepted if it is taken as such.

***

Chapter 1

What is 'awakening'?

Stacy

'Awake' means we have seen through the illusion of a separate self. Ideally, this also leads to seeing through other illusions, such as body, time, memory, free will, control and other concepts.

***

Marieke

For me awakening is the unshakeable knowing of Being prior to experience.

***

Erick

Grace upon grace, light upon light, love upon love. There is nothing else, and this too is Nothing.
   Big question, best approached from several angles.
   It comes in stages. I experienced two distinct 'forms'. First was recognition of the Absolute, the non-expressed Existence at the heart of all experience. This was experienced as a Nothing that accompanied all activities. It was recognized as pure existence, the precursor even to consciousness. Its dwelling was in the eternal moment. The world concept of a time-space continuum was replaced with a direct cognition of the only thing there is – this eternal moment. All events in all time and everywhere take place in this vessel. All the past and future are coiled

Chapter 1 – What is 'awakening'?

up inside it and are only expressed as experiences in this moment. Now is all there is.

There is another phase where the absolute existence falls upon the changing world and the two become one indescribable wholeness. This is absolutely natural yet exquisitely sublime. Joy is ever accessible, though the waves of all emotions continue to wash across the awareness in daily life. Nothing is separate yet we are all our natural, individual selves. The sense of silence versus activity is fully resolved; they are fully integrated and at home with each other. Amazingly, each has given up its identity to create this greater whole. There is no silence and all is silence. There is dynamic action yet nothing ever happens. I sensed that I had returned to where I started … a simple, innocent child gazing upon the wonder of creation.

***

Marianne

Awakening is a profound and undeniable shift in one's identity or sense of self, from the egoic, mind-made, separate 'person' to the vastness of our true nature as Life. As This. As Now-ness. It is awakening to our natural state.

For me, the actual awakening was an expansion into an infinite spaciousness, stillness and freedom, which all at once was both the background and the substance of all. Once that was seen, it could not be unseen.

However, after the initial awakening there was a continued shedding of the conditioning that habitually tries to recreate a separate self, as well as a continued deepening into the Mystery of what we are.

Awakening is not a mental conceptualization or understanding (however profound), nor is it an altered state of consciousness, spiritual high or mystical experience. It is also not an experience of *samadhi* or Kundalini.

***

Kiran

My husband asked me, "So what did Awakening really do to you?"

I remember not being able to answer his question immediately, but after a while I said that it had changed my inner address and that this perspective was becoming increasingly clear within me.

The profound announcement of awakening is that the whole of existence is without any separation. It's all just ONE, the same at every level and in every speck.

Along with that realization, a massive formless door opened through which all that carries any structure and form continues to drop and drop into oblivion, into that which seems unknown but is so deeply known as I am and we all are. Awakening brings a shift in our world view and becomes a ground of allowing the flowering of true loving, kind and compassionate humanity.

Awakening is the experiential knowledge of Oneness settling into beingness as the fundamental rule of functionality (world of form and duality). Through that fundamental rule, every form slowly shifts into Oneness; consciousness keeps awakening to itself, increasing the spacious capacity of awareness.

This evolution doesn't happen without facing difficulties. For me, these stretches of pain and suffering seem like blessings as they keep opening me in a larger and deeper way.

The awakened one is a living groundless ground of being, within whom all experiences and forms sooner or later diminish as they are slowly disidentified with.

Life starts living itself with ultra-fineness. Such supreme management could be perceived as chaotic or hazardous, but it is so deeply entrenched, organized, and effective that I call it Higher Management.

***

Michaela

The word 'awakening' could be used for every step that brings an understanding on a deeper level and strips away some of our false beliefs.

The 'awakening' we refer to in this book, is a final realization that strips away *all* beliefs, so that there is literally nothing left. It is a simple yet profound shift. It also removes the core belief of a separate identity, so that reality reveals itself as one life, one source, one 'I' in endless forms. Time as we know it collapses and we realize that past or future are non-existing and merely projections of our minds. All we are left with is pure presence, where reality is seen without any labelling – as it is.

Pure, miraculous, wondrous happening.

Chapter 1 – What is 'awakening'?

***

Maureen

I've been struggling with language, worn out by words. My goal for this chapter was to come up with something simple, brief, and experiential. Not about words or definitions, but about being, and falling into language.

What is it to awaken?

I awoke to the reality that I was consciousness itself, dancing in human form.

***

Richard

My initial experience of awakening came prior to any knowledge on the subject. I had no language for it and could only have described it by saying something like, "I know Heaven exists." For that reason, I'm very open to people languaging the experience in many different ways. Although now I could give a far more detailed description, when it comes to conveying the essence of it, I'm not sure I could improve on that initial effort.

One area where I may differ from others, is that I don't experience awakening like a light switch; either on or off. Nor do I see it as a permanent state; once touched always present. I can't separate such ideas from psychological projection and perceive they have overwhelmingly negative consequences. I'm referring to people frustrating themselves by trying to reach a state of perfection that doesn't exist, and in doing so, missing out on what does.

***

Timothy

Awakening, as a noun, I define as an experience or meditative event that is beyond what is considered a normal (average) conscious experience, which may, or may not, be permanent. It doesn't have a common reference nor can it be explained in common language.

I originally called it 'the light', and referenced it by saying, "When the light came everything changed."

***

Amy

When I discuss being 'awake' I can best describe it as being Inwardly Rearranged. The person that I had been and the way I perceived everything (All of Life) was turned upside down and inside out. Within this experience exist multiple layers of accountability, ethical responsibility and openness. It includes not having an agenda.

It is not an elite, knowing-more, or better-than-others experience. It is a recognition of sameness with the world and everything that is.

***

Sarah

Spiritual awakening, is when we realize through direct experience what we are/we are not. It's primarily about one's existence and identity.

This can happen in stages. First we might realize we are not what we thought we were, and directly experience ourselves as something deeper, vaster and eternal. Later we might realize through direct experience that we are everyone and everything, and that there is no separation and never was. An even later realization may be that we never existed to begin with. And even further, that all of it is happening simultaneously: existing and not existing, being a someone while being nothing.

Spiritual awakening seems to be on a spectrum that isn't necessarily consecutive. A person might jump to a 'later' realization while skipping 'earlier' stages.

***

Lisa

My definition of awakening is the disappearance of the entity we call 'ego' or what we usually perceive as 'me'. It includes the realization that there was never such an entity in the first place. The 'me' is seen as a tangle of memories, concepts, thoughts, ideas, experiences, and trauma, which upon awakening, is untangled and released. The dissolution of the illusion of 'me' also dissolves the illusion of separateness; hence the word 'non-duality' is used.

Instead of a 'me' there is now a beingness without a center or a core;

Chapter 1 – What is 'awakening'?

there is no one 'in' the body anymore. However, there still *is* a body, a mind, feelings, thoughts and a personality with its previous traits and preferences.

For me, awakening also includes the realization that ultimately, all that is not love, is an illusion and that love is everything, eternal and indestructible. So for me awakening is also the absence of fear and a profound experience of peace; like the stillness at the bottom of the ocean even if storms ravage the surface.

Awakening is not an attainment or an experience of the 'me'.

***

Ben

I see awakening as gaining an objective understanding of reality on top of the subjective experience of it we already have.

***

Andrew

Awakening is like an optical illusion. It is simply a different way of seeing what is already there. If you can't see it then I can't make you see it. All I can do is tell you what I see. You may think I am nuts (and you might be right), but if a lot of people say similar things you might take another look. Nothing changes with the image on the page; it is what it always has been, but your way of perceiving it is different. Everything changes and everything stays the same. But once you see it you cannot un-see it.

An interesting thing is that before you see it, anybody that mentions it seems to be more knowledgeable than you because they say they see something you don't; you want to see it because you might be missing out on something.

Once you've seen it for yourself you know what it looks like and you can recognize people who have seen glimpses but not the entire image. People who have seen the full image may describe it in totally different ways to yourself, but you still know they've seen it.

Using another analogy, I can't describe to you the taste of strawberries and ice cream so that you can taste what I tasted. There is no language for it. If you've never tasted it you will have no idea what I'm talking about if I only use words to describe the taste alone. If you've never had anything cold and sweet you would probably think I'm nuts. If you have tasted it, then there is a chance you will recognize it from my description no matter what words I use. There is no language for taste and no language for awakening.

Aside from that broad justification for why I can't tell you what it is, I'll now tell you what it is! Awakening is simply being able to see what is, as what is. There are no filters overlaid of what it should be like or what is right or wrong about it. It is what it is, and I am what I am.

***

Georgette

While 'awakening' has a variety of common meanings, such as "arousing from sleep", "opening to new ideas", "a revival of religion", it is a term that also refers to the possibility of Awakening to our True Identity as Consciousness Itself.

Awakening is a verb, a process. We awaken layer-by-layer from a separate-self-sense into individuated unique expressions of the One Light through infinite waves of expansion and contraction, birthing Light into human form. Simultaneously, our human skills and capacities continue to evolve and express as naturally as breathing.

Life's evolutionary impulse carries us to actualize our human potential on pathways of development as Leaders, Peace Makers, Artists, Builders, Change Makers, Care Providers, Scientists, Mystics and Healers. Even though we know conditional reality is a dream, we become Lucid Dreamers playing our encoded parts.

As the Great Light illuminates the human being along each of these developmental pathways, a myriad of fundamental misunderstandings, conditioned limitations, unprocessed karmic patterns come to the surface of awareness for healing. Energetic contractions unfurl and expand back into free unbound creative life energy, clearing and strengthening the human instrument for the next phase of Awakening.

Most of all, the Great Mystery of Consciousness Awakening to Itself is beyond any human definition but we do love to try!

***

Chapter 1 – What is 'awakening'?

The Bliss of This

by
Amara

Sometimes …
It's more than enough
To Sit
With the bliss of This
The fullness
Here
Interrupted only by
The wanting to share

***

Chapter 2

Stories of awakening

Maureen

In the Buddhist tradition I practiced, awakening was taught as something that might happen in some other lifetime, and there were things we could learn to help that come to be. There was absolutely no expectation that it might happen in this lifetime. I was drawn to the spiritual life – always pulled deeper and deeper. Adyashanti said (I think I have this right) that we can make ourselves more grace-prone. That's what my practices seemed like, in retrospect.

I found a quote from Adya that exactly catches it for me: "When you get down to the simplicity of it, there's just you, your yearning, and the stillness that beckons you." So I meditated. My mind became quieter, kundalini energy started moving in my body, and I learned to let go.

A few years ago I had a sudden vast insight of the nature of the entire cosmos, as a pool of energy out of which emerges all things – Buddhist emptiness and fullness. My first reaction was "Holy shit!" My next was "What now?" I felt as if I'd stepped through a doorway and found myself on Mars. Everything I knew to be true was flipped upside down.

The Buddhist organization I'd been involved with for 15 years had nothing to offer, so I started reading and listening to Adyashanti. His book *The End of Your World* became my lifeline.

I had about six months of loveliness (what Adya calls the honeymoon period), and then the suppression lid came off emotional baggage. It was clear working with that was the next task. I've been clearing and learning how to embody awakening ever since.

***

Chapter 2 – Stories of awakening

Lisa

My awakening began with a classic NDE (near-death experience), when at five years old I almost drowned. I let go of my whole human self, my body and my life. There were feelings of profound peace, absolute freedom, bliss, and an all-encompassing unconditional love, which permeated all of existence while at the same time also being my core. It included an other-worldly journey to a world of light, where I encountered beautiful beings of light and was taught about the nature of Reality.

This experience transformed both me and my whole outlook on life. But as a small child, it was impossible to integrate, so I repressed the whole thing and then began to subconsciously search for 'something', but I didn't know what.

My childhood and early adult years were difficult. I felt like I didn't fit in and that I was different in some way. I was interested in things no one else was: what death really was, existential questions and the paranormal. I was never drawn to mainstream spirituality and considered religion utterly meaningless.

In my mid-twenties, I 'accidentally' met a therapist/teacher who had also experienced an NDE. This was the beginning of the more conscious part of my journey.

I did experiential psychological and existential work with him for about ten years and worked through a large part of my personal history. Additionally, there were experiences of the kundalini process, memories of past lives and trauma, out-of-body and paranormal events, and unity and bliss. I also went through a very scary ego-death experience connected to reliving my birth trauma.

There were no techniques practiced during this work, apart from some healing and painting. It was simply based on letting go and working with whatever came up. It also didn´t rely on any conceptual spiritual or psychological framework, only on the teacher's own experience and intuition. All I went through during those years came up spontaneously as a result of a deep letting go and trust in the therapist/teacher.

Many times during those years I felt divided, like there was an unknown deep part of me directing and controlling the process, while my 'everyday self' continued to resist even though it was completely powerless to stop it. During those years, I learned to let go and to accept whatever came up. I found that the more I resisted, the more I suffered.

This therapist/teacher became extremely important to me, even somewhat of a guru. But crucial as this relationship and work was, it also included destructive elements of projection, inequality, dependence and turning over my power to the teacher in an unhealthy way.

After all that inner work and spiritual experiences, even though I did go through periods of joy and bliss, I was consistently feeling worse instead of better. After a few years I began to question the teacher, the nature of our connection and the work we were doing. Finally it all ended with an unpleasant breaking-off, which led to my complete breakdown.

That was the beginning of a dark night period that went on for years. I suffered with extreme anxiety, deep depression and excruciating loneliness. My outer life came crashing down as well with work-related issues. I also became very anti-guru and decided all spiritual teachers were on a power-trip and that enlightenment/awakening was either a fairy tale or a hoax. I had read a bit about non-duality but found it uninteresting. I couldn't comprehend what the 'no-self' business was about. I thought the whole point of psycho-spiritual work was that the self ('me') would feel better and have a better life, not disappear! There had been a lot of deconstruction, but I thought it was a deconstruction of ingrained trauma patterns and non-authentic ways of living and relating to others, not a deconstruction of myself!

I worked through the 'guru years' in ordinary therapy and took my power and autonomy back. I felt better, met my partner and had a family. For about 10 years I led a pretty ordinary life and didn't give spirituality a second thought. Almost automatically I kept on accepting whatever came up, letting go of the past and focusing on joy and love in daily life. The powerful spiritual experiences had stopped and I felt normal and okay on the whole.

Then one day, without preparation and without noticing anything in particular beforehand, the final ego knot quietly and undramatically snapped. I wasn't looking for it, didn't believe in it and didn't expect it. Boy, was it a surprise! I thought, "Bloody hell, all that inner work, accepting and letting go was the undoing of myself! Who would have thought?"

There was such tremendous relief. There was a surge of exhilaration and the thought that it was so f***ing good to finally be rid of Lisa. There was a profound, deep peace that I recognized from my NDE but that I never expected to feel while still in a body. But I also wasn't 'in' a body any more. Rather, the body was in me.

There simply was no 'me', no center any more. There was still some sense of self, but everything just occurred. 'I' didn't speak, speaking happened. 'I' didn't want to do something, doing happened. Emotions happened. Choices happened. All in an Emptiness, that wasn't empty. Fear of death completely disappeared. I didn't care anymore, because there was no one to care. All feelings of loneliness or incompleteness disappeared. This state of being was completeness and wholeness itself. All feelings of being awkward or shy or uncomfortable around others disappeared. My perception of the body changed. I perceived everything as part of 'me' and 'me' as part of everything else. The body was not a barrier any more.

One of the most beautiful realizations of the 'transition', as I call it, was that all the trauma in my life, all the events that were so painful for me, everything that had not come out of love, was an illusion, even though it had previously felt very real. All that had been without love in my life disappeared like a puff of smoke, like a fading dream. Of course I still remembered events in my mind, but the emotional charge, the suffering and the judgement connected to them, had gone. From where I stand right now, Love is Reality. It is being awake. All else is illusion. All else is dream.

And lo and behold, suddenly that 'enlightenment' stuff also seemed to fall into place intellectually. I 'accidentally' came across Adyashanti and read his book *The End of your World* which was very helpful. I had become a bit removed from others and ordinary reality and in his book he advises to 'keep going'. So I 'kept going' and immersed myself in it completely. After a while I reached a kind of plateau or resting place. Here, I can still perceive my whole personality that I used to call 'me' but I'm not identified with it anymore. It's like I've transcended the whole thing and grown into a much larger skin. I don't bathe in eternal bliss of any kind, but I do feel that there is a lot of unconditional love, through me, around me and in me. There is deep peace. There is lack of fear. There is a profound sense of wholeness and freedom. But there is sometimes also sadness, anger, loss. Whatever arises, is. I'm sure this is but another part of the journey and that there will be more to come. Deepening, or even more deconstruction, or maybe something I can't even fathom yet.

This is a journey into the unknown, a journey without a return ticket.

***

Georgette

How in the world could I describe something that ended the one who could describe it? The mind goes blank. Deep velvety silence engulfs in response to such questions now. The story of the dream becomes so translucent it's barely remembered. Everything feels like sand passing through my fingers even though I still fully participate in life creation processes ... just so strange, and wondrous too, this adventure into the unknown as the unknown.

It all started as a girl of 12 when an Indian Guru touched my forehead with a peacock feather and gave me a mantra. After this I began to meditate in my bunk bed each night relaxing into a state of natural bliss before falling asleep.

There have been many, many glimpses and awakenings over the years since then but the one that changed everything happened like this:

On the way to a week-long spiritual retreat, I was driving alone up Mt Madonna Rd, near Santa Cruz, California on a very narrow gravel road that went up and up ... and on and on ... for miles with many blind turns. For most of the drive, I was worried I had taken a wrong turn after losing GPS access. My apprehension and anxiety had already hit a high pitch when I saw the car barreling directly towards me!

All I can now say about that moment is that when the collision happened something radically changed. The body-mind was shocked into a deeper state of Unity Consciousness than ever before. It felt as if everything happening and everyone involved, every part of the experience, were all expressions of this one thing. As soon as I saw the driver's frightened face, my heart burst open with so much love and compassion for him, myself, our vehicles, for everyone who would be impacted in a stressful way. I felt strangely overwhelmed and disappeared in an explosion of LOVE.

Simultaneously with this beautiful GIFT of a deeper realization of Love and Unity, the accident also dramatically brought to the surface a collection of my fear-based conditioning. Even in the most traumatic moments of this experience, as the scene unfolded, there was awareness of living out the fears I'd experienced on the drive up the mountain. Fears such as traveling alone in unfamiliar territory, breaking down on the side of the road in a remote area, being alone with intoxicated male strangers, not to mention getting into a car accident! At the root of all these fears was a separate entity afraid of the unknown. And, this is what dropped away.

Even though I totalled the car, it screeched terribly and shook like crazy, I was able to drive very slowly the rest of the way to the retreat. Within a short time of checking in, my roommate arrived who I hadn't met before. I explained what had just happened. She told me she was a "Somatic Trauma Specialist" and offered to help the body unwind from the shock right then and there. Another gift from the Great Mystery on this adventure of Awakening. My sense of self and reality have never been the same since.

***

Kiran

I came to this world with an active pilot light (the spiritual impulse). It was years before this was recognized, perhaps due to my psychological baggage.

As I grew up, I was surrounded by religious philosophy which created a profound desire for God/Truth.

I participated in many rituals such as prayers, chanting and singing hymns all with the intent to unite with God. The belief that unification could only happen to a chosen few, left me feeling unworthy of it. My feelings of unworthiness were a substantial part of my psyche.

Over time, the sincerity and dedication I devoted to my 'purpose' took over my life and I spent hours daily in the pursuit of Truth. While I experienced much disappointment with my lack of tangible results or changes attributed to my practice, something deep within was stirring; although I was not aware of it, the process of refinement had already begun.

The difficulties and pain of life pushed me further and further; the pursuit of Truth and Peace became my sole purpose in life. I gave up my career, which I had worked hard to build, in order to follow my deeper instincts. The pilot light had become a raging fire and I was ready to throw my 'all' into it.

Gradually, help (Divine or Universal) started coming my way, initially in the form of Buddhist meditation, and then later in the form of a teacher who did not support meditation. Regardless, I remained resolute and willing to do anything and everything that was asked of me.

Over the course of four years, I endured much difficulty and harshness from my teacher, yet I never gave up. During this time, I did recognize the 'me' (the egoic entity) that was in my way. Through religion I had heard about this entity all my life. I came to clearly see its patterns, desires, judgments, likes and dislikes, resentments and resistance and much more, yet I felt totally helpless. I didn't read many books or seek any therapeutic advice during this period of intense self-inquiry. This helplessness took most of the 'doer' away and transformed it into surrender.

Then one day in October 2012, everything inside of me began to melt. I found myself drowning in a pool of something that I had never imagined Awakening would be like. It was a strange mix of nothing and everything; an empty fullness.

The same state carried through when I went to bed that night and into the next day. I felt disoriented and absolutely absent as self or person, yet my body was fully functional, as were my senses. It felt like I was the embodiment of a vast and endless heart full of love and compassion. I couldn't see anything wrong anywhere. Dissatisfaction or all resistance had disappeared; the One who would normally experience such things, seemed to be absent. It was one unbroken, undivided No-Self. Although I could not know what it was yet, I knew it was Sat Chit Ananda.

Prior to this event, I'd had several spiritual experiences, but this time I realized my inner address had changed. Something had shifted; everything that had happened in my life had contributed to this point.

Although I experienced a distinct taste of union and oneness, I found this change disturbing because it shattered my old view that awakening was a finish line; I knew that there would be a long road ahead to walk. I no longer saw everything only from the place of identification, yet neither was I completely united nor one all the time. While I doubted things often, I knew that this sprang from the remaining forces of the psyche or egoic entity surfacing every so often.

This was a blessing. It was the embodiment of learning to 'live' the Awakening; opening more and more petals of the lotus. All of it came from the peace and truth I had experienced during Awakening. Now, 'living' was being shaped and restructured and thus, it feels so harmonious.

***

Timothy

Ever since I was a child, I had the feeling that there must be something more to life than what other people told me. It was a hobby to question and look for answers to the bigger picture of existence.

In my teens I started reading everything I could find on the subject of higher consciousness and self-improvement. In my mid-twenties I found a small bookstore packed with literature on these subjects. I discovered many meditation techniques and tried different ones for about two years.

I had been doing an imagination technique for a couple of weeks, when one night, in my sleep, I had a dream I didn't like. I began altering the scenario, which I'd never been able to do before. It occurred to me that the changes I was making were impossible. Realizing that I must be asleep and dreaming I suddenly lit up with light. I was without thought and felt weightless in a brilliant sea of perfect peace. I dissolved into a fearless and total oneness with everything. It wasn't anything like I could have imagined. Who I thought I was vanished and was replaced with nothing. I was empty, and at the same time full of an energy that could only be described as love. When my body awoke I got up from my bed with this new condition still present. It's been persistent ever since.

***

Marieke

From the time I was a small child, I was interested in finding the truth: something deeper, less false and less confused than what I encountered in my surroundings and in myself.

As a teenager and up until my early thirties, I was terribly unhappy (major depressive disorder, and social and general anxiety disorder), so sought truth in psychology and lots of therapy.

At 29 I was introduced to spirituality and after reading Eckhart Tolle, became quite captivated, even though I didn't understand much of what he said. I snooped around in Buddhism, did some meditations, did a Taoist course and some more meditations, but only ever for a few weeks at a time, never regularly. The only thing I practised almost daily, for two years in a row, was mindfulness meditation. This helped me to disentangle from my identification with thoughts and emotions, and I recognized the witness there, but I wasn't awakened yet. I also learned to really feel and to recognize the felt sense of the body.

Those years I was also into non-duality as there was a great podcast and community that spoke about it in a fun, relatable way. My mind became clearer, as I sensed this non-duality was what I was looking for. It had such a ring of truth to it! It was really captivating. I read a lot about it and watched satsangs and interviews online for a few years.

And then, suddenly, after a five-day meditation course I felt some energy moving in my body. I had never felt this before. It felt nice. It was a stream of energy through my arms and out my hands, sometimes also in my legs and out my feet. My teacher said it was *prana*. I had just come off anti-depressants so I attributed it to that. But after a while I felt very carefree, with no problem in the world. Life was in a flow and very gentle for weeks on end. This was new and pleasant.

And then came a point when I had my realizations. I popped out of my ego bubble and saw it from outside or above. I saw through the illusion of the self and my conscious 'I' was now very different. I was in *samadhi* for long periods of time. However, on an existential level I was confused and desperate. It felt as if I was dissolving, dying and there was no ground to rest on. This went on for five or six months.

During this period I was so completely lived by this higher force (which I learned was called kundalini), that it seemed weird for me to 'practise' anything. I was no longer a circumscribed person with a personal will that could do a practise or have a purpose. I was on a completely different plane. I had nowhere to go, no goal, no say in it. My instinct or the kundalini led me and told me what was good for me. For instance, I went to satsang with my beloved friend as much as possible, I walked around in nature to ground the energy, I regularly lay down and let the energetic movements and the energy turn inward and inside itself. I also went into all kinds of altered states where I encountered different dimensions and sometimes beings. This was four years ago.

The knowing of the Ego or small self as an illusion has persisted and my mind has become a lot quieter. I am not so interested in social talk and social conventions anymore and I am manifesting myself more and more from this true place of Being. I recognize the energetic ground of everything and in this, the perfection of every life situation. This has made my life so much more peaceful and content.

***

Richard

I drank whiskey for the first time and the following morning woke up in a transcendent reality. I experienced the absence of consuming thoughts about the future and past, leaving me with an intense appreciation of the present moment.

I spent the day outside, in awe of the life in the grass and the trees and the blueness of the sky. I had very little language to describe what was going on, so I fitted it into my vaguely Christian framework. It felt to me as though I knew that Heaven existed, knew that this world was only a small part of a much greater one beyond, one from which we come and to which we return. I also knew that the greater world beyond was infinite in time. This allowed me to drop all my worries about life, leaving me able to appreciate being in the moment. I cannot overstate what a contrast this was to my normal existence.

I was technically too young to purchase whiskey at that time, so I couldn't just rush out and buy a bottle to repeat the experiment. On the times I would drink it however, this space would open up again. Eventually I started making the connection with things like consciousness and meditation, and my journey to recapture this state began. Around that time the effect of drink to induce it started to diminish. Now all I get is a headache. I've never met anyone else who reported this nor, to this day, do I have any explanation for it.

***

Silvia

"The dark night only grows larger when you ignore it." This is a quote from Eckhart Tolle.

My dark night started when I was 20 and, with some long breaks, went on for more than three decades.

I was diagnosed with 'unknown' neuro-vegetative disorders, daily panic attacks, and heavy incurable depression. For years I wasn't able to sleep more than two hours a night. In the meantime I had to raise my two children alone and do my best not to lose my job as a teacher. The night of the soul seemed unending!

I had a strong fighter's identity. My conditioning was that a person should have control over life and fight situations when they seem adverse. I never learnt anything about acceptance!

I was taken to see a number of doctors all of whom (with the exception of one who admitted that he was confused by such strong symptoms along with such a clarity of mind), hammered the label of 'mental illness'. I kept saying that the pain and anguish were somehow NOT mine and that even though they were felt in my 'body-soul-mind' they didn't come from me. I suppose this made me look even crazier but I knew what I was saying. Everybody wanted to look for trauma in my past (and for years I let them search) but I have NOT had a traumatic childhood, rather I enjoyed myself greatly as a kid!

As an adult, of course I experienced some difficult 'outside' situations. The father of my kids left when they were very small and my daughter was abused, but the truth was that the dark night *had already started* prior to these events. Only two friends stayed close to me during those difficult years but they were unable to understand.

I often had the feeling I would go crazy. I felt a strong energy 'inside' as if my body was about to explode! I pushed this energy back with running, I kept it down with 'meditation', I battled against it with all my might. I was terrified. I often wanted to commit suicide; everything was planned ... it would seem like an accident. I understand now that the one who had to die was basically just a thought, but during those difficult years I could find nobody to help me see that this was *not* madness but a movement of Consciousness that would lead towards *real life* and that 'on the other side' there was peace ... and love ... and joy!

I desperately tried to find a solution through thinking THINKING until it seemed I could think a thousand things at the same time. My mind wanted to explode. In addition my body had started shaking vigorously, especially at night, sometimes for one or two hours. I was unaware that I was functioning from resistance mode. Then came a time when I wanted to surrender ... but how can one *do* the surrendering?

Until ... enough was enough ...

One day I decided I would give the fears, anguishes, death thoughts not one more ounce of attention. I had actually tried this a few times but I had never been so coherent about it. Since all the fighting had not given *any* results I decided I could just as well stop making any effort!

Due to exhaustion, surrender took over. I finally allowed things to be as they were, which in this case, was desperate! I decided I would practice 'pulling the attention back' every time it was drawn towards *any* worldly object. I don't know where I got this idea. Perhaps it came because I had had enough of worldly experiences. I just didn't want to give attention to anything anymore! I'm sure that to the eyes of others I must have looked like a zombie.

By this time I had already lost my job and was considered incurable, so I had plenty of time to do my experiments. In the past I had even locked myself in a completely dark room without food for three days and nights in order to get to the bottom of things ... without any result. So for about three days I did this practice constantly: every time my attention would alight on an object, or thought, or feeling, or experience I would *pull it back*. I wasn't sure of what it meant exactly, it was not some technique I had read of, it was just something that had come to mind.

Chapter 2 – Stories of awakening

And then ... suddenly ... one morning it happened! I was in my room when, all at once, everything was still and silent. There was stillness even in movements and silence even in noises. Suddenly the curtains, the floor, the walls, the furniture were made of 'I'. It was seen that I was everything and everywhere! My view was not from a 'point' of view anymore, it was universal. I realized that the world is *made* of silence ... that silence is the very substance of everything! And that it *is* me! Such a peace! Such a subtle peaceful joy! Tears streamed! I have no idea how long I stayed there ... this was outside time! Then I started seeing that I am not only the 'substance' of which the universe is made but that I am also the 'source' of it. I saw that in the black nothingness there is a sort of movement ... and that this very movement is *Love* ... and in this way 'light shines the world through'.

All this was *seen*; it wasn't a *thought*. In fact for what seemed like eternity not a single thought crossed my mind. The first real thought came after seven days. I was concerned for a friend to whom I had written a desperate letter some weeks before ... I wanted to let her know that I was well.

During those blissful days more and more clarifications came. They felt like they were showered down from nowhere.

Well, this is basically the story of my *long* dark night of soul ... which from my current perspective doesn't even seem long anymore ... and of its *end*.

I hope this might help another despairing soul, shorten their journey.

***

Elizabeth

I entered in in an awakened state. I was both aware and balanced at that early age. It is the most natural state for all human beings.

I fell asleep around middle school and then had my first re-awakening experience in college, around 1996-7.

I was sitting on the floor with several books spread out in front of me: Carl Sagan, Jung, the iChing, and James Redmond's book (I forget what it is called) when quite suddenly 'I' was gone and my consciousness expanded throughout the cosmos. It was a bit like an explosion.

The little bit of me that remained eventually attempted to locate my body and what I'd referred to as myself, but for quite some time, was unable to. I came back into the egoic self, altered. Not fully awake, but that was my first big bang. Then automatic yoga postures began occurring. For example, at random times my arms would shoot up, or my body would contort into a new pose while I was sitting with friends.

Throughout the years I've had a number of 'awakenings', each different from the other.

***

Stacy

This is almost a trick question. Yes, something happened. I'm more awake. Awakened? Maybe, maybe not.

How? I haven't the foggiest idea.

In Truth, it just happened.

Permit me one quote, which I find attributed to three or four different teachers, so I don't know who first said it, "Enlightenment is an accident. Meditation makes you accident prone."

All my life there have been transcendent experiences. But a transcendent experience without some understanding and a context and you simply go back to sleep and long for the ease and bliss of those moments or days or weeks when everything was clear and beautiful. Seeking continues.

I can't say there was absolutely no context, either. I listened to Alan Watts on the radio in the 70s. I meditated. I was a *Course in Miracles* student for 25 years. I practiced The Work of Byron Katie. I read books by teachers. I went to workshops.

I could not say when I first experienced this more awake awareness. Maybe marijuana, acid or mushrooms. Some of the first flips into more awake-ness were through sex. Sometimes through meditation or watching cottonwood leaves in the wind or a stream running under a bridge beneath me.

As one of my teachers explained it, there is a kind of relaxing in and back.

In 1985, I experienced this awareness through a breathwork group. From then on, I looked for it and wanted to teach this awareness to others. I found quite a few things that 'worked'. I wanted to be with other people who were finding this same awareness, but like most of us have found, too many people just wanted to talk about it, not do it.

I started to find that there were current books about it, such as *Translucent Revolution* by Arjuna Ardagh and *Waking Up: Spirituality without Religion* by Sam Harris.

The 'biggest' shift happened around April of 2007. I was lucky to be a participant in a one-time meditation weekend. It was recorded. We learned about a dozen pointers over three days. They all 'worked' for me, so I spent most of three days feeling connected, clear, light, peaceful and all that Good Stuff(™) that people search for.

There was some context. Some understanding that it would come and go, that it doesn't mean anything, that I could relax and stop searching, that there was no 'I' or 'me'.

It lasted for weeks and weeks.

I felt I was 'done'.

... and then I got into a relationship and it 'slipped'. She ridiculed my 'awakening' in light of other personality habits and 'faults' I still had. That was tough, but it did not take away my certainty. It just made me sad that she didn't share it.

That was maybe 2009.

I still felt 'done', but in 2016 a friend told me about Liberation Unleashed (LU). I knew I didn't 'need' to wake up but I still craved the company of like-minded 'others'. So, I was guided online in that context and again found this 'awakening awareness' thing. This time there was a small community, some more context, some more cognition to go with the blast of bliss that would eventually become a new normal or fade or whatever it does.

My guide gave me only one exercise: Look for the place where the chair begins and your butt ends.

Other pointers about there being no self, about direct experience, about the non-existence of control, free will, and decisions, about the body, about time and memory are given at LU. All deepen both the experience and the comprehension of what is. I began to guide others, partly to continue my own awareness, partly to give back what had been given to me for free.

Was any of this what I expected? Yes and no. In a way, it is always surprising to deepen in awareness and loosen the sense of an identified 'me'. In another way, no. This is normal. This is reality. Or truth. Or whatever you want to call it. Somewhere in my being it is known that this is it and always has been.

***

Amara

In the summer of 2013, a friend introduced me to sungazing. With this process, I would wake early, stare into the rising sun for 10 seconds with bare feet on bare earth, then meditate. I added 10 seconds each successive day. By the end of June 2014, one year later, I was gazing into the rising sun for 36 minutes and my practice had evolved to chanting before sunrise for an hour, chanting during the sungazing and meditating after the gazing for at least an hour (usually more), with a contemplative practice thrown in as well.

By this time, there had been quite a few insights and experiences, and even extended bouts of bliss. But still I was at a point of desperation. In my contemplations, I found myself making the heart-felt declaration, "I would give ANYTHING to know the Truth of my Being!" Then I would wait for the "Yes, but ..." Yes, but my daughter ... my husband ... my home ... my business ... One by one, with emotional release, I let them all go until I could declare without exception that I was willing to give my very life. I realized I couldn't live a lie anymore. It was just too painful. It was seen that the basis of my life as it was being lived was a lie and that I had no idea what the antidote was.

That whole year of Sadhana had been effortless in a way – it had taken no discipline – it was just happening. But after this plea to the universe to reveal the truth or take my life, it all just stopped. I stopped waking up early. I started sleeping in. I stopped chanting. I had to *try* to meditate. The magic of the previous year had fallen away. I was oddly okay with this.

About a week later, the morning of July 2, 2014, I awoke from sleep, and a spontaneous inquiry arose directed towards the idea of self: Who was I really? Before my mind's eye were arrayed all the selves I took myself to be – higher self, lower self, ego, body, mind – where was 'I' in all of this? About a week earlier, after re-reading Tolle's *The Power of Now* I had created a 'witness self' to assist in moments like this. I wasn't in a place to consider that I might actually be 'THE Witness' – so I made one. The mind is complex and holds many delusions! So, with this question that appeared as I awoke and even before I had opened my eyes, I decided to move into this 'witness' self I had created to sort it all out. As I was 'moving' toward this witness self, a new question arose. "Wait a minute ... How did I create this 'witness' and what did I create it *from?*" And I turned back to look. That was it. I watched as all these 'selves' became brittle armatures and I instantly knew them to

Chapter 2 – Stories of awakening

be empty constructs. They were actually all NOTHING! So Empty! Just constructs! Then, as if not able to stand the pressure of truth, they all imploded – shattered into dust. Then … There was only shining black Aware Stillness. 'I' wasn't 'in' stillness. That's all there was. Aware Stillness. For an eternal moment.

Then there was laughing. Then there was moving out of bed. Then there was staring out the window. Then a thought appeared: "This is IT. It's been right here all along. This. Is. It. There's no place to go, nothing to do, no future magical state to be had. How silly was that thinking! This is It. It's right here." Two other things were also completely and irrevocably understood: "Everything is profoundly and eternally Okay." (For anything to not be okay is an impossibility.) And, "Now I get to start." It was seen that all interpretation up until then was confused, complicated, fallacious pseudo-understanding. Everything was different yet it was all the same. It was noticed that all tension had left me. Leading up to that time, no matter what I was doing, there was the sense that I should be doing something else and that whatever I was doing wasn't right. Now there was only perfection, only peace. All of this understanding and underlying peace has remained an undercurrent ever since, even through the challenging first few years of intensive releasing of conditioning and subsequent re-arranging of my life.

There were a few glimpses to follow, most in that first year. On coming out of a particularly deep meditation, there was a glimpse of Beauty that sent my body into hours of convulsive grief. It was seen that the Beauty We Are can never be expressed in form. For some reason, my body just couldn't bear this. If all the beauty in all the worlds on all the planes of existence was somehow gathered up, it would seem as a grain of sand compared to the Beauty We Truly Are. And yet, the Totality tries, in a way … it tries and tries to express What We Are. Impossible. Not even a wisp of the Greatness We Are can ever be expressed in form. This was experienced as an exquisite tragedy.

Another glimpse was the classic 'me awaring back at me'. I was watching a video of my teacher, Francis Lucille, and something 'popped'. Suddenly everything was me, Awareness, shining back at Awareness. There were no things, there was just 'me' everywhere. I shot up off the couch and jetted out the door and walked and walked and walked. The trees were me, the mountains were me, every particle was me … all without a sense of there being trees, mountains or particles or a 'me'! Something that was baffling, and fun, was that the words 'behind me' came to mind and I couldn't conceive of what they could mean. I knew that I had been able to understand that concept in the past, but now I just couldn't grasp what 'behind' meant. Because it was all 'me' there couldn't possibly be a 'behind me' – it was 'me' all the way to forever! Then, about 20 minutes in, I sat on a rock and watched as my mind reassembled a person with a perspective. I sat helpless, really. I knew if I fought it, this experience that I knew to be much truer than ordinary reality, would leave me sooner. I didn't lament. I was glad for that 20 minutes of lived Reality. At least, I now knew the potential of this body-mind to welcome Reality as it truly is and was happy for it.

***

Michaela

I grew up in a communist dictatorship, in a society where we all knew we lived in a lie, but feared the consequences of speaking the truth. Most of us felt like prisoners, but at the same time we felt safe. We knew what to blame for not living in happiness. The reason for our misery was obvious: it was the oppression of the political system. So when I moved to a free country at the age of 25 and the happiness I expected to come with the freedom did not eventuate, I faced my first serious depression.

I started looking within for comfort, while at the same time being scared of that unknown endless dimension. Playing my musical instrument, sometimes I would almost panic as I watched my fingers moving so fast: "Who is doing this? It is not me! I am not fast enough to consciously control all of those movements!" And the questioning went on: "Who keeps breathing when I sleep? How do I walk? Who controls what I do?" These were terrifying, paralyzing thoughts, as I could not find the one final 'I' that was in charge.

My biggest fear at that time was that I would lose my mind. I envied people who could believe in God, as they were seemingly at peace. They lived in trust and faith. But as much as I tried, believing in God was not possible. I was unable to buy into any stories that were not objectively or scientifically proven, and not my personal experience. With no solid position to hold onto, my state of mind was one of constant questions, doubts and fears. I was desperate to find wisdom and to know the real values that I sensed life must contain. In this chaos of insecurity I had only one virtue to rely on, sincerity. I never put on any mask of pretence over my ignorance; I stayed vulnerably open to all.

After some very intense, busy years, traveling and performing worldwide, at the age of 33 I was profoundly shaken by a strong relationship. The situation was complicated and made me seriously investigate: "What is truly love? What is conscience? How do they relate and which of them is of 'higher value'?" I was close to losing my mind on that self-made riddle, while at the same time trying to justify my feelings and make sense of the situation. I would allow myself to make a choice only if it left me with a clear conscience. Whirling in that dilemma I experienced the first glimpse of truth, when I suddenly realized that what people refer to as God is simply love!

I then took a crucial step in a new direction by seeing through and resolving the strong victim mentality from my childhood. I took full responsibility for my life and was able to start a conscious journey towards the truth. I read philosophy, psychology and also the teachings of Maharishi, Papaji, Osho, Anthony de Mello, mystics from my country of origin and many, many more. It was clear to me that self-inquiry was the direct path to truth and salvation. Finding an answer on the question "Who am I?" became my deepest leitmotiv.

This period lasted for many years. I knew intellectually that God must be the same for all of us, ever-present and therefore reachable for everyone everywhere. So I searched on my own and never looked for any community. Life of course sent its teachers (like my husband, who was the result of that strong relationship) and I learned eagerly everywhere, wherever I sensed wisdom or human qualities present. I tried hard to rid myself of any egoistic agenda, let go of old patterns of conditioning and dissolve any feelings of pride or superiority. I would almost welcome sacrifices in my life and see them as necessary purifying lessons on the road.

In 2006, I had everything I could wish for from life: a beautiful family, children, and a successful career. Yet at some point the old fears showed up again with renewed strength and soon took over. I knew that in spite of all efforts I was still missing a basic understanding of myself. I had several health issues at the time which allowed me to slow down my activities and dive deeper into the inner dimensions. The progress was slow and I fell into despair.

At some point I typed a spontaneous cry for help on my computer: "Enlightenment NOW!" A man called Eckhart Tolle showed up. At that time he was not well-known as he is today, but some lectures in German were available. I was immediately captivated. Here was someone as ordinary as me, yet 'enlightened'. I could connect with everything he said and sensed the dimension of truth he talked from. I started to follow his instructions very seriously, trying to go into the inner body and calming down my mind on every occasion. I gave up all worldly desires and my only focus was on breaking through the invisible barrier that was keeping me from experiencing the shift. Yet to my despair, nothing happened.

One day – a date I would remember – an old friend called me after many years, to ask how I was doing. He apparently expected the talented young girl he once knew, to be enjoying a great and successful life. Totally exhausted from my search I started to cry. "What is wrong?" he asked. I told him that I felt miserable because I still had no idea of who I was, why I was here and what my mission in life was. He listened and then burst into laughter. "What are you saying? What is it you are looking for? Every single person in my street knows who they are and what their mission in life is. It is just walking the steps in front of your nose. That's all there is to it!"

Though I would doubt that the whole street was actually enlightened, the energy of that statement still had an unexpectedly powerful effect. I suddenly felt like a total fool. Here I was, an adult, a mum of two kids, searching for a non-existent idea of enlightenment, while everyone else was living a real life. I gave up. There was no more place to go. I had tried every possible way to get 'THERE'. My hope was gone and I was left alone in an emotionless desert.

Next morning, like a little robot, I baked some cookies for my kids and drove to another city for a scheduled meeting. Deadly calm. My last unfulfilled longing, the longing for truth, had gone and I didn't want anything anymore.

Driving that grey rainy January day, a tree on the side of the road suddenly caught my attention. I looked at it and at that very moment my perception shifted. Gently but monumentally! I saw that tree and all its magnificence, absolutely alive in Presence! My last thought was, "This is it! This is what all the Buddhas refer to! This is NOW." Then thinking stopped and all that was left was a total indescribable peace. Nothing could be added to it and nothing taken away. It was accomplishment itself. Within it was the realization that what until now I had seen as 'me' was only a dream story. There was never any real 'me' as there is nothing but One Life. I remember wondering what should be done with the body that was driving the car. It was of no need anymore as it was not real, so what should I use it for? And an answer came from deep within, "For the others".

This experience was the strongest and most real of all that I witnessed, yet it was so utterly simple that I could not say anything about it for a very long time. Only in retrospect, would I 'classify' it as the second step of awakening. While in the first step I took full responsibility for my life, in the second I gave it back to Life, after I saw there was no 'me' and no such things as 'my' responsibility, my 'will' or 'my' life. It was all just One Life happening.

This was not the end, but rather the beginning of a very intense and painful period. I was thrust into totally unexpected situations that required making strong choices, which I was unable to make because I had given up my will and felt myself to be a mere instrument of life. My old self did not really matter anymore. What mattered now was to do things right, in accordance with Life/God's will and for the best of the whole. But in the dilemmas that I faced at that time I could not hear what this 'right' was. I felt completely abandoned, without any compass or inner guidance. I constantly pondered the theme of unconditional love: a real true love. I wrote pages and pages of reflections on that theme, contemplating the biblical story of Abraham and Isaac and its powerful message of sacrifice as the key for transcendence to absolute love. Since my meeting with the divine I already knew who I was not. But I still did not know who I AM.

My life situation got increasingly complicated as a result of the dramas going on within me. Life was not responding with concrete answers, but rather, with painful lessons. One of them made me realize, that in spite of all my talk about absolute love, I was still hurting others. I realized that shouting out loud what I might consider as true, is not The Truth, and that a person who protects a loved one with a lie, might be acting with more love than me with all my sincerity that I was so proud of. But could a lie be compatible with truth? The dilemma of a lie versus truth played a big role in those final stages. It was again an unsolvable riddle for a mind that could not yet cross the limits of dual-thinking logic and grasp the 'paradox' of reality.

Finally, I saw that all I had ever done was from an 'ego'. Even the search for God was coming from an egoic fear: ego looking for its benefits, for self-affirmation, for survival. Seeing the ego's game everywhere in my past, I knelt on the floor in tears, asking for guidance and still not hearing any answer.

It was around Christmas time. I was composing psalms about Jesus' crucifixion while going through an inner process of psychological agony. At some point I went to visit Eckhart Tolle's page to find some relief in my darkness. I saw he recommended a book that I would normally never pick up, as it was written as a channelling of Jesus. It was called *A Course in Miracles*. I found it in a local library that same day and with curiosity opened it at a random page. Tears started to roll down my cheeks as I felt with all my being that this book was alive and talking to me! I was finally getting the answers I prayed for! It was addressing exactly my situation: the giving up of free will, the struggle for making right decisions. Everything I went through was explained and fitted so perfectly, just as if it had been written for me. I knew that I was never forsaken. All this was a part of the learning! God was alive and talking to me.

I slept with that heavy book on my chest that night. And next day a miracle happened. As softly and effortlessly as the first time, the divine dimension opened, emptied the confusion and provided me with previously unknown clarity. It revealed the absolute purity and innocence of all creation. It revealed the nothingness of all.

I saw that I am the one creating this illusive world. There is no past, no future, no time. All are mere thoughts appearing in Presence.

The mind was liberated from its conditioning and a total forgiveness took place. Not that I was blaming anyone before, but this was an experience of profound knowing that there was never anything to forgive, as all is pure and all is love. I realized that Christ is not an entity outside of myself, but a perspective of forgiveness and love and the only way to know him truly is when looking with his eyes as one.

The search was over. I saw that there is nothing but Love. I am it, we all are, as there is no separate you and me. The simple riddle was finally solved. I knew, that the only Truth is Love and that I am That.

***

Erick

I was washing the dishes. It was an early spring evening – nothing special about it. As I was quietly thinking, I don't remember about what, I noticed something. I noticed that which was always here. I recognized, for it truly was a re-cognition, the essential element of life which was consistent throughout every experience. It was a seeing of not only the consciousness of this being, but the very existence at the heart of the universe. That existence aspect was so interesting – before consciousness expresses itself existence *is*, and that is what we are. I remember a clear sense of being undeserving, but then, no one can ever earn this awakening – it is already owned.

Immediately following this recognition I was thrown into a deep transcendent experience, a sort of witnessing of the active self. I sensed the presence of my guru's teacher with whom I had sought a personal connection for three decades but which had eluded me. There was a brief exchange of thoughts:

"Where have you been?"

"I've been here all along. I just don't get mixed up with the Relative. It keeps my message pure. Welcome."

"Oh."

I let that go and continued washing the dishes. Experiences come and go but I knew immediately that this recognition was different. I also noticed that it was not what I had expected; based on decades of deep meditation I had pretty much expected that the transcendent expansion of meditation would eventually become steadfast. But I'd actually pretty much given up on that, because I'm not that disciplined in my practice. I meditated twice every day but did not follow all of the prescriptions of the guru (which were many). I no longer attended long retreats aimed at deepening that experience and had pretty much drifted away from any formal spiritual study.

There was no significant harbinger or precursor to the awakening – it just occurred.

Sure, I had practiced meditation with the intent of awakening and I had spent most of my twenties in deep pursuit of spiritual knowledge and experience. But then I went on to live a regular American life – wife, business etc. … nothing notable or special in any way. I suppose I could assume that the awakening was brought on by my regular meditation practice, but apparently the great majority of those who have engaged in a similar endeavor have not seen what has come to me. Maybe I could say that the meditation was excellent preparation but not necessarily a precipitating factor.

My mother had given me Adyashanti's book, *My Secret is Silence* recently and in there is a poem called *Wake Up!* about a transcendence addict. That really shifted my thinking about awakening – opening my awareness to other possibilities than that which I had expected from my earlier spiritual studies. Perhaps it was that openness that brought me to look elsewhere for Reality. It's hard to say. Looking for causality in the Causeless is a ludicrous exercise. Still, I feel that Adya's subtle influence was probably the tap that cracked the egg.

I had also been studying the law of attraction and had noticed a deep correspondence between my thoughts and feelings and the outward events in my life. That inquiry led to a significant break in my view of reality, in that I did not see causation as material anymore. The world turned inward and was much less tethered to the standard view of how things work. Perhaps you could say I was broken open. There was no world view to negate my noticing of pure existence some months later.

There is no way to fully prepare the mind for the flip in reality that awakening is. Perhaps the best thing for me was to be familiar with the anecdotes of the experience from others, observing the descriptive characteristics and having those descriptions in memory when my experience became radically shifted. I read scriptures, great poetry, spiritual texts, and classic literature. I also followed the science of human evolution to get a feeling for the landscape in modern terms. Finally, I kept an open mind, not doubting my own experience and using that as a primary reference.

The experience was sufficiently unfamiliar to require some guidance from others. I hung out in the discussion forums of *Buddha at the Gas Pump* (batgap.com) and found it very enriching to discuss the descriptions of the interviewees' awakening with others who are awakening or awakened. In particular, the descriptions of awakening in Rick Archer's interviews gave me a touchstone against which to gain foothold in understanding my own experience. It took many interviews over several years but it did eventually come around and the full knowledge became my own.

I haven't gone into experiences of bliss or witnessing since they are tangential to the experience of Reality in that gritty, primordial sense that true awakening is. Awakening is so much more than our expectations would have it be, and it is so much less.

***

Jennifer

I was in Ubud, Bali and I heard the guidance, "You need to have sex with him." I asked, "Why?" and heard the response, "Because you need to experience it." He was someone I had met at an organic restaurant and we had talked for hours about spirituality and enlightenment. If we ran into each other we talked. We disagreed a lot. I had a healthy amount of skepticism. He had been a student of Ramesh Baleskar who had been a student of Sri Nisargadatta. I had been traveling in Australia for a few weeks and had just returned. I didn't know if he was still around.

A few days later I ran into him. He initiated coming over to my place that night. I knew he wanted to have sex with me. Until that year, my entire adult life (20 years) I had only had sex in the context of a love-filled, monogamous relationship so this felt a bit strange. I had never received any guidance like this before.

He came over, gave me a massage and before I knew it we were having sex. I had never felt anything like it. It was like there was nothing solid anymore and we were completely merging with each other. It was like there were no physical boundaries or edges of bodies between us ... almost as if we had melted into each other. The whole experience was deeply soft and sensuous, as if we were made of honey. It also felt wild and primal like there were no individual selves present. Interestingly, there was not a lot of heart or a deep quality of loving the other, as there had been with previous lovers.

The next day when I was in meditation I remembered a suggestion he had made. During a previous conversation, I had told him about how Mooji told me to "Remember that I am (we are) God." He said, "Why don't you skip the remembering part and just be God." I had no idea how to do this or even what it really meant but I set the intention to do it. As I did, I could feel my presence expand out further and further and further and ... The next thing I remember, I was walking down the crowded streets of Ubud looking deep into people's eyes. Many of them were Balinese and they had a knowing in their eyes that was God looking back; God recognizing itself. Interestingly there seemed to be degrees of this Godness; some eyes shone brighter and stronger with this Divine quality. They looked into my eyes as if they knew me ... as if to say, "You know and see too, and we know and see you."

The streets were packed and in the past when my body got too close to a man who was giving me unwanted attention, I would contract. On this day, I felt no physical boundaries with anyone because my whole being was completely open; the opposite of contracting in every way. Everything was perfect just as it was. Everything felt so deliciously alive and pleasurable. The sunlight. The water in fountains. The growing green plants. Even the things I had previously disliked were beautiful. Car horns. Loud noises. Odors. It all washed through me and I through it. It was like being intimate with all of existence. I remember feeling pleasantly surprised that I had no real preferences or aversions to anything. It felt so amazing to simply be in a body walking down the street. It was deeply sensual. Ecstatic and simultaneously very relaxed. Just to be in a body and move was the best feeling in the world. Nothing was personal. Nothing. I saw a friend at a coffee shop and wasn't sure if I'd be able to talk coherently. He asked me, "How are you?" and I said, "This is one of the best days of my life." He said, "Wow that sounds really good, how come?" I had no real answer. It was simply an ordinary day.

***

Chapter 2 – Stories of awakening

Opening

Photo taken by Silvia in Africa.

Chapter 3

What advice would you give your newly-awakened self?

Ben

The euphoria of the initial breakthrough will drop away. Don't go looking for it again, it was an indicator of change, not the point of it. Sustained bliss is found in being able to revel in the normal.

***

Kathy

- You probably have a preconceived notion of what awakening is, and soon you will realize it's not what you originally thought or believed. Let those stories go. They will not serve you now.
- Share discriminately what you have discovered, or others may question your sanity. That said, try to find those who have had awakenings to walk this path with you. Face-to-face connections are best, but there are also various places online to look.
- Take time for yourself to enjoy the beautiful newfound silence.
- Ground yourself and stay in the body. It will be easy to want to ignore it.
- Write things down. During this period, you may continue to have experiences that could take significant time to fully understand. Although they may feel so vivid now, they will most likely fade.
- Also, don't make major life changes until things settle. You may feel clearer than ever but making major life changes may not be wise.

Chapter 3 – What advice would you give your newly-awakened self?

***

Sarah

To my newly-awakened self:

There will be deeper realizations to come, my dear, revealing the broader dimensions of what you are, what others are, and the totality of it all. But this is just the beginning.

Through it all you will have no choice but to hold in love that which has been suppressed and which you were not able to be with prior to this. There will be no more places to hide, and this will bring forward whatever is ripe, to fall and smash to the ground in a mess. Hold these knots, these tender places, these arisings, in the vast loving expanse you've now realized yourself to be. Go forth and get therapy and specialized trauma support; face the embedded holdings in your body. Plant your feet on the earth and dig your toes into the dirt. This is what's meant to happen, dear one. Nothing is wrong.

It will surprise you that as this process unfolds you will drop deeper and deeper into being human. A vulnerable, feeling, flawed, ordinary and awake human.

Even though you know with every day and every breath that you are the Universe, you will still feel lonely sometimes. But you are not alone in this. You never were.

***

Andrew

Don't stress. The process of awakening will happen when you are ready and it will never be what you think it will be.

But I wouldn't have believed me anyway! So maybe my advice should be to just do what I want because it'll happen when I'm ready.

***

Amara

This is just the beginning. Take your realization of "Now I get to start" to heart. Your body-mind is now in a marvelous process of undoing, bringing your life into alignment with what you now know to be True. This is not for you to do or not do, it simply IS and emerges from, and as, infinite loving intelligence. Muster as much love, patience and compassion for yourself as possible and just let go, let go, let go. Trust, trust, trust. No one presently in your life is going to 'get it' so relax about that and let this just rest in you and be yours alone for now. You'll find a teacher who can fully meet you, and you'll find your people, eventually.

***

Stacy

Don't get into a relationship with someone who doesn't get what is going on, particularly not someone who is skeptical or condescending about it.

***

Timothy

Enlightenment is a private journey. It's likely that no one you know will understand or believe you when you tell them what has happened. There's no need to share your experience because without a point of reference, people aren't going to comprehend the immensity of what you've experienced, nor the changes that will be borne of it. This is like a new beginning, a new adventure.

Before you follow the idea that your presence is of any beneficial influence to others, give yourself space to grow first. As healed as you may feel you've become, there is more clearing to come before you can try to help others understand.

Invest your time in joy and freedom. Go have fun, explore the new world and let your light shine of its own accord.

***

Lisa

In hindsight, everything seems more or less perfect and exactly how it was supposed to be, even the painful and difficult parts. But if I look at it from the perspective of diminishing the pain and hardship for myself that awakening and the path to awakening included (and there is probably more of that to come in one way or another), I'd mainly say one thing: try not to resist. Go with the flow. Don't resist the pain, don't resist the love or the happiness, don't resist the anger, don't resist the anguish. Don't resist the outer circumstances of life either. See it all, feel it all, don't act on it all, be mindful and careful, but embrace it all with all your heart. It is all Being, it is all learning and expressing the consciousness and the oneness that you are. It is all blessed, even if it's painful and difficult. I'll try my best to follow that advice as I go along myself.

***

Silvia

Don't get attached to bliss. It is bound to subside. And when it does, don't start thinking something has gone wrong. That would be identifying with a thought. You just saw that you aren't your thoughts! You aren't anything ... any 'thing'.

***

Jennifer

No matter what changes or falls away, you are safe. Trust the process.

***

Erick

I wouldn't give myself any advice, since it all plays out perfectly, but there are a few words of descriptive guidance:

This bears little resemblance to what you expected; your expectations were wrong. There is more settling in to come. You will find the comradery you are looking for, but not where you are looking. There is no need to teach. Just Be.

***

Richard

In spite of my often fervent fantasizing for a time machine, I don't believe I'd tell him anything. Life has forced me to conclude that I am moved by currents beyond my control, on an ocean whose very nature is goodness. To want to go back and add something to myself would reflect a lack of faith in that goodness, so I'd keep my mouth shut.

That's not to say the fantasy doesn't arise. My time machine does offer great insight into what's going on inside me now. At times I've wanted to go back and advise myself to be a little more worldly and pragmatic. This arises from my current sense of shortcoming in materialistic areas, a felt sense of lack, and my fear of a future where the goodness evaporates and I am truly cast adrift.

If I did go back (perhaps if I could go in disguise) the one thing I might do is listen to myself, as I certainly recall a hunger for that at the time. Listening seems like an axiomatic good which changes nothing and everything.

***

Michaela

Actually ... nothing.

Newly awakened, I was in some ways better off than I am today. The newly awakened self was totally connected and intuitive and as such perfect. The liberation and joy of finally arriving home was enormous and the direct connection with source seemed unbreakable. It was the most fantastic period of 'my' life.

Perhaps the only thing I would say ... in that period I could hardly take anyone's problems seriously, as it was all so clearly mind-made. With time I became more careful and considerate, ready to meet others where they are and not trying to convince them that their suffering is not real. Compassion is growing ever since.

***

Maureen

Ironically, the advice that triggers the most resistance: practice surrender. Resistance to what is happening will cause pain; surrender will lead to flow.

***

Chapter 3 – What advice would you give your newly-awakened self?

Kiran

If I had to give myself any advice, it would be to trust. Be in Trust, however and wherever it takes you. There are many uses of the word 'Trust'. In my experience, Trust connected me with my capacity to allow everything to be as it is. Trust also allowed me to move forward through phases in which I initially lacked clarity with regard to where or what I was.

Although my sense of trust had developed in this way from the beginning, after awakening I believed I would always experience pure undifferentiated *Sat Chit Anand* (Truth Consciousness Bliss). When I transitioned from this absence of 'I' to the 'regular grind' of life, and I was at times thrown into distrusting my own experience, it was trust that was the only saviour.

At that time, I didn't realize that everything needed to be embodied and that another type of journey had commenced. However, along the way, the deepest whispering of *Sat Chit Anand* was always present and ultimately guided me to live that which I had experienced.

***

Georgette

Don't worry darling, disorientation is natural. Nothing was ever as it appeared to be anyway and never will be. Be at peace as the 'person' you thought you were recedes into Aware Being-Existence, breathing in and out this magnificent life.

Many (or all) of your cherished beliefs about who you are, what life is, what God is, what anything really is will begin to fall away. At first this might feel destabilizing, frightening or even terrifying. Try letting go of the riverbank for a moment and relax into the river of life. The current will take you further and further into the unknown washing away the self you believed yourself to be until you become this profound, beautiful, flowing river of life.

***

Marianne

The advice for my newly-awakened self, is something that in retrospect would have been of great value:

Stop. Take the time to smell the roses for a bit. Take the time to live the change in perspective that has occurred. Take the time to feel what this is for *you*. Become familiar with it. Don't go rushing off for validation or to teachers. Don't go rushing off with thoughts of completion and enlightenment. Awakening really *is* just the very beginning of the true spiritual journey. There will always be more of this Mystery to live and to deepen into. There will be time for teachers. There will be more pain and contraction to open to. But for now, just stop. Breathe. Take time out. Take time off work. For now, just live this simply into your days.

And stay humble. Always humble.

***

Chapter 3 – What advice would you give your newly-awakened self?

See Through

by
Amara

There comes a time when what we are
Begins to see through ...
Through the character
Through the situations
Through the sets
In the play we took for real
These constructs that made it all seem real
Once so solid, believable, certain
Become transparent, empty, weightless
Like armature with clay fallen away
There comes a time when what we are
Turns ... naturally ...
Just turns, to see what's Real
And falls into the Sweetness
Of This

***

Chapter 4

Identity

Stacy

The shift in experiencing identity is everything and nothing since awakening. This is why the Buddhists call it the 'gateless gate'. It looks like something right up until the moment you realize it is nothing, has always been nothing and will always be nothing.

This makes no sense at all if you haven't been there.

Because we are taught, conditioned and inculcated with this thought of and belief in identity, many will never consider questioning it and even those who consider it will often rebel, give up or run away from the idea that there is truly no self. And that is fine!

However, for those who do question identity and find none, there is nothing more peaceful or blissful to find in this world. I'd like to say that it's the whole point, but I don't even believe that any more. No one has to find that they don't exist, but if you're drawn to it, well, there is nothing to compare.

Paradoxically, we continue living, loving and interacting with seeming 'others', even after we wake up. I can't explain it and have found no one who can. It just is. 'Meaning' is a construct of the mind, of thinking. Back when, I thought meaning was the end all, be all, but not any more. Meaning is just more thinking and 'what is' is more than that, more than we can even talk about.

Sense of self comes and goes to the degree that we are looking at what is true and not at what is made up.

All aspects of identity: gender, sexual orientation, family roles, profession, membership in any group or club, astrological sign, or any personality profile of any kind? Meaningless stories. Fun, as long as they aren't used to separate. The story of separation from each other, from the

Chapter 4 – Identity

whole, is the original lie. Truth is one. There is only one. And even that, using words is a lie.

***

Ben

I am endless, boundless creation and I am Ben, a form of that creation that allows me to view and experience myself.

***

Richard

My initial awakening experiences coincided with a breakdown in my sense of identity. Prior to that, one of the first things I ever used the Internet for was to acquire a copy of René Descartes' *Meditations*. His *Cogito, ergo sum* ("I think, therefore I am") had provided me with what I felt was something solid to stand on. I knew I existed.

Then that solidity started to dissolve.

I turned 18 and technically became an adult. I was old enough not to have to lie about my age in pubs anyway. I was coming to the end of my school life and yet somehow felt I was the same as on my first day. I'd rather expected a more profound change to take place, and yet everything seemed like it had changed. I was a different person in most ways from when I was four, so what was this part that felt so consistent?

The next blow was the realisation of something so obvious it astounded me that I'd missed it. I was in school one morning bemoaning the fact I felt groggy from not getting enough sleep. Then it hit me how strange it was that this 'thinking thing' I took myself to be was so transient; it moved on the whims of chemicals or sleep. More than this, it actually disappeared altogether for several hours a day!

The final blow came later. My initial awakening experiences, although powerful, hadn't brought about any reflection on my sense of self, but as a result of starting meditation, I saw one day that it didn't exist. Descartes was wrong, or limited at least, there was no 'thinking thing' at the root of it all.

This was not a happy insight. Rather it felt like the rug of my painstaking philosophical efforts had been pulled out from under my feet. I was distraught! I don't remember it lasting however. I can't recall exactly what brought relief, but I suspect as I read more Zen I discovered that this was in fact supposed to be a virtue and not a vice.

There was an episode of depression that was kicked off through a later investigation of identity. I've mentioned it elsewhere in the book so I'll skip it here.

My experience of identity now is: if I sink within I experience a dissolution into a field of awareness that feels like it's 'me' on a transcendent level. Out of this field a stream of thoughts and feelings emerge which form my more superficial and transient sense of self.

I would like to finish by saying there's a lot of emphasis in spiritual circles on losing one's sense of identity and moving to a place of 'no-self' or identification only with that transcendent awareness. Personally I don't think this is the whole story. If you think about it, an actor expends a vast amount of time and effort going in the opposite direction, attempting to *take on* an identity. They can do this because they feel secure in being able to step back out of that persona once the play is over and know it wasn't really them (even if it leaves them changed in some way). Likewise, when we feel secure in our true identity, more freedom to play our character opens up.

***

Erick

I am Infinity. I am Light. I am Love.

I am a guy form New York who works a factory job and plays music for fun.

I am the flow of Infinity upon Itself.

I am Nothing.

***

Maureen

What is my identity?

That's such an interesting question. I am the vastness of the universe, the oneness of energy, expressing in this human form. Sometimes I remember one more than the other. Mostly living in human form is foregrounded, but the vastness is always there. Always

I have a sense of past lives, of other forms, human and not, which are more like ghostly filaments that float around me, sometimes drawing attention, mostly not. This affects my relationships with others, who may have been in relationship with me in other lives, in other forms.

There's a softness to it all, holding it all lightly, and behind that, a vast strength and power. That has not been explored yet. I am an explorer, more than anything.

> **Who Are We?**
> We are pseudopods
> of the great amoeba of energy
> source of all being.
> Extrusions of joy and creativity,
> we are pseudopodies dancing.

***

Kiran

When I look to myself to answer this question, I see two types of identity.

One is always deeply quiet with a sense of self that is vast, unlimited and inclusive of all contents; everything as is. In this mode there is no need, want/desire or conflict with what is, inside or out. There is no categorization of good or bad, right or wrong, only serenity and peace. I identify with this still, silent spaciousness.

However, I do view myself as an ordinary human form having opinions and also freedom from those opinions. I interact with the world normally and nothing seems out of the ordinary except that there is no solid ground from which to attack or be attacked; to give hurt or get hurt. (Saying 'no one is being hurt by my presence' could however be a false statement as only the one who gets hurt would know.)

However, both types somehow know how to work hand in hand naturally without a 'me' knowing when the hand changes. This is different from years ago (pre-awakening) when I was an ego entity fully attached and identified at a personal level, and being driven by beliefs and patterns.

***

Andrew

This one is huge and worthy of a book to itself. Well, actually there are probably a few hundred books on the topic of identity or ego and anything I can write here is nothing in comparison, so here goes nothing.

Ego is not a dirty word (apologies to Skyhooks for stealing their lyrics) and should not be killed. You cannot become whole by killing a part of yourself. Just understand it and work with it.

Ego is simply the process of identification. That's it, no more.

Once you truly understand that and see it in action in almost everything you do, then you realise how it has become so powerful and misunderstood. The process is there to protect you so it is designed to be powerful for your own safety. Beautiful isn't it?

Ego identifies your hand as yours and will stop you putting it into a flame. Ego will identify your thought as yours and will use it to help you navigate a safe path through life. This also is for the positives as well as the negatives. Ego will chase positives to enhance your life. Ego will tell you how good you are and encourage you to do things that make you feel good. Ego identifies your reputation as your reputation.

If you didn't have an ego you wouldn't be chasing enlightenment or reading this book. Give your ego a pat on your back. Ego will also identify you as enlightened. This will feel nice but may also prevent you from seeing the action of the ego in identifying this state as yours. That may be a blockage to true enlightenment. Just be aware of it and how it works. Once you know how your machine works it no longer controls you from your subconscious but it simply behaves in your conscious awareness.

The mind is a terrible master but a wonderful servant. I'm not sure who said that but the way to stop it being your master is to be aware of how it works.

***

Jennifer

Dathun
I am
the aspen trees, sky.
I dance the new snow silence,
Sing the dawn light

> on the faces of mountains.
> My heart kisses the cold wind
> I am nothing …
> and everything is me.
> Celebrating simplicity.
> Fiercely alive.

***

Marianne

Prior to awakening I spent some considerable time wondering about this 'thing' called 'identity'.

I recall a party when I was a teenager. It seemed that everyone 'knew who to be'; they knew how to be teenagers. They were playing roles of laughing, drinking, talking loudly, rebelling, flirting, boyfriend, girlfriend, pretty girl and comedian. But to me these didn't seem real; they were pretence, overlay. I didn't want to pretend. I was shocked that a couple of my close friends were acting in ways that I knew were quite contrary to the ways they would normally have behaved. I couldn't see the point of that. At many different times throughout my life, that same basic scenario played out.

Perhaps there was some fundamental 'lack' on my part … perhaps I hadn't been able to establish a strong-enough persona to 'believe in'. I don't know. But I did take on identities to some extent, particularly those of suffering, of seeking, and also of being a musician, an artist.

Perhaps a year or so before awakening, I had been inquiring quite deeply into 'identity'. Sexual identity, identity as a woman. What was it? As much as I looked within I could not find anything that could be classified as an identity. It was a strange thing. All I could come up with was an 'emptiness' underneath everything, so I assumed I had taken a wrong turn in my inquiries.

The awakening (as described in the preface) was actually a collapse of identity: I saw all the identities I had ever been (daughter, sufferer, partner, lover, musician) and knew without a doubt that I was none of them. Then, a couple of days later I expanded into my true identity and immediately 'knew' this as myself. It was what I had always been and it was blindingly obvious.

There are no words to describe what I am, what we all are … vastness, emptiness, Life, Thisness are okay. But still they point to 'something' and there is nothing to point to. There is no self. And yet, there is a verbing ... there is laughing, womaning, daughtering, walking, eating ... how can that be? I don't know. It's a mystery. And I'm completely okay with that.

There are times I catch sight of myself in a mirror and it is odd that the 'Lifing' has made this form that people look at and will think of as 'Marianne'.

***

Kathy

With a glimpse in the mirror, where eyes met reflected eyes, it was revealed or seen. The person I thought myself to be was a long series of layered beliefs and mind constructs of which none were real! Many of these beliefs were the cause of great and lifelong suffering. Laughter and tears arose as this truth was seen through.

A honeymoon period followed where mind became quite still and quiet.

Three and a half years later, life goes on, stories are sometimes created, yet they no longer carry the weight or seriousness that they did in the past, and no longer can be believed as ultimate reality.

***

Lisa

The identity before awakening was a tangled-up bundle of memories of past experiences, pent-up feelings, thoughts and concepts. The more I untangled this mess (a process that included therapy, releasing feelings, inquiring into thoughts and concepts, and finally, for a few years, just accepting whatever was left) the less of this identity there was. Until that final little strand of tangle snapped I didn't have a clue that I was actually 'undoing myself'.

At first, after awakening, there was nothing, which was a little scary, or unfamiliar. But after a while, when I got used to the silence and emptiness, there was Being. It's not "I think, therefore I am", or "I feel, therefore I am", or "I perceive, therefore I am". It's I am, therefore I think, feel and perceive. We usually identify with the tangle of past stuff and the thoughts, feelings and perceptions, but the beingness comes first. Everything, including the body, is secondary to Being.

Now, there is everything there was before awakening – thoughts, feelings and personality – but there is no 'little man' sitting in the head or anywhere else, who pulls the strings. I don't have a 'sense of self' anymore. There is a beingness and stuff arises somehow and flows through it; it appears and dissipates. You could say that instead of a sense of self there is a sense of being. 'I' don't have a good or bad self-esteem anymore. I don't feel worthy or unworthy, important or unimportant. I *am*, which is neither good nor bad, worthy or unworthy, important or unimportant. It just is.

This is the way my social identities are felt at the deepest level too. On a more superficial level, I am a 'mother' to my daughter and I do the stuff mothers do. But on a deeper level, we are two specks of Being connecting through, or sharing, our beingness.

***

Michaela

Oh God, I have no idea anymore! Smile.
Well, I am definitely not what I think!

***

Timothy

For about a year after enlightenment I didn't have any sense of identity. Then slowly, and somewhat awkwardly, my previous conditioning came forward when I needed to act in the world. I appeared to others to be my prior self in most ways but I felt completely different, more expansive and less of an individual.

Now, 37 years later, I feel as though I can easily use what I've found to be my inborn personality. Prior conditioning rarely comes up but when it does it doesn't last long, and it seldom appears more than once. It's like I know the individual that is present, and that person is just a part of the bigger picture – the best of both realizations.

***

Silent allowance

by
Kiran

Silent allowance is the vivid and unchallenged answer
appearing gently to the question what am I.
The pull and gravitation of this Silent allowance,
nothing less than marvel.
Unimaginable amazing miracle
turning a tiny little spark into all engulfing fire.
Shedding the old skin, reeling wheeling and moving
through gateless gates of this Silent allowance.
Mystery of its quality of no quality
yet felt and sensed with undeniable astounding clarity.
Engulfing, rerouting every conscious speck
into its silent abode resting into effortlessness.
The melting of awe, amazement, bliss,
gratefulness or devotion and love
into formless nothingness.
The ultimate formless, silent allowance.

***

Chapter 5

Myths and misconceptions about awakening and enlightenment

Michaela

You could say, that anyone who has not had a 'personal' experience of awakening has misconceptions about it. I certainly had. We cannot know what we have not tasted. In spite of always being it, only by totally leaving behind every mind concept and idea, is the naked truth revealed. Afterwards it is beautiful to see those spiritual concepts in a new light and recognize what they were pointing to. I loved suddenly understanding the truth hidden in symbols, myths, legends and religions. What an awe to see how many had arrived at that place behind the 'me' curtains and what a joy to recognize them.

One of the most common misconceptions and also a reason why many don't claim their inborn divinity, is the idea that it is something very exclusive reserved for special kind of 'saints', not ordinary people.

Also the seeking mode itself and planning to find God/Truth in the future, whether in the afterlife, the next life or just on a good day, is a misconception that keeps many from not recognizing the simplicity of it.

***

Jennifer

The biggest misconception about enlightenment is that it is only for the special ones: the spiritual ones who renounce everything and have been meditating in caves for years, the ones who did all of the right things in past lives as well as this one, the ones who are part of a particular tradition and, the one which was hardest for me to swallow, only men. I was in Thailand in the forest on my first ten-day silent meditation retreat and the Buddhist nuns and monks were teaching this. I have no idea why awakening happens but I do know that women are quite capable of awakening.

***

Ben

The biggest misconceptions …

That there would, in some way, be an 'end' to the process rather than it being ongoing.

That it would prove my worth, and only the 'worthy' could possibly hope for it.

That it would be so obvious to everyone else that I had 'got there' that they'd be like, "Wow, he's so wise, I really respect him!"

Basically, for obvious reasons, everything my ego thought about it/hoped for from it, was a misconception. Haha.

***

Marianne

- Awakening or enlightenment is only for other people, not for an ordinary woman living in suburbia.
- Awakening and enlightenment imply some sort of perfection, rather than it simply being the natural state.
- There is an end point or a sense of finality, after which life is forever easy or perfect. Although seeking *does* end, the deepening never ends.
- Awakening is the end of the spiritual journey. In reality it is just the beginning.
- I'll be able to pick and choose what to keep and what to discard. I had no choice in the matter and I didn't care that I had no choice. It is total destruction.
- The mind/ego can know Truth. No it can't! Ever.
- I'll have to become a teacher. I think this stems from the fact that the most visible awakened/enlightened people are teachers. There are few other role models for awakening. I hope this book will address that to some degree.

- I'll be special. It is actually seen that I am completely *un*-special.
- There will be a continuous state of bliss. Bliss was irrelevant.
- Spiritual 'experiences' or *siddhis* are somehow important. Spiritual experiences have nothing to do with awakening. I used to think that if I had the most amazing spiritual experiences I was somehow further along the path. I tried to develop and exaggerate these *siddhis*. They were fun but proved to be a hurdle.

***

Timothy

I feel very fortunate that I didn't get 'taken-in' by any hype or ideas about enlightenment. I was taught to never believe anything I hear, and only half of what I see. I definitely didn't trust any description; others' stories didn't hold much weight for me because I know everyone is different. Besides that, memory is often subject to inaccuracies. I figured I'd just find out for myself.

Of course I knew that something had happened for me but I wasn't sure if it was *the* enlightenment that others had alluded too. I didn't take long to realize that it must be enlightenment, but even if it wasn't, I didn't care. I knew I'd never, in all eternity, want to go back to the way I was before, and that was good enough for me no matter how it was defined.

***

Stacy

Myths, expectation and beliefs about awakening. That you will:

- get rid of ego, I or self
- relieve boredom
- become 'special'
- escape from your life
- achieve some 'high' or altered state of consciousness
- attain some kind of esoteric knowledge
- think the 'right' thoughts
- become a righteous, good, moral, better or superior person
- have eternal happiness or peace of mind

- escape feelings or strong emotions
- fill some perceived emptiness
- solve emotional problems
- have perfect relationships
- get rid of depression or other emotional issues
- resolve conflicts
- attain perfect health
- change, stop or get rid of thoughts
- eradicate some sort of story of self
- acquire wealth or possessions
- improve some self
- become free of physical pain

***

Richard

For me, the essence of awakening is the realisation that I am not a person.

By contrast, my biggest misconception about awakening was the belief that I am not a person.

***

Lisa

Many times my path progressed somewhat backwards; I was doing or experiencing something, or was transformed in a way that I knew nothing about and had no intellectual understanding of. Sometimes I wasn't even conscious of a process in motion at all, until it was completed. I guess you could compare it to a caterpillar crawling around and munching away on a leaf, not having a clue about some strange beings called 'butterflies', nor having any interest in becoming one. And when my little caterpillar-self became a bit more conscious, it sure picked up a lot of misconceptions about what becoming and being a butterfly actually meant. No wonder, because the difference is huge and impossible to imagine from within the caterpillar perspective.

One thing I mistakenly imagined, was that becoming a butterfly would make me - the caterpillar - special. Needless to say, the caterpillar 'me' first turned into an unpalatable mush, before disappearing altogether, so not much specialness there!

Chapter 5 – Myths and misconceptions about awakening and enlightenment

Second, I thought being a butterfly must be magic, and that they were some kind of supernatural beings with supernatural powers. Flying does understandably seem like something supernatural to a caterpillar, but from the butterfly perspective, it's perfectly natural and fits within the ordinary physical laws of nature. A butterfly might seem supernatural to a caterpillar, but it is simply a different kind of being, a perfectly ordinary one.

Next, I thought butterflies didn't have problems. But of course they do; they're just not the same *kind* of problems. A caterpillar sees the world from the ground and so only sees a little bit of the world; even though they seem like a caterpillar's whole world at the time, its problems are small. From up in the air, a butterfly sees a bigger picture, a larger perspective. But even if they see a lot more from this larger perspective, it's not only beauty and wonders they see. They also see clouds gathering on the horizon. They also see more ugliness and danger and pain.

I haven't been a butterfly very long, so there are still many things for me to explore in the butterfly world. And it might very well be that this isn't the last transformation into a different kind of being. Maybe next time, I'll become something even stranger and more wondrous … something I can't even imagine yet.

***

Andrew

Enlightenment is a myth. There I said it.

If you think it is a 'thing' you can achieve or obtain then you will spend your life chasing your tail. Many people do that and they really seem to enjoy the chase and anybody that tries to stop the chasing will have hell to pay.

One of the biggest myths about the state of enlightenment is that somehow it will reach down into your DNA and change everything about you. It is not a miracle cure. I know people who desperately want to be enlightened but at the same time are afraid of becoming 'nice' and not enjoying their life any more. The reality is different.

***

Kiran

One of the myths or misconceptions I recognized after awakening is with regard to the 'seeker', the one who searches for enlightenment or further improvement. It is not the seeker who awakens, rather, the seeker disappears. The seeker turns out not to be real at all. The disappearance of the seeker leaves a great spacious quietness in which all old beliefs and patterns (of the egoic entity) get settled.

Another misconception is the realization that this awakened/enlightened being is not in a state of perpetual joy and bliss. In fact, I realized a state of sheer void/nothingness exists which is, at the same time, extremely alive and intimate; more intimate than the skin on the flesh. This alive nothingness is beyond even quietness or deep inner silence; it is beyond differences of duality, totally undivided, unlabelled. This seems the realm from where form and its manifestations arise. In this true way of living, 'wow' type spiritual experiences don't carry any more weight than a painful experience; both are part of the moment unfolding itself. There exists a misunderstanding about the high value of spiritual experiences; this is because of our labelling based upon categorization and differentiation.

There was a big childhood myth I held, that once I met God I would know it all; I'd become all-knowing like God. In my current reality, I see myself to be clueless and not-knowing, although, as the moment unfolds, I never fail to respond exactly as required or as the situation demands. I surprise myself when I experience that and wonder where this knowledge comes from. It strengthens the trust in intelligent awareness.

I feel the journey or path, if it can be called that, is all about dropping our misconceptions which can indeed restrict and choke us. This opening of ourselves is really a continuous journey of liberation; a never-ending awakening with no destination.

***

Elizabeth

I became obsessed with enlightenment in my late teens. In college I read everything I could find on unraveling the mysteries of our human depths. Most of what I read was about swamis who performed magical feats such as walking on water, levitating, producing *malas* (meditation

Chapter 5 – Myths and misconceptions about awakening and enlightenment

beads) out of thin air … I came to believe that gifts (*siddhis*) such as telekinesis, telepathy, clairvoyance and clairaudience were par for the course for enlightenment.

I was born with psychic gifts and did end up with a guru who seemed to display some gifts. However, I also spoke with several others who were awake who had very few or none of these. I was disappointed at this. I had thought that I would finally find my ilk, so to speak, by spending time with these awakened individuals.

However, by the time I discovered that most others weren't like this, it didn't matter as much to me. While my personal journey did involve the *siddhis*, and some have told me that these *can* naturally occur with deepening, it ceases to be important. In fact, as things have unraveled more and more, at certain stages it has proven to be bit of a hindrance. If it had all been removed from my experience, I suspect that things would've gone along much more smoothly (and quickly).

Although I still possess some of the *siddhis*, I'm more centered and more shrouded in the essence of awareness. I probably see/hear/feel more than most, but it's gradually become less intense. The more I sink down and ground as the Absolute, the more it somehow loosens within me and dissolves into Itself.

I know it is a process. I know I am not done. Perhaps the awakened teachers and friends I spoke with who do not have *siddhis* are not done, either. Perhaps it really is a part of awakening and it just happened in a topsy-turvy way for me.

What I have learned from the whole experience (and the initial dashed expectations) is that having psychic awareness just isn't that important when one is in the flow of awareness.

***

Kathy

Before awakening:

There was a belief that awakening was only for the special chosen few. I never thought it was possible for someone like me. If by chance awakening happened, I was sure all my problems would disappear, I would have to become a spiritual teacher, money would no longer be needed, health issues would vanish, patience and unconditional love would be my temperament, there would be an eternal sense of peace at all times thus leaving no room for anger or sadness, and I would have great spiritual knowledge and ultimate understanding of life.

The reality:

Life is incredibly ordinary, more ordinary than before. There is no interest in becoming a teacher of any kind. Problems still arise, but they are not taken as seriously. Money is still needed, and I still need to work for it. Health issues still need to be addressed, yet there is less attachment to the outcome. There is more peace and acceptance, less reactivity, and more capacity to feel all feelings without labelling or judgement. There is no knowledge, only direct experience and a fascination with the magic of life.

***

Chapter 5 – Myths and misconceptions about awakening and enlightenment

Silence of the Forest

Photo by Michaela

Chapter 6

What has been awakening's greatest gift and/or surprise?

Silvia

Awakening's greatest gift has been dropping the search for life's meaning and for the ultimate Truth or God. These questions were with me since I was about twelve. Sometimes the meaninglessness of existence had felt unbearable. Now, it is not that a meaning has been discovered but that there has been a shift of perspective which has made the question fall away.

In a sense, as a human, I could say that the most profound meaning of life is recognizing everything is God. This can happen initially as a profound 'seeing', but then it has to be recognized moment by moment. This is why the process is endless.

***

Maureen

The greatest surprise was stepping through the doorway of awakening, as Adyashanti calls it, and seeing the nature of the universe. Holy shit!

The greatest gift is knowing myself as oneness on the one hand, and in human form on the other, and holding the knowledge of both at the same time, like two hands clasping.

***

Chapter 6 – What has been awakening's greatest gift and/or surprise?

Richard

The greatest gift is simple. It is an antidote to nihilism. Not an intellectually reasoned antidote (although that may be there too) but a direct continuous experience that life is so very very meaningful.

Upon this foundation, all else can be built.

The greatest surprise has to be the exact same thing – that God is good and life is so very very meaningful. Who would ever have predicted that!

If I were to go for a bonus greatest gift and surprise, it is that it did not consume my individuality, as certain spiritual systems had threatened it would.

***

Erick

Other than the complete inversion of every sense of reality, I have been surprised by the very 'outward' direction my activities have taken.

I have not become a contemplative recluse wallowing in bliss, rather I have addressed the weak points in my personality by flowing into the activities presented to me, with 100% of my mind and body. This has included a massive expansion of my social circle through my work as a semi-professional musician, and diving deep into manufacturing engineering as the general manager of a small defense manufacturer (we make windows, not bombs).

In both areas I am flourishing because nothing is holding me back from being totally present. The takeaway is that whatever your expectations may have been, you will flow into where you belong, wherever that may be and your natural gifts will be allowed to flourish.

***

Kiran

The greatest gift has been the realization of this *Trueness* and *Oneness* and the door that this opened for me. I am always surprised by the continuous refinement process: for example, how can subtlety become *more* subtle and refined? How is it that there is always *more* that unfolds; *more* to be included and embodied? How is freedom to be understood as an ever-expanding process? How is it that lines of division can disappear, compounding the present emptiness, silence and stillness?

A different source of wisdom is revealed to be the gate that allows anything and everything life brings to pass, regardless of what it is. Anything that comes in the way or doesn't pass easily, is only about 'me' and 'my' preference.

***

Lisa

The greatest surprise for me was awakening itself. I didn't believe in it, or seek it. I looked for it for a little while, many years before it happened, but decided it was a fairy tale or a hoax made up by people wanting an easy job as a guru. Then, I forgot all about it.

And many years later it suddenly happened. What I always thought was 'me', just quietly snapped and disappeared. And I was like, "Hey, where did Lisa go!? And what is this here instead!?" That was quite a surprise!

The greatest gift for me has been the peace. It's what I always wanted, even though I'd given up on ever finding it. But it was real. To finally have peace from all the turmoil of egoic life is priceless. Not pleasure, not bliss, not joy, not even happiness, just peace: the peace that passeth understanding. And the absence of fear. There is no fear of people any more. There is no fear of life, nor death. There is no fear of failure, nor success. There is no fear of love, nor lack of love. No fear of pleasure or of pain. No fear of being, nor fear of ceasing to be.

***

Timothy

The greatest gift of enlightenment for me is the courage and freedom to venture out into the world and explore the things that deep down inside I had always wanted to do.

For instance, I started learning to play guitar when I was eight years old and always wanted to be a professional musician. Post-enlightenment I became a solo singer, songwriter and recording artist. I have written and recorded three studio albums (CDs) and I've performed more than a thousand times at over two hundred locations around the country. I even did some stand-up comedy and had twelve professional appearances in Chicago. I don't think this would have happened prior to enlightenment because I could barely speak on stage much less perform my own songs.

***

Marianne

The greatest surprise is that the sages knew what they were talking about! We really *are* Truth. In every moment. And it *continues* to surprise me. There are times I live into a teaching I previously hadn't *quite* understood, and I think, "Oh WOW they *were* RIGHT!"

But there is also the surprise that this is possible for an ordinary human being. I had truly thought that enlightenment was a fairy story, not a real-life possibility.

Greatest gift. The end of the search. Peace. Home. Oneness and Love. And rather than being something special and other-worldly, realizing that these 'qualities' are the very essence of our natural state.

***

Jennifer

The greatest surprise was how my entire cosmology changed. Prior to awakening, I saw God or The Divine as a separate source I would bring into myself, in order to create or heal with. After awakening, I saw myself and everything *as* God/The Divine. Everything was sacred and precious. All things were already perfect as they were.

Right now the thing which comes to mind as the greatest gift of awakening are the moments of direct experience: truly experiencing all that is unfolding in a moment, just as it is.

***

Georgette

Biggest surprise? The shift from separation into unity happened but there wasn't anyone to notice. Like falling asleep on a car ride and waking up hundreds of miles away from where you started without a memory of any journey.

Also surprising and a gift to feel this PEACE ... while at the same time empathetically feeling so much through the body-mind as sensation, changing like the weather, while the flame in the center remains steady and undisturbed by calm or storm. Actually, everything is surprising. That anything IS. And everything is a Gift. It is a surprise and a gift to be here tuning into the face of love as it participates in this book.

***

Kathy

Time was my portal. Upon the realization that time was completely a concept and not real, it was astounding to enter the place of timelessness. From this place it was so clear that 'I' was never born and could never die.

Upon realizing that the world as I knew it was built on beliefs which were ultimately not real, there was freedom.

The greatest gift of all was there was nothing more to search for. Seeking stopped.

***

Michaela

The greatest gift that I sensed immediately was TRUST. Only after I felt it, was I aware that I had never known it before. I had known hope, I had known belief, but only in the Now that opened in the awakening experience, did I meet real Trust.

After that came a very profound YES to life. It was so strong, that if I could, I would have changed my name to "Yes", as that was the only name that was true to what I was experiencing. Following that, was GRATITUDE. Like trust, it was new. Or qualitatively different to any glimpse of gratitude I might have felt before. Here was seemingly no reason and yet *all* was the reason; existence itself was the reason. There were tears of joy to see the beauty that was always here, but only now, perceived as a miracle.

Surprise ... Well, 'I' did not imagine it would be so simple and so 'me-less'. Up until then, my identity had been built on a story of emotions, but now there were no emotions. At the very moment that the all-encompassing profound peace took over, the personal projections collapsed and were erased. I imagined awakening as some kind of blissful

Chapter 6 – What has been awakening's greatest gift and/or surprise?

ecstasy, but there was nothing like that. It was only clarity and peace. All was accomplished in that instant. There was no more to add, no more to change or to strive for. It was a total accomplishment itself.

***

Amara

The greatest gift is Peace, pure and simple.

The greatest surprise is that peace can deepen infinitely. Okay, I don't know if it's the GREATEST surprise, but I no longer hold the perception of awakeness as some static state. Maybe the greatest surprise is how dynamic the absolute can appear. Everything is included and it's ever fresh and new.

***

Andrew

Greatest surprise....

It was nothing like I thought it would be.

Greatest gift....

It was nothing like I thought it would be.

There is an old story that seeking enlightenment is like riding an ox in search for an ox. I like to add that it is like riding the ox backwards, and then when you think you've found it you lean forward and give it a kiss.

When you have truly found it the ox disappears and the search is over. There are no more questions. I thought awakening would be the answer to my questions. Each time I found an answer a new question arose. My life was full of questions but now there are none. There are plenty of answers but I realize I don't actually find answers. All I can do is make up a question for an answer that is already there. No more searching, no more stress over finding the right answer. If I want to question, that's fine. Contentment.

Nothing like I thought it would be.

***

Stacy

Peace.

When I was *A Course in Miracles* student for 25 years and still had some kind of belief in a god, albeit a panentheistic one ('God in all things', a term Matthew Fox, the priest, coined), I used to pray for the peace of God. No more. Peace showed up - or rather I made myself available to it.

Peace is.

That happened during my longest phase of intense bliss in 2007. I date my awakening from April 2007 when I was privileged to attend what turned out to be a one-time meditation workshop. I sometime still use the pointers I learned there, both for myself and my Liberation Unleashed clients. My teacher did not want to do the guru thing and stopped teaching. SO grateful I was where I was, when I was.

He offered a lot of pointers to reality-based thinking. Liberation Unleashed did that, as well. Their definition of Actual or Direct Experience was a huge refinement of my cognition about (*waves hands in grand opening gesture*) all of THIS.

***

Ben

The biggest gift was reconnecting with the sense of peace that is ever-present deep within us, whatever the life circumstances. I always suspected that maybe the concept of 'true inner peace' was just a sales pitch for Buddhism but thankfully it is actually part of what we fundamentally are.

***

Chapter 6 – What has been awakening's greatest gift and/or surprise?

Finding beauty in a thistle patch

Photos by Maureen

Chapter 7

What has been awakening's greatest challenge?

Kathy

Finding heaven on earth then realizing that the messier human part is also included.

Walking in unknown terrain without a map, compass, GPS or guide.

Learning to love my human self.

Letting go of the stories and beliefs of what I had believed awakening was supposed to look like.

Learning how to keep one foot in each world at the same time.

Realizing everything is included, not just the perceived good, but also the shadow side of myself, others, and the world.

***

Amara

One challenge of awakening has been the impossibility of sharing this revelation with others in my life. An even greater challenge is having such a different perspective on myself and the world and re-learning how to relate with others from this perspective. There was no longer a desire to commiserate, complain or resist what was happening around me – the usual ways that people find connection. I mostly stood silent as people tried to find their way into a conversation with me.

I naturally want to freely share of myself, but learned early on the inevitability of the blank, disconnected stare of someone who wasn't ready for this message. In the beginning it was heartbreaking. Five and a half years in and I'm still learning discrimination with regard to when to talk about it and when not to, and just how much to say or write.

Chapter 7 – What has been awakening's greatest challenge?

My teacher says that to share the Truth with someone who isn't ready to receive it, is an insult to Truth. It's challenging, because it's so very simple! SO very simple. And yet, it just isn't shareable with maybe 98% of the population on the planet. A respect and love for individuals right where they are in their unfolding is one of the greatest lessons learned. And there's also a tremendous admiration for the masters who can offer the message using allegory or other pedagogical tools and speak to all levels at once with a transmission of Love and Presence.

As for the sense of alienation when wanting to relate with others, I've learned that if I speak from and as That Presence I Am, to Presence as other, all is well. Any suffering in this regard was the result of coming from that sense of a separate personal self.

Of course, all of this is aside from the relentless wave-upon-wave of conditioning, beliefs and stored trauma that arose to be seen and released which pounded and carved away at the shores of my sense of a separate personal self for the first two years – and the five-plus years re-aligning 'my life'! Yeah.

***

Lisa

Biggest challenge so far is that it's also a beginning and not an end, that I haven't 'arrived' anywhere and probably never will, and that there are still many lessons to learn and challenges to meet. Oh, and that there won't be any fanfares or Nobel prizes for being 'enlightened'. It would have been nice to get at least a little itsy bitsy teenie weenie fanfare, but the universe says "No!"

***

Marianne

There have been numerous challenges along the way.

One of the most deeply felt challenges was languaging. Not just the languaging of the Wordless, which is in itself difficult, but the fact that I felt no movement at all to language, to talk, to have opinions, and to share conversations in the socially accepted ways. Words felt narrow and heavy and loaded with meanings I could no longer partake of or even understand. But over time, I have come to see words as a tool. Sometimes I choose to use them and sometimes I don't. And yet, many relationships have fallen away as a result.

The return of conditioning after a two-year 'honeymoon' period was a challenge. I didn't want to go back to therapy and rehash past trauma; I had had enough of that. But I knew it was essential that some of this material be revisited; it was from the broader perspective of awakening that it could find its true healing.

But there was also a point, when I needed to let go of any notion that there was a 'person' here, with a history, who needed therapy. Therapy had been a big part of my journey and much had been worked through prior to awakening. But now I could see that the mind would continue to come up with never-ending 'stuff'. I had to make an internal switch. The 'stuff' didn't need more therapy, it needed to be surrendered. Just as our heart beats, our lungs breathe, so does our mind continue to produce an endless string of thoughts with almost no substance or relevance to reality. "There is no true thought" was my mantra. But thought is immensely powerful and over and over I found myself caught. The challenge was to stop. Stop everything. Surrender everything into Mystery and freedom. Always a work in progress.

***

Ben

Moving from knowledge into consistent practice of that knowledge; understanding into consistent being of that understanding. Old habits die hard.

And a second challenge: the concept of eternity. When I'm back in identified thought, my mind can't cope with what the reality of existing forever (and being continually conscious of it) might actually entail. I end up thinking about being eternally alone and feeling it would be hellish. Then I realize that this is a separated and human way of viewing it, and go back to trusting the feeling I feel when not identified. Still, it freaks me out when it comes up.

***

Chapter 7 – What has been awakening's greatest challenge?

Stacy

I am extremely extroverted. It is challenging not to be able to connect and talk with other people about how things are. It just kills me. And not. Especially my partner.

Even 'spiritual' people are kind of asleep about all of this until they're not. My very least favorite conversation is the one that ends with the other person saying, "Well that's your truth. It doesn't have to be mine." Truth really is global.

***

Kiran

My greatest challenge is navigating the paradox I experience between entanglement and freedom, suffocating and breathing.

Periodically, I find myself entangled in the 'dream' or 'identified state'. Whereas the heaviness of the surface is unbearable, the deepest connection is intact and alive.

As refinement and embodiment continue, although each little speck is more visible and every deviation is louder, the inner light and clarity is actually intensified. Greater transparency reveals that this is such a being and becoming ... a true paradox.

This is such-ness in its working. This is how the truth of awakening is embracing me. Embodiment doesn't seem to have any finish line.

***

Marieke

My biggest struggle in awakening has been extreme loneliness, and the fear of being alone and never connecting again. It kept me from surrendering more into the path, even though I knew it was clearly not in my control.

From one moment to the next, my experience of the world and everything in it had completely changed and I felt unable to communicate. At first words literally hurt, because they were so far from the immediate truth. This passed, but the feeling of being unable to communicate with others stayed for months and years. Nobody understands what is happening to you and when you try to explain, people don't get it. I wanted to be alone because it was too hard for me to act 'normal' according to the social norm, but this also left me very lonely at times. I felt alienated from my friends because they still had their 'old' interests and mine had almost all fallen away, so we had nothing in common any more.

***

Maureen

What has been awakening's greatest challenge?

Pre-existing health issues have been magnified, as a constant fatigue. It feels as if the universe wants me quiet, with lots of time in bed - flat time, I call it. The depth of fatigue is hard on me, it's hard on my family, and it's hard on relationships with friends. It's also a beautiful gift - the gift of silence, stillness, and depth.

This process is hard on relationships in other ways. As I work to clear my own emotional baggage, I see more clearly, and am unable to play dysfunctional games any more. Dysfunctional relationships fall away, or, as with my childhood family, are deeply strained, as I no longer respond in the old family patterns. This is another gift. I don't do dysfunction anymore, and that's a daily joy.

***

Georgette

Greatest challenge 'so far': for a couple of years I felt unplugged from the life force. Physical vitality and any motivation to create or contribute diminished to a very low ebb. This was a shocking change for someone who'd lived a life of constant mission, creative expression and giving. It seemed Life had come to an end but there was nothing wrong. Nothing had the meaning it once had and previous sources of comfort and stability became inaccessible, or the energy it would take to reach out just wasn't there.

It was challenging to keep doing all the activities required for a functional life and yet, somehow, everything was accomplished miraculously ... even more beautifully than ever before but there was some anxiety in the not-knowing-how.

Chapter 7 – What has been awakening's greatest challenge?

Another challenge was the inability to express this radical shift of perception of self and reality to my closest friends. The loneliness expressed by others here was, and at times still is, an echo. Also, the limitation of ego function in this human system and in others became extremely obvious and all I could see was the never ending human stream as patterns patterning.

***

Silvia

Awakening's greatest challenge is that there is no way you can avoid anything that comes up. Old patterns, old traumas ... everything is exposed. The intensity of 'difficult' emotions seems unbearable to the everyday self. Yet they come up to be seen with compassion ... and to be included ... because everything is made of what I am.

This was certainly not what I had imagined before experiencing the big shift, nor even for the few months afterwards when I experienced total freedom. I didn't know then that conditionings such as identities, beliefs and traumas, can hide in dark corners. It is challenging to be patient and give the process TIME ... particularly as I had seen that ultimately time does not exist. It is challenging to see that what is known deeply is not automatically translated into everyday life.

It is also challenging to interact with people, particularly family. In spite of knowing we are all the One, there is sometimes the feeling that there is no common ground any more. Sometimes words come out of my mouth that people can't understand, and I can see that they are bored, envious or even angry, particularly if they are not interested in Truth. So many friendships fall away.

***

Erick

- Slipping and sliding, as the conceptual groundwork of my worldview was pulverized.
- Reaching for a branch on the cliffside as I tumbled in freefall, yet not falling at all.

- Looking for fellow climbers falling alongside me to ask of them their thoughts.
- Accepting the guidance of a tumbler who had landed.
- And, finally, giving up my 'awakening' for completeness.

***

Jennifer

After awakening, I saw myself and everything as God/The Divine. All things were already perfect as they were. This also simultaneously made everything extremely ordinary and took away a lot of motivation for action. The concept of 'me' and any personal wants or desires became insignificant. I had no idea what to do. Nothing made sense. Everything in my life had been built on a foundation of achievement and improvement, but now that was pointless because nothing needed to be done or changed. The loss of my God, motivation and the magical experiences attained through bliss-chasing broke my heart and brought with it so much grief and confusion. Few people understood what I was going through. The feeling of isolation as a result of this was deeply painful.

Another challenge was the sheer terror of feeling like I did not exist and had no personal agency because life just happened regardless of me or my will. I know the mind or ego can play tricks to turn the idea of pure awareness into something bad or insignificant as an attempt to fight the process of awakening. It wants to continue to exist and works hard to destroy that which it thinks will destroy it. I could not meditate on my own for years because of this unbearable feeling of terror and panic, so I attended lots of silent retreats. Sitting in silence with others felt 'right' and a lot less lonely.

A fleshing-out process of my relationship to it all is still happening, even though it has been years.

***

Michaela

After the realization nothing seemed a challenge. Whatever happened, I only felt compassion as the answer. I enjoyed a state of total innocence. Everything felt perfect and effortless, even situations that might be seen as a problem for most people around me.

Chapter 7 – What has been awakening's greatest challenge?

The big challenge came later, after perhaps two years of living in this effortless state of joy, purity and peace. One day, pollution came into the system and the old drama showed up. I knew it was not me, that it was not true, that it was not good for anything, and yet it seemed to grab me. The more I tried to escape it, the more I got involved. Of course, "Whatever you resist, persists!" That sudden loss of the precious world made me fall into its direct opposite, self-hate and depression. There was again a bad guilty 'me' who had not succeeded in maintaining the new heaven. And I even started to doubt that awakening itself is the whole truth. What if it was just an illusion of escape? The pain felt real and I could not deny it.

It passed, but now I knew, it can actually happen: there is no permanent guarantee of not falling out and gliding into that mind-made turbulence.

As disappointing as it felt, this was also a good experience. It took me down from the honeymoon and back to 'work', learning humbly how to integrate the two dimensions within, the timeless and the human.

And the challenge is still here, simply to stay alert.

***

A Little Story

by
Silvia

Here is a little story I wrote for my daughter quite some time ago. It is dedicated to all those who, like me, still have identifications being burnt and wake up at night with fire in their chest:

" ... in the darkness of the night, sitting by the light of the fire which revealed the shadow of every illusion, the young woman asked the old wise man what Love was.
And by the elderly man she was told that Love is No-thing disguised in all possible ways.
The woman was sitting very close to the bonfire ... and in a flash, before she could actually reflect on the old man's words, without anyone being able to prevent her, she was swallowed by the flames.
Everything happened in an instant and in the utmost silence. The fire flashed more alive than ever and an echo reverberated in the mountains.
The story tells that some of those present swore to have caught a clear precise sound in the midst of that rumble, shouting and sighing:
"th...a...n...k...y...o...u...u...u..."
And while, around the fire, the whole village was desperate, the old wise man smiled."

***

Chapter 8

Languaging, communication and words

Andrew

Ha ha! Words are so hard I have given up trying to use them. I have learnt the hard way that you cannot describe the indescribable. The simplest analogy I use is to ask you to describe the taste of ice cream and chocolate topping so I can taste what you tasted. There is no language for taste. The best we can do is point to it, hence the old saying not to mistake the finger pointing to the moon for the moon itself. If I've tasted it before there will be a recognition of what it is and we can discuss the flavours and textures and smells. But we still can't taste it the way the other tastes it.

Short answer: People will either understand so there is no reason to tell them, or they will have no concept so there is no reason to tell them. I still try, and I guess one bonus is there is less frustration when people don't get it. I just move on.

***

Ben

I found it very hard to communicate at the start, especially communicating this great revelation. I don't feel much difficulty any more, not because I've found the words, but because I've found specific definitions to be increasingly irrelevant. I also have no desire to 'convert' anyone any more. I might offer advice, but I generally avoid using spiritual language as it puts a lot of people off.

It's not particularly surprising that people don't want to hear about it. Imagine a great TV series and someone is enjoying episode 4. But you have seen episode 10, the season finale, and you start telling them all the plot twists. Then you ask them what they think it all means and what they think is coming up in Season 2 ... it would be understandably annoying! Hahaha. And to stretch this analogy a little further ... if you come across someone watching episode 4 it might actually be a good opportunity to watch it again with them, and remind yourself what was in it. With the knowledge of what's to come later you might see things you missed first time around!

Being understood externally is nice sometimes, but largely irrelevant in the grander scheme. I seek groups of people who share this interest, so if I want to dip in and discuss something, I'm not imposing myself.

***

Jennifer

I have had a difficult time talking about my experience and the shift in perspective which arose out of it. People often think they understand what I am saying based on their point of reference but then when they share a little more I realize that they actually don't. I don't know how to respond when after a few attempts of clarifying, they think I am talking about something completely different than what I am trying to communicate. I usually just let the conversation go. Perhaps better discernment about when and how to share would be wise on my part. I trust that we all know 'this' because we are 'this' but speaking to it can be challenging to say the least.

But there have also been many who do understand and they have been a blessing along the way.

***

Erick

I can't view others as not awake. I struggled with this at first. I was almost desperate to find others who shared my vision, to the point where any slight indication of awakeness from another made me jump into assuming they were fully awakened. Further conversations generally led me to a different conclusion which I would arrive at fairly reluctantly. At the core of this behavior was a deep perception that it is only awakeness that can speak through anyone. Any consciousness in any being is *the* consciousness, there is no other, and though the person may be acting as if shrouded in limitations, they are, in fact, pure Liberation.

It has taken me a while to grapple with this 'understanding vs. perception' dilemma. Even writing about it for this book has helped me to clarify what it is I am doing. I feel now that the only way to resolve it is to speak directly to the awakeness in others. This both respects their supreme status and eliminates the barriers that my mind might put up by distinguishing between the awakened and the pre-awakened. It also enlivens that level within them, which is probably the best thing I could offer anyone. Trying to translate this experience into common terms only leaves me dissatisfied and feeling like I am underscoring, rather than passing through, interpersonal barriers. So, I really try not to think about any distinction at all, rather perceiving another's nature directly and letting Truth speak for itself. The joy and love that can pass silently between eyes is the deepest form of communication. Attempted descriptions of the indescribable are just stones in the road.

***

Kiran

With respect to 'languaging', it's relatively easier to talk with people who already possess this 'understanding' or who are either seeking or have moved beyond seeking. For those who are living this dream as their only and entire reality, the task becomes difficult.

Their topics infrequently interest or attract me and so I listen to them in silence, which doesn't seem to bother them … at least most of the time …. not *every* time. Most people like to be heard; listening and paying attention to them with no agenda, helps both of us.

People generally draw their own conclusions about someone who doesn't participate actively in conversation. If questioned directly, I use words like, "My life took a different turn from my usual way of living" or "The way I am leading my life now, was really attractive to me and I followed my interest". Yet, they seem to be either confused or make assumptions. Although they may say they understand, I feel there is wide gap between what I am saying and what they seem to be understanding.

At the same time, I recognize that for both of us our communication is confined or liberated to the extent of our capacity to comprehend, perceive and articulate.

Usually, most communication is characterized by some level of recognition. For instance, individuals (especially my relatives) are surprised at how I can be so restful and centered in different types of circumstances.

In the past, I tried to motivate people to walk towards their inner truth. That desire has considerably faded now, so the requirements of 'what to say' and of 'how to say it' have drastically lessened.

Life is living itself in a simple way, yet anyone who needs help or guidance in this direction, receives it naturally, without me doing anything special or specific.

I do see that people around me such as family members, close friends and relatives are impacted. Their lifestyles are changing. They're becoming more aware. I feel that the deepest levels of honesty, integrity, clarity, heartfelt compassion, and a lack of fear and judgement, are required for truth. Sometimes, I feel that I fail with respect to compassion of the heart. At the same time, I feel compassion of the heart builds progressively over time.

***

Stacy

Maybe my favorite metaphor for this is Plato's allegory of the cave: we have been out of the cave into the sunshine, and now we're trying to explain that everyone is only seeing shadows.

Let me put it this way: if all the great awakened teachers and authors, including, but not remotely limited to, Jesus, Buddha, Mohammed, Richard Bach, Adyashanti, Tolle, Katie, Jason Shulman, Sam Harris, Ilona Cuinate, (this list could get very long!) can only use metaphor because Truth is Wordless, indescribable and frightening to those who are still asleep, how could I do any better? And mostly, why?

I try to be attuned to when it's right action, but that can be challenging when I want my loved ones to join me. That's one of my dark places to clear.

***

Lisa

My daughter is currently going through a Harry Potter phase, so I read the books and saw the movies with her, and actually thought to myself that this is kind of the way it is: there are Muggles, who just don't get it, and there are wizards, and the two live in different worlds.

On the other hand, we are actually *all* wizards and the Muggle-identity just conceals our true identity. Since the wizard identity is still there even if for most it's hidden, I feel I can communicate with it even in Muggles.

I've recently written a book about Near-death experiences (NDEs), which includes both my own and others' stories. Since a lot of people have heard of NDEs and it's a pretty well-established concept it makes it somewhat easier to get across what I want to share. But saying to someone, "Hey, by the way, I accidentally got enlightened the other day" is out of the question. I don't know anyone who wouldn't think I'd gone completely bonkers if I said something like that. So when talking with people one-on-one, I adapt to their understanding and way of communication, and don't bring up anything they won't understand or be interested in. There are so many associations attached to words like 'enlightenment', 'God' or 'spirit' which can make their use feel clumsy and wrong. Most NDE-ers feel that the NDE is basically ineffable, and the core of awakening and what we are talking about in this book, seems to me to be similarly ineffable.

So even if sharing with words has its place, I feel the main purpose of this process is its *embodiment*; letting it express and live itself through me in each and every moment of my life. If and when it includes sharing in words, like now in this book, that's fine. If and when it includes something else entirely, that's fine too. I don't feel any need to be 'understood' in a personal sense.

***

Michaela

Discovering the true meaning of words such as Love, God, Truth was a crucial part of my journey; I would not give up until I found their absolute meaning. And it was of course painful because I was trying to find an answer within the mind. Only after its 'collapse', falling into the silence beyond the language, did the essence reveal itself. The words then came alive and I was able to use them free from previous misconceptions.

I became generally more careful and conscious and tried to speak in a way that was not in conflict with the truth. In the beginning this seemed really tricky. There was even 'conflict' as to how I should answer the simple question: "How are you?" How could I be in a 'how' mode? I just *am* ... with no labels attached. My content changes all the time, so which thought should I refer to in this endless field of non-existing time? Even just to call myself 'I' is not true ... So instead of 'I', I would generalize as much as possible, and use the word 'one'. I often finished my reflections with "and yet ..." in attempt to leave a space for all that is unspoken.

However, with time I found myself sounding too 'alien' and detached from others' perceived realities. I more or less accepted the traditional way of communication, just like we accept other concepts and traditions, knowing that these are just relative appointments, or games we play.

***

Sarah

I spend time with a lot of people who don't know or even care about this stuff, and many who have heard of enlightenment, but have ideas about it, as most people tend to.

I simply say, "I went through a radical inner shift and I experience myself and the world differently now." If people are curious I tell them what the fruit of such a shift is, which seems to help them get it. For instance I'll say: "Well, my mind stopped spinning and it's quiet in here now. I used to have anxiety and that's gone. I feel connected to you and this table and to everyone here; there's naturally an underlying love that's always felt. And there is a core of peace that is unshakable, no matter if I temporarily feel a wave of sadness or frustration or fear. I always feel at home and as though all is well. It's pretty f***ing cool."

I learned to share it this way when, early on, a friend was curious. I shared with her how I had realized that ultimately there is no self, that time and space continue to collapse, and that I was the doorframe and the sky and the dirt and that it's all one thing. She looked at me, fascinated, and said: "But how does that translate into your life now?" She wanted to know the nitty-gritty of how things are different in a lived, human, day-to-day way. I found that to be wise of her.

***

Timothy

I've told a few friends I'm enlightened. So far, only one has had an emotional outburst that included telling me I needed psychiatric care. In that moment I asked him what his point of reference was and he couldn't come up with anything. He's since relaxed from that standpoint.

Another friend has also found enlightenment and she occasionally calls for validation or to ask questions.

When non-awakened people find out that I claim to be enlightened they usually don't ask me anything about it. If someone has a more advanced or specific type of question I usually try to expound on the subject. If they're beginners and say things like "I've always wanted to try meditation" or "I'd like to become enlightened", I reference my book as a starting point. If they can get through my book with a good idea of what I'm talking about, they're not beginners anymore.

For the most part, I help if I think there's a chance that what I say might work for someone. Otherwise, I tend to stay silent. I don't want to be a guru, especially among those who are asking questions but not listening to the answers.

***

Richard

It's difficult for me to answer the question directly, as I don't conceive of people as being 'awake' or 'not awake'. I don't know what anyone else's inner experience is, so I can only really contrast my own at different points in time and say I'm more 'awake' now than I used to be. I'm also aware of my capacity to be a self-absorbed jerk at times, so I'm not sure what a claim to be "more awake than ..." would really amount to.

Whether we see ourselves as being basically the same as, or fundamentally separate from others has important implications, and will greatly determine our capacity to communicate with them.

With all that being said, I certainly recognize and struggle with the problem being raised here.

I've found that it's much easier to talk in terms of "being interested in a philosophy", rather than attempting to describe transcendent inner states of being. People are usually intrigued to hear a bit about the former, whereas the latter just weirds them out. I might then say a little about the basis of *advaita* and throw in a comparison to René Descartes (because everyone's heard of him) and people go away happy.

The important thing I've had to remember is that in these situations I'm not being asked to give an esoteric initiation. I find that people interested in awakening (myself included) often feel that they *should* be able to offer anyone an in-depth explanation. People in other areas of human endeavour do not subject themselves to this sort of pressure. I have a friend who's a Maths professor, and whenever I've asked him to explain his research he just looks at me aghast. I don't feel there is an onus on me to be able to convey this stuff. I aim to give people what they're really asking for, which is usually just polite conversation.

***

Marianne

Post-awakening I have struggled with languaging, most particularly with the spoken word. When I write, I can take the time to feel for what is true in my heart, take the time to let the words come, and I know that the faceless audience out there will simply take it or leave it. But when I have someone in front of me who is asking questions, either out of politeness or interest, it is completely different.

It is difficult to find words for the wordless. Whatever I can call it, it's not that. But situations sometimes demand words and it took a long time to find some that felt even vaguely 'right'. I don't have a natural 'gift of the gab', so there was (and at times still is) a lot of fumbling around and experimentation. I tried different words on for size. I tried to find words that might fit with others' perspectives. I had to allow myself to make a mess, to say the wrong thing, to be uncomfortable, to watch others' eyes glaze over. It took practice. Lots of practice.

The words that fit most with me at the moment are either Life or Natural State. That's what this is: the utter ordinariness of what we simply *are*. I might say: "It's about finding what we *are* when we let go of all our ideas about it. It's our natural state. It brings a simple peace where previously I felt turmoil and anxiety." And yet I'm not sure these words suffice for those whose perspective is wholly within separation.

I'm beginning to feel that the 'ego' needs to believe that anything beyond itself must be really quite *grand* before it will take an interest in or commit wholeheartedly to the inward journey. "Wow I'm going to be *really* special (or free, or enlightened, or liberated … or whatever word)!" The 'ego' can only ever be seen from beyond the 'ego', so perhaps words like spirituality, God, Wholeness, Liberation, Oneness, Unity, Consciousness, Awareness are necessary for a time. They're good words and descriptive words, but they can also have a slight suggestion of specialness or something *other* than the simplicity of *This*.

Only when the 'ego' drops does one realize that there is *absolutely nothing* in this for the 'ego'. But saying that to someone who is looking from the egoic point of view and is wondering if there is anything 'more' to life, is meaningless ... and frankly the ego can even make its own destruction sound like a pretty special thing. So I always try to sense into another's perspective and use words from within their framework, while carefully adding a few of my own. But there's no perfection here. It's trial and error every time.

Over time I have opted more and more for silence. At first I probably did feel a need to be 'seen' or 'understood'. I no longer do. What this *is*, cannot but 'speak' (communicate). It speaks through silence, through one's presence, one's smile ... and yes, sometimes it speaks through words. But there are also some out there, who are so busy making noise that they are unable to listen. That's okay, and it's also okay to politely move away.

But I have also made considerable effort to meet up with those who share this post-awakening perspective; a shared space in which it is understood at the very start that the words are irrelevant. That shared space is a great gift.

***

Clear Clear Water

by
Marianne

Here
now
is
clear clear water
quenching every thirst
every longing.

Beyond colours
or fanfare,
beyond studied words
or embellishment,
beyond thrill
or beauty.
Beyond.

Here is indescribable transparency.
Simplicity.
Clarity.
A quiet
and unadorned bliss.
Absolute purity.
Clear clear water.
No separation.

I abide as that.

***

Chapter 9

An ordinary day. An ordinary life

Kiran

My life is ordinary. It is the opposite of what it used to be and also the opposite of what I expected when I was seeking. It is a simple way of living that arises from deeper nothingness and deeper contentment. It is not looking to satisfy any desire or accomplish anything, other than what life brings.

It amazes me that life itself knows how to live. That is why I refer it to as Higher Management … and its management is very impressive. At times when there seems to be chaos, it shows me that I was caught in some kind of idea or belief, however subtle.

If I look back ten or more years ago, life was lived mostly from conditioning and judgment, which resulted in extreme dissatisfaction and resentment. Life is now seen from the very different vantage point of emptiness, which allows all experiences to move through without being caught, and so without losing openness or freedom. This shift has made life relatively smooth and peaceful.

As I mentioned, even when chaos appears (which can include hurt, pain or anger) the deeper peace and silence is unbroken and always there. The connection with that peace and silence helps me move through chaos relatively easily. Although identification may be evident at the time, it is short-lived and there is no establishment of a separate entity.

The awakening now seems to have established on all three levels of mind, body and soul as I feel no internal conflicting energies. Inner flow is smooth and gentle yet aware and alert. All form is transcended, bringing formlessness into form and enlivening it with the power of pure awareness. The awakened state in the ordinary life of form, embodies this wholeness and feels unobstructed by any form. All areas within the body are completely open; it is as if an extremely gentle breath rises from the bottom of the back (root chakra) and up through the empty spinal cord. The undercurrent of peace and harmony, love and compassion, is blissful.

Any given day is full of a variety of things, comparable to anybody's day. I am a wife, mother, grandmother, relative and friend to many around me. Even though I am retired from work, life is always bustling with varied activities. Fifteen years ago many of the same activities would have felt very trying and difficult.

The world is welcomed in, in exactly the way it presents itself in any given moment. There is a deep surrender, a very warm surrender, without any effort as such. 'I' is not living; life is living itself. The need of the 'I' to change experience in any particular way has dropped significantly, and continues to diminish, allowing life to flourish as it is.

***

Erick

Ordinary life is more ordinary. There are no more era-defining dramas. No more dreams to be fulfilled that dominate a chapter of my life. Gradually the frustrations inherent in the limitations of living have dissipated. I'm a helluva lot more pleasant. I see my relative self for what it is – a natural form moving in a beautiful world.

There is the forever Now – that which is and is indescribable. It is the hum of the universe that underlies all mundane events and experiences. I know that absolute Nothing is what we all are. I feel like Infinity pretty much all the time. And I'm just a regular guy.

I can love a stranger deeply and I can still curse out a distracted driver. I can feel the flow of Infinity and still be writing a technical manual for the Navy. I can feel the passion of accomplishment in the material world while living a solitary existence in Silence. There is nothing to do and everything to do. I can see into the Infinity that surrounds and pervades us and I can look at a stone as a stone.

A river of exalted joy runs through my silent moments. Taking a walk feels like flying.

I cannot hate myself. I cannot turn on myself in anger. I cannot love myself above others. I cannot suffer. Suffering requires a self to judge and there is no place for that in my existence. I cannot judge the Universal that we all are – there is no one to judge and no reason to judge. I can't wallow in self-pity. When all is right, where is the injustice?

Chapter 9 – An ordinary day. An ordinary life

The loss of the ability to dive into self-loathing was a distinct change from the moment of awakening. The old patterns of judgement would try to kick in but there was no object to apply them to so they eventually just atrophied. Suffering, as an emotional state was dissolved. I could see the mechanics of the immunity, the turning away from the old world view and the identifying with the Nothingness of Pure Existence.

Time no longer exists as a limiting factor. I see infinite possibilities and I am only this moment, nothing more. I have the patience of eons, and I can push very hard to get things done on time. I've had to learn to do that last thing post-awakening.

***

Stacy

The biggest differences between before awakening and after awakening are that I am no longer seeking and no longer interested in life's seeming dramas.

From about the age of 12 or 13, I looked for some kind of spiritual truth or reality. I read books, listened to speakers, sought out workshops and classes, and basically spent all my spare time looking for well ... awakening. Part of this took the form of what you would call healing from the effects of my childhood and of incest, but in truth, nothing 'bad' happened. I'm fine. My family is fine. I would not condone incest, but hanging onto it is just stressful.

I had many experiences of seeing clearly, most of them short, maybe a few hours, via breath work, sex, and a handful of experiences with psychedelic drugs. After a well-contextualized and longer time of seeing that there is no self, no problem, no ... anything ... in 2007, there was no more seeking to do. Even though the intensity of that time faded, none of that mattered any more. There have been some other times of intensity since then. My current understanding is that when I'm embroiled in some area where I still hold on to lies, my awareness of truth and joy recede. When I clear one of those pockets of lies and truth re-emerges, I see clearly again.

The second big difference is that I am no longer interested in life's seeming dramas. Through my 20s and even into my 30s, problems seemed so important and so life-threatening. No more. You could literally tell me that I have cancer and my response would be pretty neutral. I have another awake friend that says he'd be excited about it. It would be something new to learn.

Do I have so-called 'problems'? Yes. It still appears that I have chronic body pains, as well as difficulty relating to this man I'm living with who has no clue and no interest in these awakening matters. But none of it seems particularly serious. Pain comes and goes. Maybe this relationship comes and goes. I have no idea.

This life is completely ordinary. I work in an office. I live with a boyfriend. I have a cat. My inner sense of it is that none of it matters. We've written about death in another chapter. That's the one people sometimes throw at me when I talk about being awake and how death seems. They say, "But what if your mother died?" I say, "Well, it hasn't happened yet, so we'll see, but I doubt it will make a lot of difference. She will be where she has always been – in my mind. I can't imagine feeling separate or feeling loss. She will still be around."

I never did fit in with regular people – whoever they are. I've always been different, and I'm still different. I just have no interest in all the dramas that seem to occupy people. Even reading a book or watching a movie is sometimes challenging. I do get a little exasperated because I can see that if one thing were communicated truthfully there would be no story. Our lives are like that. If we just communicated truthfully, with ourselves and others, there would be no drama at all, just an overflowing beautiful sense of being.

Postscript: A few weeks after I wrote the above, my mother graciously died and now I can complete this thought and confirm that it was a 99.9% neutral experience. It didn't make a lot of difference. She IS still in my mind. I think of her about as much as I always did. Yes, I cried for about a minute, about 10 minutes after I received the call saying she was gone. Then for a second or two a couple of other times when I thought I wished that I could tell her something or that something was different. Sadness only shows up when I wish something were different. I'm pretty content with the experience and the fact that she is dead. I'm okay. She's okay. There is nothing that needs to change.

***

Lisa

An ordinary day for me after the transition is full of paradoxes. For starters, there are no ordinary days anymore, and yet they are as ordinary as they ever were, and as ordinary as anyone else's.

Now, every day is a miracle. Every step I take is a miracle. Everything

Chapter 9 – An ordinary day. An ordinary life

I see, feel, think, know, do and experience is a miracle: having a headache (which I have today), going on the subway, writing a post in a Facebook group, breathing, being alive. And yet, it is all perfectly ordinary.

To me, awakening is still a process and the further along I go, the more I find the distinction between 'good' and 'bad' is disappearing. I'm not enjoying my headache, but yet I'm revelling in the realization that I am a conscious being who can experience a headache. I am both the whole and a part of the whole at the same time, able to experience a headache! That is miraculous, unfathomable and beautiful. And at the same time I'm a bit annoyed and don't like having the headache. It is all there simultaneously.

The same goes for all other 'negative' experiences in my everyday life. Being tired. Feeling sorrow. Being impatient with my partner. Feeling horrified about climate change. The 'good' feelings of joy and love in an ordinary day are still more enjoyable than a headache, but in a fundamental sense I find everything I experience equally miraculous and meaningful. As the mystic, Julian of Norwich put it, "All shall be well, and all shall be well, and all manner of things shall be well."

After the transition, the outer circumstances of my everyday life haven't changed much. I have a partner and an 11-year-old daughter. We have a small publishing company. I have a couple of non-life-threatening, but uncomfortable, chronic illnesses. I do some service work and some volunteer work. I love and enjoy animals, reading, helping others, and learning new things. I have the same political views, the same likes and dislikes as before, but it's all a lot more fleeting and superficial now. In the depths there is peace, acceptance of what is. Whatever is.

I increasingly live in the now. My thought processes are different than they used to be. Thoughts arise, but they don't linger or evoke feelings or imagery as they used to. I don't obsess about things. They are there and then they are gone. When there are no particulars I need or want to think about, my mind is mainly silent. I experience it as a tool, like an arm or a hammer, whereas previously is was 'me' and a source of suffering and obsession.

I do all the things I used to do, but at the same time I go with the flow of life and I'm prepared to follow it wherever it leads me. There is basically no fear in my everyday life, regardless of what happens. Life arises in the moment. It might be a 'small' everyday thing like doing the dishes or a 'big' thing like helping a friend during her illness and physical death from cancer, which I've recently done. I might be led to share my experiences and my journey, like now, and at other times I'm led to keep them to myself.

'I' am not living my everyday life anymore. Life is living me, in me, through me.

***

Maureen

Oh, this is such a juicy topic! Anything dysfunctional became intolerable and has mostly fallen away. Most of day-to-day life goes on as before.

In another way everything has changed. While I am primarily conscious of the world as Maureen-human, awareness of beingness-allness-oneness is always present, as a steady background. Sometimes it is pushed back a little more, sometimes it is more foregrounded. It is never absent. This creates an odd vision, where I can see a situation from many perspectives.

There's a need for quiet and solitude, but also an isolation because so few people understand. It's hard to find people to talk with.

I see differently … the way aspen leaves spin and rustle, light shining on a newly opened peony. I love taking photographs, trying to catch the light, that exquisite moment.

The biggest practical change is how I take action. While I have to-do lists, what I do moment-to-moment is what arises, the next right thing. Sometimes I consult my inner guide. Sometimes I stand and let my body lead me. It takes practice to listen, to allow myself to let go of all control, step into flow and let the current take me where it will. But when I do? Oh, what a ride!

***

Michaela

The shift did not make me a more disciplined person in my everyday life, as I would have hoped for! My routines (or lack of them) did not really change.

What changed was the capacity to sense and cherish the extraordinary beauty of 'ordinary' life. The silent majesty of Nature became my church and could easily move me to tears. Every single leaf on a tree was seen as a miracle and a touching encounter. I had to hug trees, melting in love, even though I had never heard of 'tree-huggers' before. The same with sun, without knowing of the existence of so-called 'sun-gazers', I became one myself, adoring the beloved source of light. Also my love for animals went to a new level. At some point I was clearly shown my responsibility for their well-being and I immediately changed my eating habits, so as not to cause more unnecessary harm.

My life has not changed much on the surface, still it is a different world of wonder I live in now.

What I also enjoy as a great benefit of awakening is the clarity that is always at my disposal and allows me to see through most of the human nonsense and madness. It is such a joy not to get hooked and be free.

***

Timothy

I used to suffer from not fitting in. I wasn't able to understand how I was expected to act in order to be accepted into a group. I couldn't even understand what my supposed motivation for conforming should be. This inability was obvious to everyone I met and as a child I was picked on a lot. I'd lie awake all night trying to figure out what I had done wrong the previous day and why people treated me the way they did. I wanted to die and get it over with.

When I turned eight I decided I was never again going to let someone make me feel as if I wanted to kill myself. After that I only did what I wanted to do, no matter the consequences – although I did try to stay out of trouble. This included trying to figure out who 'I' was, why 'I' was here, and how 'I' wanted to be, even though people thought this was strange.

At 26, enlightenment happened. I suddenly realized who I am, why I'm here, and that I could just relax into being myself moment-to-moment, without effort. I began to understand that the motivations of others also brought them suffering and made them feel empty.

Now, everything I experience is simplistic. I make observations, rather than judgements, about what I detect around me. There is no longer any distinction between myself and the rest of the world. My body occasionally has moods but I don't give them the full attention I once did; they just happen, then fade. I have dropped all interest in labelling and attaching to my feelings, and make no determination about them.

Random thoughts still appear, but just like my emotions, they don't seem to be of any particular importance. I do not desire anything, so I'm never driven to acquire possessions or achievements. Often, if I do imagine I could use something in my life, it just becomes available. I only actively think about things when I want to. For instance, if there's a problem to be solved, or an association to infer that might be helpful. I remain partial to doing only what I want to do, but now it's more that I'm being led to the things I most resonate with.

My average day is fluid and relaxed. I still enjoy meditation and continually explore the inner world. I take an active interest in the societal ambiance of the day, and frequently write about it. I play guitar and sing when I'm led there. I craft posts and reply to comments on social media about various subjects ranging from ancient spiritual theories to more scientific endeavors such as microbial fuel cells. I occasionally create things with my hands, usually in leather, wood, or beaded jewellery. I make herbal remedies for my family and friends, and frequently go out into nature to look for wild medicinal plants.

From the viewpoint of others, my life is happy and blissful, but that's only in comparison to their own experience. I forget because I'm no longer actively aware of inner peace, I'm just used to it.

**

Ben

I find a lot of things funnier than I used to: general quirks of existence and human nature.

I am so much more alert and receptive to my senses. Rather than stepping away and disconnecting from the physical world I engage in it much more than I did, although without putting any value on it. It's more like a game. For example, the sense of touch has become a particular fascination to me. I don't know why. Before awakening, I didn't focus at all on how things felt. Now, on a day-to-day basis, I touch everything: a brick wall, tree bark, I turn the shower from hot to cold and back again. The sensation of skin-on-skin, whether erotic or platonic, is beautiful.

I don't believe other people's suffering as much as they do themselves, but I find that makes me more compassionate towards them, not less. I'm more patient because I don't find their pain a threat to my peace like I used to.

I have no fear in expressing myself, as the fear of judgement has gone. There is nothing else to do *except* express myself, however that may present in any given moment.

There is a deep sense that everything is okay regardless of the surface level 'threats' that the world presents, whether political or social issues. It is the same world as before, only different. I feel 'lighter' in it. It isn't as 'sticky'. But it still remains fascinating and fun to indulge in things like work, achievement or possessions, even though I don't take them as seriously.

And finally, I don't know why, but the things I spent time desperately chasing in the past, have effortlessly started appearing in my life, even though I gave up focussing on them post-awakening. And this is happening to a weird level! It is an incredible gift and one of those quirks of existence I mentioned at the beginning that makes me laugh.

My day-to-day life is blissful to be honest, but in the most ordinary way.

***

Marianne

When I had newly awakened I puzzled about how to 'live' it. The only 'example' of awakened living available to me at that time were teachers, either in person or on the Internet. These teachers were usually seated comfortably in a chair or on a *zafu* (meditation cushion), and presented themselves as articulate, perfect, exalted and special. They seemed to have their lives totally 'together'. I was certainly 'awake' but my life looked nothing like that.

In his radio broadcasts, Adyashanti was occasionally asked, "But what does your everyday life look like?" I'd prick up my ears in anticipation, but his answer of "just life" felt disappointing. And yet that's how I would answer that question now. Just life. Literally.

When I get up in the morning, there is just getting up. When I make a cup of tea, there is making a cup of tea. When I have a shower, there is having a shower. There is checking emails, eating muesli, watering the garden. There is the sky blueing, a tree leafing, a body walking, an ant crawling. It's a verbing of this Mystery of Oneness, of Being, of Life, without an 'I' trying to separate itself out. There is no story, narrative, drama, meaning, motivation, manipulation or opinion. When there's a headache, there's a headache; it's not good or bad. It's certainly not pleasant and sometimes my eyes water from the pain, but it's just a body paining. I might take some aspirin, I might put some heat on my neck, massage my neck, but I'm not bemoaning it. It's not a drama. There are times someone might say to me, "Oh I'm *so sorry* you have a headache" and I am taken aback. I understand their beautiful intention, but for me there is no 'sorry'. It does not occur to me to be sorry for myself or sorry for What Is.

In this Oneness, this living business, this mystery – in the knowing and living of this – there is an underlying current of bliss, of okayness, of clarity, of strength, of silence, stillness, openness, knowing, dynamism, compassion, love ... the list could go on. It is always there. It's what we are.

I cannot remember much about living wholly from separation. I recall the sense that I was never 'at Home', that I was living a lie, trying to pretend as best I could to be a 'Marianne'. I remember feeling that I should somehow be able to live in 'my natural state'. Because that's all this really is: our natural state, our natural birthright. The struggle stops. The fight stops.

Here in this simple being-ness I live in a house with my partner and our two dogs. There is laughter, there are some tears, cooking smells, trees, birds, fresh vegetables from the garden. I enjoy hiking in the bush, I enjoy having a body. I am passionate about nature conservation and photography, and enjoy inspiring others with my passion. I run this Facebook group and I'm putting together this book. I mentor a few people in spiritual matters. Things happen ... so much better than before really. Friendships fall away though; relationships change and there's a sadness about that. I actually don't see 'relationship', but that's perhaps a topic for another chapter.

However, there's no ideal of perfection. There are times I still feel the jagged grasp of separation. Mostly it is simply let go. If not, it is met with uncompromising honesty: What is *actually* here? There is nothing else to do. Truth is truth.

I think of Basho's famous haiku, about a frog jumping into a pond. Splash! That's how it is.

***

Richard

I was 16 when I had my first awakening experience and 18 when I figured out what was going on. I'm 37 as I write this so I suppose a lot would have changed anyway. I no longer have to make up excuses about homework for a start! With that being said, I can certainly disentangle the effects of awakening from plain old growing up.

There was a ten-year period, from 18 to 28, in which I came to understand and ultimately recapture the blissful state of Being that had

Chapter 9 – An ordinary day. An ordinary life

spontaneously arisen right at the beginning; when I arrived where I started and knew it for the first time, to paraphrase the poet TS Eliot. Prior to this I was anxious, on both an existential and personal level. I had cravings, holes I tried to fill with things the world told me should be satisfying, but which always came up empty. I was also capable of being quite unpleasant; I lacked compassion for people. Inwardly, my thoughts raced continuously. I drew my sense of self from them; a limited and imprisoning sense of self.

The process of awakening led me into a greatly expanded sense of self. I can directly perceive myself as the consciousness in which the universe is arising. I can also experience the nature of that consciousness as being love. This brings the most immense sense of bliss and security, but it has not – to my surprise – diminished my interest in the character of 'Richard'. I can still feel the full range of human emotion and experience both passion and stress at the dramas of my life. This beautiful drama just takes place in a wider context; inside a loving mind which both holds and guides it.

***

What's Awakening Really Like?

An ordinary day

Chapter 10

The stabilisation of awakening: 'maps' of post-awakening life, the unpacking of implications, and working with conditioning and trauma

---

Maureen

Stabilisation? Does that happen? For me, this has been a time of ever-deepening change. It started with an ah-ha-omg-holy-shit moment. This was followed by a honeymoon period, a wild and amazing six months that could have been scary except I was totally open to it.

Then the suppression lid came off all the emotional debris we avoid. It's as if the universe said, "Here, my dear. You've come so far, you can handle all this now." I discovered traumas I didn't know were traumas, and dug deep into family dynamics to understand my childhood, totally shaking up childhood family relationships. I'm three years in now, and still working on clearing.

I feel I am now fumbling into a new stage, finding a way to exist as an energy being in human form, to be both at once, like two hands clasping. I've not quite got that clasp yet. I bounce from one to the other; sometimes the hands touch.

***

Marianne

I once heard a teacher, perhaps Adyashanti, say that the real spiritual journey begins after awakening. I think that's true. Before awakening I was drawn to spirituality and to truth, but I had no idea what was being pointed to. After awakening my perspective changed completely. Physically everything was the same – the same house, the same partner, the same bed at night – but in every other respect everything was new. Adyashanti talks about total destruction, and that's how it is. In a way, you're starting again. You've seen what Truth is, you're a 'Buddha', but you're a *baby* Buddha. You're learning to walk again. You're learning not to poop in your pants.

One aspect of the post-awakening journey is unpacking the implications of what has been seen. There is so much here to write about; a whole book would not suffice. For instance, if I have seen that my true nature is infinite, what does that actually *mean*? What does that mean for my everyday life? What does it mean for the spiritual journey? Infinite really is infinite ... there is no end to the unfolding, to the depth, to the understanding, to the living ... no end! Mystery!

If I have seen that there is no separate self, what does that actually mean? All my life I have functioned as a separate self, and now, all of a sudden I have seen that there isn't one. So if there isn't a little 'me' in my head or in my body, what on earth is going on? How is it that this body is moving? How is it that there is still this amazing 'verbing' of Life going on without a 'me' to control it? If there is no separate self, then what does that mean for my relationships? What does it mean to know that there is no 'other'? And not just no 'other' human. There's no 'other' anything! It's big stuff.

And then, if I have seen that Truth cannot be known by the mind, what then is the mind used for? What even *is* the mind? Are all thoughts rubbish? How can I live without using my mind to work everything out? How do I relate to others who are firmly entrenched and identified with their beliefs?

More and more questions. Lived questions. They can only be 'answered' in the living of them, and that takes time. Lots of time. Interacting with others, discussing with others, reading, staying open ... living, more living, deepening ... it all helps.

Another aspect of the post-awakening journey is the arising of conditioning. For two years after awakening I experienced what is called 'the honeymoon period'. It was a time of bliss and ease. But regardless of the relief of having seen the nature of reality, the old patterns of operation still existed. Some do drop away quite quickly, but others may be persistent. Some may even be completely beyond awareness. This is extremely frustrating. Why do I still react from identification when I have so clearly seen that this identification is false? Great humility and sincerity is required.

In addition, some patterns, particularly of trauma, can resurface after awakening. I had done a great deal of therapy before awakening – it had been enormously valuable and in essence had emptied me out – but post-awakening there was a need to revisit this material when life circumstances became difficult and I was pushed to my limits. It was only from within the vast view of awakening that the imprint of trauma could come up for its true and final healing/holding. An awakened therapist was necessary for this.

But I also see a 'danger' in working with conditioning. Yes, it does need to be understood in order to be released, but for me there also came a point when it was necessary to simply surrender it. Let it go. There was no longer any need to meticulously explore each branch of the 'conditioning tree' before lopping it off. The tree could now be cut off at the ground. I knew without a doubt when that point had come.

This post-awakening journey is so very different for everyone. We each have a different perspective, a different life history, different insights and understanding, different places where we are still blind. In addition, after awakening, the play of life doesn't stop ... there are illnesses, global crises, pandemics, there are children and partners and parents, there are money difficulties or job difficulties ... and so the deepening never ends. I find this extraordinary and always surprising.

For me now there is a trajectory into what I can only describe as a true Oneness and freedom. Initially when one awakens, it is into the bliss and 'wow' of transcendence (the 'honeymoon' period) and one can think that this is the entire view. Then one comes back to reclaim this world and one's functioning in it. Now, I feel a movement beyond this ... I cannot but see it all as the same thing. This is not a mental construction in any way, but simply my lived experience. There is no world beyond the Self ... words fail here ... it is completely natural. Peace. The natural state. I am the eyes of a caterpillar ... I am a yellow coral fungus by the roadside ...

***

Kiran

After the awakening experience everything was bliss and nectar; the presence, the love, and the peaceful calming energy of formlessness took over everything that was once considered 'I'. Following that amazement, there was disbelief that there was still so much sleepiness there and the old self could come back. The hidden belief that there is a delete button that erases everything unholy and impure was totally shattered.

However even during the honeymoon time, there *was* a sense that it was only a beginning, a step into a life where the control button was not available in the same way as previously.

Awakening was an offering to the Divine. It was a point of no return: no return to a controlling and self-serving life, no return to the agendas which aimed to fulfil the desires of ignorant ways of living. Many of these mechanisms were protective and had developed because of traumas encountered from very early childhood until late into marriage, and from riots and migration to another country. All these energies had been held in the form of memories or subconscious material, and it was now the time to empty them into the innermost stillness.

Whenever old patterns took over, it became easier and easier to see which part of the ego entity was active. Bringing this part to heart in the presence of innermost quietness, allowed that part to settle down and dissolve. This process became intense, but was always supported by deeper and wider clarity. I referred to this process as an "inner classroom with an invisible teacher"; its message was always clear as bell and its guidance is there today.

Each episode took a different amount of time, but I also became more patient and tireless. Even when a pattern repeated itself many times, the openness within was always ready to embrace it. I must admit that earlier on, self-judgment, self-blame and criticism continued to play, keeping the separation intact. But later on, as that gap started to come increasingly into awareness, it was very quickly and seamlessly filled.

All this changed the so-called 'me' in my surface behaviour, and in my many friendships and relationships. I could not continue in the same old ways and outside attractions dropped away. This brought feelings of loneliness and sadness. But there was a very sure sense of trust, respect and love in it; not love for me or for anybody, but just Love. However, there was always more and more emptiness within to realize, and each time there was a new challenge to embody it.

Now that the formless is living in an almost detached way, movement above this depth has no impact and no influence. Occasionally if I get drawn into it, it withdraws itself right back into silence, into One.

***

Chapter 10 – The stabilisation of awakening

Lisa

My experience of the journey towards awakening and also the place I stand at the moment, is much like Jeffrey A. Martin describes in his book *The Finders*. I feel it's a kind of continuum more than a fixed spot of 'before' and 'after'. The sense of self, as the little 'man in my head' I experienced 'before', disappeared 'after', but I still don't believe this is the end. There was a transition that definitely made a big difference, but something tells me there will be more transitions. So I prefer to talk about "the spot where I stand at the moment" knowing that this spot will probably change.

The spot I find myself in after awakening is an all-the-more deepening present. I think, feel and do, but when the thought, feeling or action has run its course, in the next moment they're gone. Each moment is a finished life, so to speak. Each moment and what is contained in it is born, and then it dies, and something else is born. It's like the cycle of life. Or like in quantum mechanics: we can be both a wave and a particle simultaneously. When we're a particle, we're fixed, but in our wave state, we're ever-flowing, ever-changing.

When it comes to trauma, so far nothing more has come up for me after awakening. I did psychological and therapeutic work for 20 years before awakening and think I'm done with most of it. Sometimes I can see where something in my personality originates, but doesn't carry the traumatic imprint of the past. Maybe something more will surface in the future, I don't know. The way I work with everything now is to let it be as it is and let it run its course.

Something that keeps deepening, is my understanding of and ability to express love in different ways. My personality is still there and it expresses itself as 'Lisa'. But the underpinning, the current that flows beneath it all, I'd call love. And I keep being surprised as it moves me in different directions.

Something else that keeps deepening, is a kind of human-ness. It's being immersed ever more deeply into the physical life, in the human experience, with its joys and sorrows and beauty and ugliness and the love containing and embracing it all. Awakening to me is definitely not to be removed from ordinary life, it's the opposite: being fully immersed in it in each and every moment.

***

Timothy

I believe that some conditioning, some 'programming', by parents or by society in general, is necessary for survival. Many times I had to be reminded to "Look both ways if you cross the road because the cars may not be watching for you", "Mushrooms are poisonous", "Don't talk to strangers". There were many of these learned directions for ensuring that I wouldn't accidentally die, either because of my inability to 'pay attention' or from my innocence about the motivations of people I didn't know.

I became rather proud of my survival skills and learned many more on my own. Growing up, I was picked on a lot and often thought of permanently running away to the woods. I identified with being one of the few kids I knew who could go out into the wilderness and disappear from society. This was 'who' I was: a survivor extraordinaire.

But enlightenment showed me that I'm not who I 'think' I am. I now feel that I'm 'one with everything' so I'm not limited to just having thoughts about myself. In the innocence of the first year of awakening, every bit of non-functional conditioning fell away. Any idea of 'who I am', perished. I still remembered practical conditioning like not crossing the street without looking both ways, but anything that didn't have a practical function, totally dissolved. I was a blank slate.

I even found it difficult to determine what other people might be thinking, and nearly impossible to figure out what their conditionings were; this had previously been a hobby of mine in order to avoid the bullies. Eventually I found ways to associate with people without depending on past conditioning.

Occasionally, conditioning that was no longer useful in my life would emerge from deep within. It was as though it wanted to be reviewed so I could find out whether it was still necessary or not. When I looked objectively at each specific issue and did some reading about self-improvement, the old conditioning usually evaporated.

Then I got married and past experiences that I was not actively remembering were triggered and came flooding into my daily activities. I felt the light of awareness beneath the onslaught but it was very difficult. The challenge had such an impact that I was sure that if I couldn't resolve it, I wouldn't want to continue living. It felt as though the experience was trying to drag me out of the light and down the rabbit hole.

I sought help from professionals and was able to get a handle on the 'what, when, where, why and how' of this confusion; it was based on traumatic experiences from my childhood. I had not previously considered them because I assumed it was the way everyone grew up. Recognizing that I had a strange home situation was a big part of processing the old conditioning.

Being married to someone who also had hidden conditioning was the instigating factor that triggered my personal challenges. Had I not gone deeply into that relationship I wouldn't have been gifted the opportunity to explore and eliminate the childhood trauma. Her dogma was chasing my karma, so to speak, and I, for one, benefited from that. I just hope we're karmically even now!

Overall, I see the journey from enlightenment to reintegration into the world as being one of perspective, similar to growing up. For the first year I was an innocent infant with starry eyes, living in a predominantly blissful plane of existence. I think that it's common for this period to taper off, and some even think they've lost their enlightenment because the bliss seems to disperse. When that first happened, I figured I was just used to it; it was as if the contrasting viewpoint of my previous life had now faded. During this infant stage, I functioned in a world that was seen through brand new eyes. Some call this the 'honeymoon phase', but I see it as a new beginning, or a rebirth.

This infancy was followed by a toddler phase where I learned to figuratively walk in the world. Then I entered a childhood phase where I began to explore different aspects of society. I made plenty of mistakes just as most children do. I think this is why some Buddhist sects say not to teach until you've been enlightened for at least 10 years. A teenage type of experience kicked in soon after, with some reflection on angst and a wee bit of inconsequential drama here and there. During this time, I made a lot of attempts at socialization and relationships, with varied success.

The feeling of being in my 'twenties' came next and things began to settle down; that's when I got married and had a son. After 37 years I'm now in my 'middle age' phase; perhaps I'm finally starting to have some wisdom to share with others. But I don't see any of this as cut-and-dried; everyone is different.

In conclusion, I think that the average person tends to age themselves in their minds as they grow older. I don't have any idea who I am in my mind so I haven't aged myself. I don't perceive time the way I did pre-enlightenment. Life is just one moment that never ends, and isn't counted for any purpose. What's important to me is that I'm still happy to be here, and I hope to have many more years to explore further.

***

Jennifer

After awakening, I had moments of extreme fear and sadness. It felt as if what I now knew meant I would have to let go of so much. My whole life had been built on the foundation of trying to get somewhere which seemed completely pointless now. It was abundantly clear that there was nowhere to get to. There was nothing to achieve. I had little motivation to continue doing anything: my healing work, my PhD, following my passions of creative expression and solo international travel, even engaging in relationships. 'Being' was all that made sense.

I could feel that my solar plexus, which had been quite strong, was blown out. It felt as if that part didn't exist anymore; it was simply vacant space that someone could put their hand right through. In those emotionally panicky moments, I was very aware of its absence. However, when I didn't have thoughts, everything was beautiful. Someone who was more awake than me, described this experience as 'flip-flopping'. A few days later I was out with a group of people at a salsa dancing show and I drank. Afterwards, I no longer felt the spacious expansive quality which felt like a relief, but also sad at the same time.

Another challenging aspect was that The Divine or God as I had known it, did not exist anymore. I used to pray and talk to God often, so I experienced a lot of grief at what I felt was a massive loss.

Even though through awakening, I had the lived experience of seeing and feeling everything and everyone as God, after some time went by, it all felt very ordinary. Prior to awakening, God/The Divine had felt so magical. I could conjure up my experience of that powerful, loving connection at any time and feel wonderfully supported, loved and grateful; it also brought me tremendous agency and comfort in the world. Even though my cosmology had completely shifted, I tried to continue to connect in this way but it didn't work anymore ... none of my old tools did. It was as though, after decades, they had expired. This was all very disorienting and disheartening. I felt lost for years. I had had a great deal of certainty (at least I thought I did) and now everything was completely unknown.

I began questioning everything and I stopped doing just about everything. I didn't know how to make decisions because I didn't have the motivation that used to drive my actions. After seeing through the illusion, there was no interest in chasing the dangling carrot. Having been a bliss chaser and pretty happy most of my adult life, this was extremely unsettling. My only impetus to do anything was centered around sitting

Chapter 10 – The stabilisation of awakening

in stillness, either alone or on meditation retreats, and discussing the impact of awakening with the two people in my life who understood.

Now that several years have passed I have found myself wondering how much suffering I could have avoided around the process if some part of me had created different meaning about what was going on. There was definitely some nihilism at play which could have been an aspect of ego trying to stomp out the light and beauty of this lived truth and clarity in its effort to not 'cease to exist'.

It has been more than five years since the awakening experience that shifted everything for me. In terms of integrating my understanding into life, I did once again pick up many of the things I had previously done, but now with what seemed to be very different motives. If it was natural or simply what came next, I did it. It was much less about achieving something but more just something I did in that moment.

On the topic of stabilization, it feels worth mentioning that I've had several other awakening experiences since then, which I assume I am still integrating. The living of these shifts of awareness feels like a magical present that never stops being unwrapped. Each layer is a new gift. Tonight as the warm wind blows through my home and touches my skin and hair, I am reminded how deliciously beautiful and full awareness is. Perhaps each one of these deeply alive, sensuous moments is a part of the stabilization process.

***

Erick

For me, stabilization was never an issue. When my experience opened to inner Existence it was so clear – like an apple held in the palm of one's hand – that the idea of it being lost was not applicable. That doesn't mean there was not a period of stabilization taking place before then, but it was not seen as stabilization so much as just the natural alternation of inner expansion and then relative integration. I was actually really surprised when awakening dawned because I was not a stellar practitioner of my spiritual path, and there were few signs of a change approaching.

I have written about post-awakening developments in other chapters, but there is always something new developing within the unchanging. Those stages may serve as milestones, but there are subtle shifts taking place all the time. The individual aspect is always evolving, enveloping more and more of the qualities of the Absolute.

Trauma is an interesting subject. I can't say that I have had much experience with that. I always thought that I had a bit of a charmed life. No sudden tragedies, no deep poverty, no physical or psychological traumas of any significance. There is one trauma ... the trauma of separation from ones true nature. I think this is the root trauma that we all have to deal with. "How did I become a limited being and why am I imperfect as such?" The implications of this ripple through every other experience, whether pleasant or painful.

In that respect, I have had that trauma and have somehow healed. I think a lot of the post-awakening development can be classified as the healing of the shock of separation. For me, I could look at the initial awakening as the realization that I was not a limited being, but a universal element. That is the core healing, but the mind and body had a lot of reorganizing to do to integrate this realization.

There was the fear of falling back into the dream of separation. That was cured over time with the slow, gentle realization that I can't get lost again. I am Existence and all I have to do is stop trying to be anything else and I will fall back fully into that freedom; the discomfort of leaning toward separation triggers a relaxation back into Truth. Old habits of thought and feeling, old shards of limited self-concepts, old stresses and weaknesses in the nervous system – these would rise up when stimulated. The cure was simply to be present, and the power of these arisings to separate, would dissipate. I felt that I had become immune to suffering, and unable to fall back into the untruth of separation.

Interestingly, for me, the fear of losing the connection to Infinity was quashed finally when that inner Oneness surrendered to the changing outer world. My mind could no longer hold the Silence as separate from the active world. Like the floodwaters breaking an artificial dam, the Wholeness washed into the multiplicities and it did not destroy them. It was sacrificed on the rocks of the world, yet the world also died as it was absorbed into a greater unity: a unity that sees no separation of self and other, a unity that is neither silence nor action, a unity that is constantly changing yet ever the same.

There was no grand trumpeting of angels, no eyes wide open in cosmic amazement. Just a sense of being right back where I started and perfectly comfortable with that. Free to be the Infinity that I know myself to be. Free to be Infinity when I am at work at the factory. Free to be Infinity when I am playing my violin. Free to be Infinity when I am on the crapper.

There is no self or other. There is only is-ness in its ever changing forms. There is only love flowing in every direction, waking up peace and joy in whatever it touches. What looks at me is what looks at them. And there is peace in the knowing that we are all in this as one great big hug.

***

Sublime nakedness

by
Marianne

Oh let yourself be crushed by the beauty,
by this majesty that wishes to be known.
Let yourself be stripped bare,
stripped to the bones
and down to those hollow fertile places
so ripe for the seeding.
Come on your knees
beautiful one.
Come in your sublime nakedness ...

Everywhere. Everywhere. Can you not see it? Feel it?

***

Drenched by the sky

by
Marianne

It is not enough any more
to only open the windows and doors
to let in
the breeze
the gentle warmth
the smell of summer rain on parched earth

they are beautiful
beautiful
yes

but if I step outside
I am drenched
by the sky

***

Chapter 11

Teachers

Andrew

The only good teacher is a teacher that teaches you that you don't need a teacher.

Until you find that special teacher in a book or in person or maybe on YouTube, then there will be many teachers that will help you progress.

One thing to be very careful of is that a teacher needs to understand you and your current abilities and previous experience. Jesus was a great teacher because he spoke in parables so each person took what they needed at their level. This is a very rare skill so just be aware that something someone says to thousands of people either in an ashram or conference or on-line may not apply to you and may be counterproductive. This also means that someone that once spoke rubbish might be saying the exact same thing that makes total sense now. You have changed, not the teacher.

Ultimately you don't need a teacher. They do make life so much easier if you can find a good one.

***

Michaela

It seems as if in the life process we either want to learn or we want to teach. And in truth we do both, as it is simply a process of exchange, of sharing life experiences. We learn best when we teach, and we teach best when we stay open to learn.

I never sought contact with a teacher during the long period of my spiritual search. Just as being a part of a single religion felt untrue and even pretentious to me; so did entering any spiritual community. I felt strongly that finding the answer to 'who you are' is an inside job and as such, I have to do the work alone. The truth is universal, but has to be discovered individually.

That said, I did read a lot of books by philosophers, psychologists and spiritual teachers. I also recognized many people that came into my life as my teachers, enlightening me on different levels. So learning was taking place all the time.

The greatest and only teacher was of course life itself, which constantly provided me with mirrors of situations and relationships, through which I could recognize the tendencies, habits and programs that were forming my personality and my way of my thinking.

***

Kathy

Right now, the mere suggestion there is a teacher and a student creates a sense of separation in my mind. That said, I have definitely been given pointers by others that have left huge imprints on me, and some may call these teachings. What seems to have worked best for me is inquiry, where one is guided back to self.

When I was a child, it was Kahlil Gibran's *The Prophet* that had this impact on me. Later Jon Kabat-Zinn showed me how to be present with my senses and go inward instead of out. He also showed me how to meet pain (physical and emotional) instead of running away from it. Later there was Gangaji. While she probably was the one I had put on a guru pedestal more than anyone, she did show me Ramana Maharshi's inquiry of, "Who Am I?" Then Byron Katie's four questions dissected my thoughts and beliefs, one by one, and continue to live in me. David Whyte's poetry had, and still has, a way of stopping the mind. Eckhart Tolle showed me how to watch the mind and to see how it feeds the pain body. And later Rupert Spira showed me via direct pointing that time does not exist, which opened the door to a timeless experience. The skilled pointing back to self, to help one see beyond illusion, is truly the only teaching I have ever found helpful. Listening to or reading countless hours/pages of descriptions of what it is like to be awake, are about as helpful as trying to understand how a mango tastes before actually tasting a mango. Impossible. One eventually has to

Chapter 11 – Teachers

taste it for oneself. And once it's been tasted no matter how one tries to explain, it's impossible.

Before my consciousness shifts, I had volunteered at a retreat with a famous teacher that was totally unaffordable for me and many people. Yet as insanely expensive as it was, it was sold out. This is a teacher who is undeniably humble and clearly not influenced by money. It perplexed me that his retreats would be so expensive. I still have no answer for why some teachers charge so much, or indeed, if they should charge at all. It has occurred to me that we all have our own path, and some people may need to pay a lot to actually allow themselves to stop and go inward. I do not know, and probably never will. I'm all fine with it now though. My own path did not require large sums of money, and my most profound moments were not at expensive retreats held in special places ... but that was my path. Someone else's will be totally different.

I recall the early days of my adult journey, there were definitely thoughts and beliefs that teachers had something special; that they were the 'chosen' ones. There seemed to be a belief that if one sat closer to the 'guru', there would be a better chance of 'getting it'. Now that seems silly, but then again, perhaps that mindset can indeed work for some. Perhaps by completely letting go in the name of a 'guru', an awakening can occur. I have heard of the same dynamic working for some people attend AA and surrender to God or the higher power.

For a short while after my series of awakenings, I was a volunteer guide with Liberation Unleashed (LU). What I liked about it was, we were anonymous, we were clearly called guides, not teachers, and we used direct pointing and inquiry with our clients.

About ethics and teachers such as abuse of power, sexual abuse, or cults, I think awake people have the misfortune of being considered saintlike. That alone can be a recipe for a lot of stuff to arise, particularly if this person starts to create a new identity from their public image. If their personality tends to be narcissistic, and/or they have not finished processing their shadow side, issues or traumas will arise sooner or later. This is something I have noticed so far on my own journey. Upon the onset awakening, it can seem that all problems disappear, yet some unresolved traumas of the past can still be lurking in the background. They need to be honoured and seen for what they are. If they are not given this opportunity, like pushing a beach ball underwater, eventually it pops back out.

I believe that this is what has happened to some teachers who have started out pure but later have 'fallen'. As they attract more followers, it seems almost impossible for someone who has not spent time solidifying what has been realized and confronting the leftover human 'stuff', not to inadvertently build up new constructs and identities, and ones that may be even harder to let go of. Additionally, past traumas and issues can show up with a vengeance. In all honesty, while I often feel repulsed by these teachers, there is also compassion for them. This seems like an almost impossible place to be.

***

Maureen

I've never had an in-person teacher. I have learned from many teachers, from books, videos, at retreats, and through on-line courses, but never an individual connection.

This seems to be the path I was meant to take. It forced me inward, to find my own path, to feel into what resonates for me, to pay attention to my intuition. I've wished for a teacher, but it was always a new, brilliant, on-line course that appeared, rather than a personal connection.

It's lonely and odd and yet ... there's something here, something about finding the inner teacher that I've found deeply powerful and rich.

***

Marianne

When I see a group of spiritual aspirants sitting on their meditation cushions, eagerly leaning forward and with a teacher sitting in front, it raises so many questions for me.

At one point, I was such a student. I had gone to a teacher to find context for awakening, and he told me to meditate. Talking was frowned on; talking was 'of the ego' apparently. I had nowhere else to go and so I stayed for two years. In retrospect I felt like the odd-one-out and didn't really understand what I was doing there or why I was meditating, but I went along with it all in the hope that one day it might make some sense. Frequently during this time, I found myself grateful for the writing and radio broadcasts of Adyashanti. Without them I would have been lost.

A few years later I again went to a teacher. Now there was a *lot* of talking. Again I persisted for two years and again I found myself grateful for the clarity of Adyashanti. But still, I 'learnt' a lot, or perhaps 'unlearnt'. After this I knew I didn't need a teacher again, either in-person or through written material.

Both these teachers were beautiful and I loved them. But they were unable to see their own failings, their contradictions. I could see they were human, and yet it was taboo to speak of that. I tried to take what I needed and leave the rest, but in the end that didn't really work. I wasn't being honest and I think both teachers knew this. It was a catch-22 situation. I doubt they ever knew the nature of my dishonesty and the reason I couldn't fully 'give myself' to them.

Prior to awakening I had an intense relationship with a self-styled 'guru' who seemed to need a lot of adulation and acknowledgement. After the relationship ended, I realized that in some ways it was as though I had been a part of a cult. I felt manipulated and angry, and took a long time to recover. But on reflection, many years later, I see that I learnt a tremendous amount from him, and indeed, much more than from the two teachers described above. He contributed to an immense deepening in my understanding of what we essentially are and ways of inhabiting the outer world, the inner world and all worlds. I doubt he was awake, and yet he was a profound catalyst in my movement towards awakening.

Teachers are probably needed at times. I think it is good to sit in front of someone and lay all your cards on the table with complete openness, vulnerability and lack of artifice. In fact I think this is essential on the spiritual path. I feel there are too many people out there, kidding themselves about their spiritual prowess or attainment. There are also too many who think the axiomatic "Life Is My Teacher" precludes going to a flesh-and-bones teacher. The ego can run riot with spiritual stuff, and it is good to have someone who can point that out to you.

My greatest teachers were actually my two therapists. Both behaved impeccably and I cannot fault either. Both had incredible depth and I learnt *so* much. And rather than making me into a 'better ego' (as some spiritual folks believe), therapy actually allowed me to let go of trauma, holding and conditioning, until I was mostly empty. This is not what I had expected, and at that time it was very painful to be so empty, but in retrospect it was essential. In my experience spiritual teachers did not have the depth of understanding that therapists did. Spiritual teachers were also all too ready to generalize their knowing to aspects of life that they had absolutely no clue about, for example, abuse, trauma and psychology.

There's no right or wrong here. I could suggest trusting one's inner knowing with regard to teachers, and yet, sometimes I learnt so much when I didn't trust it.

***

Kiran

The meaning of word 'teacher' changed as I journeyed through. I spent some time under the guidance of a teacher but cannot say it was good or bad, because it was both. Some basic aspects were revealed to me with her help, but there were also many negative results from this association. Under this teacher's guidance, I developed a lot of confusion, dependence and negativity about my personal self. I feel I would have benefited more from self-refection with the help of a therapist. But at the same time, most therapists work on the mind with the mind, and my teacher was able to bring me to surrender.

Upon reflection, I can say that my journey has been guided mostly by my inner guru and I feel that this is the right route for me. A teacher, guide or mentor can provoke the student and then connect the student with their inner guru. Once the seeking and inner guru are connected and one is aware of this connection, no external guru is required. Simultaneously, remaining open-minded always leads the student to further refinement. Anything and everything can provoke insight or inner teaching, provided one is open to learning or understanding life more deeply. This eliminates the hardships one goes through because of teachers.

There are all kinds of people out there posing as teachers, and intentionally or unintentionally they're not necessarily very true or committed. Also, how one receives a teacher is dependent upon the individual inner system and its level of readiness, honesty and commitment towards the journey. It is not the teacher who brings about awakening, it is our own innermost longing or spiritual impulse that actually does it. So much help comes our way that it feels as though the Universe has assigned all its resources to advance this cause. The way I see it now, I can sincerely say that I have not done a thing in my journey, as the 'I' that can take credit or discredit is not there. The sheer absence of this ego self has uncovered the reality. The only way we can help this cause is by seeing how ego's agenda is working in us and let that recognition render it inactive. Relaxing into or surrendering to what is, without interference from the ego's agenda is what does it. A true teacher can help see this, but I feel nobody can bestow awakening upon anyone.

Chapter 11 – Teachers

* * *

Stacy

Teachers are a tricky subject. Why? They are human. I don't care how enlightened they are or how 'abiding' their awakening is, they still live in this dual world. On top of that, we cannot expect to do exactly what they did and find our own awakening. They can point. That's it. The rest is completely unpredictable.

That said, those pointers can be very helpful. When we are stuck in our attached, this-world perspective, a teacher can say, "Hey, have you looked at it this other way?" That may be all we need to see.

Also, when we have fears and expectations, a teacher who has seen through these can be just what is needed. The handhold they give can calm our minds enough to SEE the Truth.

Yes, there are people calling themselves teachers who are not clear, not clean in their offerings. If we are desperate or not paying attention to our inner knowing, we can get into these traps. To get out, we have to check our gut feeling. "When I think of following this teacher, does my gut clench?" If so, get out of there. Or is there an open sense? A kind of chill or relaxation? If so, carry on. It's probably an okay place then.

I can't say I had any really 'bad' or 'dangerous' teachers. Even the ones I eventually saw through, had their hearts in the right place. They were trying to be helpful. They were simply wrong.

A couple of them were very attached to what a Christian might call 'idols'. You know - chakras, crystals, dream interpretation, trying to predict the future with cards or planets. None of that was useful to my awakening. Just distractions of duality.

Ironically, I had some very clear connected experiences in the presence of a teacher who was later found to be having sex with young male devotees and misusing funds given to him. That doesn't mean he wasn't awake in some form - it just means he had challenges with the power he had found. That's for him to work through.

* * *

Lisa

The way I see it, the spiritual path is different for each person, and spiritual growth can basically happen in any way and every way. Coming from that perspective, it's more or less impossible to generalize about teachers or anything else on the path. What is perfect for one person at a certain time can be harmful for another. In my experience, even something that seems to be 'bad' or detrimental at one point in the journey, can turn out to be a blessing later on.

I had a therapeutic and spiritual relationship with a teacher for about 10 years. It was an extremely powerful connection and he was a catalyst for me on my spiritual path. I don't know if this man considered himself 'awakened', but he worked with people in a way that implied that there was no 'ego' involved in what he said and did.

In the beginning, I was in awe of him and his work, and projected all kinds of wonderful things on him. There were certainly very positive elements in this man's work and these had beneficial and positive results for me. But as I grew and developed, I also began to see flaws and blind spots and these were destructive. When my projections collapsed and the relationship ended, I became very 'anti-guru' and basically threw the whole spirituality business out the window.

When my relationship with my teacher started, I was a pretty ordinary neurotic person with generally good coping skills, but when it ended I was a wreck. I had deep anxiety, depression and completely lost my power. It took me seven years of ordinary therapy to work it through and regain my autonomy.

As much as I idealized the teacher early on, I was furious afterwards. But after the transition, I could see that all of it had nevertheless been the way it had to be. After discarding teachers, gurus and mostly all of spirituality, there were no longer any intellectual notions about enlightenment or awakening for me to get stuck on and no more relationships to project my power onto. I was left with only myself as the 'guru', which I'm certain sped up the whole process immensely. Even though I wasn't aware of it, the positive results of the years I spent with that teacher were still present and kept on silently working inside of me. After the transition, I suddenly saw that what I previously thought had been harmful, had probably saved me decades, or even lifetimes, of getting stuck in searching for 'awakening' or 'enlightenment' in the wrong way, with the wrong people, in the wrong places, and as a result getting into all sorts of suffering and trouble.

So, generally speaking, the way I see it now, there are and never will be a 'perfectly enlightened' being, 'ubermensch' or teacher; someone who is completely without 'ego', flaws or blind spots. The notion of a perfect being is dangerous, unless we see that we are ALL intrinsically perfect beings. It is so important never to give up one's power, no matter how 'enlightened', wise or wonderful a teacher might seem. The enlightened, wise and wonderful person is ultimately within each of us. A true teacher will facilitate or point us back to our own inner 'guru': the true guru.

It is also so important never to mistake the teacher with life itself. On the spiritual path, we are surrendering to life and to our own higher, spiritual or true self, not to the teacher. We might need or want a teacher on the path and can certainly gain and learn a lot in the process, but no matter how confused or lost we may feel at times, we already have all we need inside. The way or the path is our own to find, and not the teacher's to choose for us.

Additionally I feel it is important that teachers present themselves with humility and show themselves to be just as vulnerable and human as everyone else.

In the context of our teacher/student and therapist/client relationship, my teacher was always strong, and so I was always weak. If he was 'spirit' I was always 'ego'. If I was asking questions, he always knew the answers. If I was wrong, he was always right. If I was small, I gave up my power and projected it all onto him. This was the basic flaw in my connection to my teacher and it led to very destructive results for me psychologically. I believe a lot of the pain, confusion and suffering which came from this part of our connection could have been avoided. Nevertheless, this too taught me much and ultimately led to the spot where I stand now.

***

Timothy

By the age of 13 I had come to the conclusion that no single person was any more qualified than another to speak about what is really true. I felt that if there is a broad truth it would be universally available to everyone, and that I should be able to find it on my own.

To that end, I took an elective class in high school entitled, 'The Religions of the World'. It gave me an overview and I recognized what all the popular paths have in common: there is something bigger than us that includes us.

Intrigued, I started going deeper, searching for more information about religions and other spiritual practices. Pre-Internet, I learned there was a great book store at the national headquarters of Unity Church in Lees Summit, Missouri. I found several publications there, the best of which literally fell off a shelf and opened to answer a question I had been pondering for some time. This particular author's books continued to present themselves to me like clockwork. Interestingly, I never met this teacher or even saw a video of him speaking, but I still felt I had found what I was looking for. I can't say for certain, but perhaps I tapped into his energy field.

From this material I learned about the ancient meditative techniques of Tantra. Practicing several of these meditations over a period of about a year or so, I became enlightened. After about five years of self-study, I met some of his other students. I joined the group, which included the option of getting a new name from the teacher via snail-mail. I wore the clothes and the regalia and generally continued to go deeper. None of the other group members recognized that I had already found enlightenment, but I didn't care.

I finally saw some videos and heard recordings of the teacher speaking. Most of the group had met him personally by this time, and I heard some wonderful stories about their experiences. It was nice to be in that energy, but I never got carried away by the overall group dynamic. I don't think it's necessarily a good thing if a teacher requires devotion and subservience; maybe for some, but not for me.

I also learned how teachers can be misunderstood by people who don't have any personal, real-life experiences to which they themselves can refer. In some cases, though, caution is justified because there are definitely some enlightened teachers who become quite pathological in their actions.

The teacher often reminded us not to 'believe' what he said because he was an ordinary person. Instead, he recommended his listeners try out the various techniques of which he spoke, for themselves. He also stated frequently that if he didn't have the answers we were looking for, to try another teaching or method, and that a living teacher is best. As I had already learned about the old religions in high school and found that they didn't do me much good, I rarely spent my time investigating the various words and writings of dead teachers. I enjoy old films of Alan Watts, for instance, because of his particular style and sense of humor, but he was speaking in my lifetime and he wasn't a guru.

I do feel it's helpful to connect with the energy of as many enlightened people as possible; feeling their energy can be a good example of what we are seeking for ourselves

***

Chapter 11 – Teachers

Elizabeth

Although it is currently unpopular in the 'spiritual' crowd, I am a fan of teachers.

If sensed as genuine, every single one of them has something to offer. I say, "if sensed as genuine" because it doesn't matter if they actually are or not (unless they are sexually or psychically abusive), because as long as we fully believe in at least parts of their wisdom and instruction, what we project on them returns to us as reality. If a teacher takes a frog and says to others, "This is a holy frog! Just blow on its back in this way and you will be healed." … if you believe in that, then healing will begin. This is because of the miraculous power of our own mind and how a little faith (in whatever!) can bring about change.

So I have always had teachers. They are not always good at all things. I have found that I usually just get confirmation on the thinking level of what was already there when I arrived. I feel I have grown the most just by being in the vibe of teachers. Some teachers are more subtle than others, so the transformation can be less obvious than, say, receiving *shaktipat*. For example, the Sufis are always a pleasant group for me – subtle, yet pleasant. The teacher was highly cerebral, and yet carried the Sufi vibe of gentle transformation.

Like Bhagavan Das in *Be Here Now*, I've tried out lots of different arms of spirituality. In the end, all the teachers seem to be pointing in the same direction.

As for teachers who have dropped their physical body … yes, it is most certainly a thing to receive teachings from them.

Many currently reject teachers and teachings and emphasize that it is all within. But to me this approach is one of missed opportunity. Maybe it's because I am a teacher by profession and have always been immersed in the education field, but in my opinion, accessing a teacher puts us on the fast track. We've lost some of the memories and lessons we accumulated in previous incarnations and now we just have to be reminded of them by those who have remembered or discovered before us this time. It's all One anyway, so what does it matter who discovers or rediscovers first? As the late Ram Dass was quoted as saying, "We're all just walking each other home." What a beautiful concept.

Within/without … it's all the same.

***

Richard

Perhaps because my initial awakening experience was spontaneous and powerful, I always had the sense that enlightenment was close at hand. It was something obvious that once seen always allowed me to slip back into bliss. This, in combination with a strong sense of independence, disinclined me towards teachers. If I could slip right into this state spontaneously before even knowing what was going on, it was clearly a simple thing that didn't require an experienced teacher. Unlike learning to play the piano say.

In addition to this, timing was a factor. It was the turn of the century when I started with all of this and scandals were emerging. The gloss was falling away from gurus, leaving a less-than-wholesome image. I feel lucky in this regard: to have avoided the whole thing.

I should be careful about generalizing, but over the years my observation of teacher/student relationships has been that they are inherently unhealthy. That sounds ridiculously strong as I write it, but my continued experience is that such relationships are based on an egoic need to be a teacher/guru meeting an egoic need to have one. The latter is strong; there's a vicarious pleasure in feeling close to someone we project greatness onto. In spite of what I've written above I certainly haven't always been above and beyond slipping into this too.

A central thought that has helped me is to consider the *Logos*, the Mind of God itself, to be our true and lifelong teacher. Human beings may mentor and guide, but no human can know what is best for another. To replace this infinite source of wisdom with a mere human is a form of idolatry.

I have certainly had people who have fallen into a kind of mentoring role for me; people whose advice and insights have opened me up, challenged me and directed me down avenues I wouldn't have seen for myself. However, I feel that to take this further and define such a person as being 'my teacher', is to introduce an unhealthy pedestal into a wonderful relationship.

Finally, given the subject matter, it would be remiss of me not to mention the other aspect of what being a spiritual teacher or guru implies. Unlike the teaching of something more mundane, there is this additional aspect of *darshan* or *satsang*, where simply being in the presence of the guru can open a person up to their own divine essence. In my experience this is absolutely true, but the ability to induce it is not the preserve of 'special people'. I've had incredibly transformative experiences gazing into the eyes of completely normal human beings.

***

Ben

I never had a teacher in the traditional sense. My father died when I was 15 which made me question the meaning of life. I smoked a lot of weed and chatted with friends about existential matters for several years. Then, out of the blue one night after discussing philosophy with a friend at university, I sat down on the edge of my bed and the next thing I knew it was eight in the morning and I was sitting in exactly the same position. My perspective rushed down to a microscopic level, then jumped out to a universal level and then back into my body. I saw and felt 'everything' and was utterly euphoric, sobbing with joy for hours and hours. I didn't know what had happened, only that it was true.

After that I looked into lots of things trying to find out what had happened to me, but no philosophy ever seemed to tell me something I didn't come to understand in that initial breakthrough moment. It was just a case of embodying what was already known. For that part I think guidance would have been incredibly useful because doing it on my own was messy and took a long time. But in the end, all roads lead home. In my experience pain teaches. Mistakes teach. Simply living day-to-day teaches. Honest self-reflection teaches the most.

***

Erick

I consider myself an odd bird by modern standards in that I only studied in depth with one teacher prior to awakening. As a teenager I had a glimpse of awakening stimulated by an illicit substance. During that experience I was discussing enlightenment with a friend who recommended Maharishi Mahesh Yogi's Transcendental Meditation. This was in the mid-seventies when TM was experiencing great popularity. I learned that and practiced regularly, eventually getting deeper into it and studying at Maharishi International University. That offered me the opportunity to deeply explore spiritual practice and philosophies. I eventually became a TM teacher and went into teaching practice in New York.

Over the years I began to sense the limitations of the organization surrounding my practice, so I slowly drifted away from meditation as the central focus of my life, to it being a regular practice but not something to think much about. I got married, dove into business and family life, all the while dreaming of awakening but not pushing too hard.

Awakening came as if unsolicited and was seemingly random. I had read some other teachings but did not take on their practices. I liked to visit with saints when they visited – Native American, Indian, American ... anyone who piqued my interest ... but only to observe and absorb. I was reading Adyashanti at the time of awakening and I credit him with cracking the egg which had been matured by Maharishi.

From the very beginning I had a strong sense that I did not want to get into a co-dependent relationship with a teacher or teaching. I steered clear of personality cults and tried to focus on my direct relationship with my own intuitive guidance. I have seen many struggle with teacher/student relationships and I had a deep sense to steer clear.

Regarding the inner guidance to Truth, I would describe it like this ... Ultimately, our internal sense of Truth is the only Guru. All other teachers are just expressions of this inner radiance. Even the frogs and gnats are connected to the inner Guru. Listening from the heart is the best way to hear the teachings that are being directed to oneself. Even the greatest exponent of enlightenment is no greater than a dirty sock when we can sense the connection each has to universal Truth. And many great teachers can work with us without us having to be physically present with them. Time and space are illusions to the Great Teaching and we can be open to messages from anywhere. When it all shakes out, it is being direct with our own nature that is the awakening we have sought.

***

Jennifer

My teachers have been a huge part of my spiritual path and awakening process. I don't know what I would have done without them.

I never knew how much I needed a teacher until after my awakening experience. I would have been so lost without the help of Adyashanti. I listened to his book *The End of Your World* over and over again. It brought me comfort to hear someone mapping out the territory I was living. Listening to him was one of the few things that brought me some peace in a world of uncertainty and groundlessness. On some level, it

Chapter 11 – Teachers

made me feel more okay in the everyday functioning of life which had become so foreign, mysterious and confusing. I had so few reference points. I felt as if I knew nothing and much of the time it was difficult to even make a decision. So much of my identity had been built on my accomplishments. And achieving or accomplishing was what had motivated most of my actions. With that desire no longer present, it was difficult to discern what to take action with. Adyashanti's brilliant nuanced writing and answers to my questions helped me navigate my life. I was blessed to attend several retreats with him. On those retreats the silence and stillness was heaven. The answers he gave to my questions helped me for years to come. They still do. The answer he gave me to the last question I asked about pain and past trauma rising was to find the 'yes' to the experience somewhere within me … to find the 'yes' to reality unfolding as it is in the present moment. I am working on this.

Gangaji has also been helpful for me. At one event, I sat with Gangaji on stage as she guided me into the terror of not existing as an individual self. With her presence supporting me I was able to meet it, rather than run from it as I had for years. I had witnessed my ego pull every trick imaginable to convince some part of me that it was alive and well. The closer I got to knowing the True Nature of existence, the harder it tried.

I have found guidance from Mooji to be helpful as well. His words "Bless everything in existence" have become a practice for me. One night when I was driving on the 101 in The San Francisco Bay area, I began blessing everything … the cars, the people, the concrete road. I felt myself fill with an incredible appreciation and love for everything exactly as it was in that moment. I have been curious about the difference between the teachings of accepting everything and blessing or loving everything as it is.

Before my awakening I also had many wonderful teachers. Most of my life I have had a deep love of learning especially psychology, spirituality, creativity and healing; the brilliant teachers came with these pursuits. I also include my own wisdom and experience as an integral teacher. It has been invaluable in knowing who and who not to study with over the years as well as what guidance to follow whether coming through myself or a teacher. My intuition has been paramount in discerning who to learn from and when. It is like a truth/wakefulness detector.

I have learned along the way that although a person can be extremely awake, that doesn't necessarily mean they have done their psychological work. The transpersonal scholar John Welwood writes about this. If the spiritual teacher hasn't done this work then it is likely they will project their pathology and shadow aspects onto the sangha or spiritual community and play out the unhealthy dynamics with them. This is one of the reasons why intuition and discernment are so important on the spiritual journey. As individuals, we all need different things at different times along the way. Ultimately, only we know what is best for ourselves at any given moment. Trusting this is one of the most important spiritual developments of my life. To follow anyone and anything blindly can be dangerous.

I also consider strangers, friends, romantic partners and nature to have been teachers over the years. I believe anything and anyone can be our teacher if we bring enough awareness to any given moment.

It also feels important to mention that there have been times when I have had the realization that there is nothing a teacher can do for me now. I simply have to be with 'what is' no matter how difficult it may be, or how much I may want to change it or run from it. I know to show up as the full presence of 'all that is' living through me. I have seen what I need to see to be open to the miracle of this extraordinary and deeply ordinary life exactly as it is.

***

Chapter 11 – Teachers

The Not-Nothing

by
Richard

In the centre of the centre
Beyond body mind and soul
Lies the Not-Nothing
Black cold and whole

Ever I approach it
And all my love runs out
For this what we truly are
It leaves no room for doubt

I run back to the surface
And face the world once more
Knowing I am empty
Of all but emptiness at my core

The knowledge of this haunts me
Day by day it drains
My secret to carry
As the life within me wanes

Is there no solution?
Have the mystics been deceived?
What's this, a miracle, a guide
Come to me in my need

In the centre of the centre
I maintained a separate self
That too must goes says she
As into Not-Nothing you delf

Arduously I march
Back down that same path
Determined to confront
Tenaciously to the last

Yet it comes for me
In the middle of the night
Waking, friends around me
One by one they take flight

Only one remaining
Then I'm all alone
I let go into Not-Nothing
And suddenly I'm home

An Infinite Ocean of Love!
Consuming and surround
No need for any outside source
When I am what I've found

Back out in the world
The veil draws down once more
Now somewhat transparent
Maintaining the adore

The mystics have been vindicated
It turns out that it's true
Not-Nothing, but everything
Waits in the centre of the centre for you

***

Chapter 12

Meditation

Michaela

I often felt a little confused about what meditation actually refers to. I observed that even some 'enlightened' people use this term with different meanings. Probably the most common way to see it would be as a state of silence, calming the body and mind, and a remembering of who we are (without thoughts). I don't really practice it, but enjoy the state of total body and mind relaxation, especially after I wake up or before I go to bed.

I can't say that I ever meditated in the classical way, such as sitting in a lotus position (ouch that hurts!), imagining light or having the body expand into the universe. Before awakening, rather than quieting the mind, I was intuitively drawn to use it for inquiry and questioning everything: my opinions, habits, emotions, all the programs. It was mind work and I would probably call it investigation rather than meditation. When I experienced the shift and saw the mind for what it is, that questioning stopped and I could enjoy the peace of the knowing that it brings.

I would see meditation today as a state of intimate connection with the inner beauty of our being. As such, I mostly experience it very intensely when playing music or observing nature; when diving deeply into beauty.

***

Timothy

Most days, I do an 'off the pillow' meditation in the morning for anywhere from a few minutes up to an hour; it is like silent inward attention.

I bought a Muse Headband and use that for an hour on days when I want to totally clear my brain-mind; it helps me maintain a more consistent meditative condition. For more challenging occasions I meditate for a minute or two periodically throughout the day as a kind of depth nourishment. I believe I'm very meditative in general, but find that doing these techniques helps my body stay in balance with the rest of my experience.

***

Lisa

I've never meditated, except for a short period when I was drawn to sit and turn my attention inward. I wondered, "What am I doing?" and then realized "Oh, this is meditating!" I had that need for about half a year and then it stopped.

***

Maureen

I used to meditate seriously, fifteen years of Tibetan Buddhist Dzogchen practices. My mind gradually became quieter, and with awakening, settled into a primarily quiet state.

Now, meditation practice feels like an interruption. Why meditate to calm the mind when the mind is calm? If my mind gets busy, winding up about something, a little practice brings me back to stillness.

I do a number of visualization practices when I feel like it, and play around with different meditations as they feel rich and yummy. I have a vivid inner life, but without a formal practice.

***

Stacy

I have meditated every which way but loose.

I lived in an ashram for three years where we meditated at 7:00 am and 7:00 pm every day. *A Course in Miracles* is 365 days of meditation and I did that for five years off and on when I was the student of *A Course in Miracles*. I have done sitting meditation, walking meditation,

Chapter 12 – Meditation

open-eye meditation, closed-eye meditation. I admit I never did TM (Transcendental Meditation). Mostly I like to meditate first thing in the morning when I'm lying in bed.

The Work of Byron Katie is a meditation if you're doing it as instructed.

Pointers are meditations. The best ones I ever experienced were created by a friend of mine here in Colorado. He taught them in a one-weekend workshop that was never repeated, but that he did record. I absolutely adore them. My seemingly longest and most blissful period of awakening was coincidental with doing that retreat and those meditations.

Due to questioning my thoughts with The Work and some of the understandings gained there, I was lucky to have a better context when a friend introduced me to Liberation Unleashed; their pointers are also meditations. By better context, I mean that I had already questioned many stressful beliefs, including the belief in God. This made it much easier for me to let go and experience the offerings of pointer-type meditations.

It is helpful to know that there are two types or two schools of meditation. One is the purification school where you meditate for years and years purifying this thing we call the self. The other is recognition meditation where you notice what already *is*. I strongly prefer the latter, and yet there's a place for the former as well.

These days I do not meditate very much. I only do it when I want to tune in and relax.

***

Kiran

Until recently, meditation was an important and regular activity in my life. Because I was never a reader or researcher, my way of meditating has always been guided by intuition. Perhaps that is why I had very little clarity around meditation. However, something within (the inner true guru) kept me pursuing it. This inner guidance in meditation moved me from chanting to quietness. Quietness then gave rise to self-inquiry. Self-inquiry resulted in much cleansing which then sank deeper into quietness.

Initially, I was very disciplined in my meditation which gave me tremendous migraines as I was waking up at 3:30 AM, showering and then sitting for over two hours minimum every morning before going to work; I maintained this practice for more than 15 years.

The hardness in discipline eventually softened by itself without compromising anything, even my perception of my progress. I worked with one teacher who didn't believe in meditation, so it became increasingly non-existent in my life during that time. However, the inner guru brought me back into meditation soon after that relationship ended. This time there was no discipline and meditation happened any time as needed within or if an opportunity to meditate with like-minded friends arose. These wonderful experiences helped enormously in the embodiment of all that was opened up by awakening.

Although I used to define meditation as sitting alone quietly, that state experienced during meditation, has now become my naturalness, my natural way. Through meditation I have been invited to seek and live/embody more and more formlessness. Accepting and following that invitation has honestly taken me to the deepest parts within.

In summary, I feel meditation helps to turn off the 'churning wheel' inside, allowing one to recognize that separateness is controlling life and one is not in unity. Sitting in meditation and then implementing the inner guidance, can allow transformation to happen. This can slowly take one towards the effortlessness and truth in which consciousness deepens and comes to recognize that there is no separating line between manifest and unmanifest.

***

Richard

I certainly never meditated prior to my initial awakening experiences. I became interested in meditation as a way to recapture the space I'd effortlessly slipped into. I knew it had to do with shifting consciousness and that seemed a logical way to go.

This was in the days prior to the Internet, so I had to order a book. I was skeptical of its recommendations because, in spite of reassurances to the contrary, it seemed to involve a lot of effort. I don't mind effort when required, but this was the polar opposite of what I'd already experienced. I saw parallels, like talk of being in the moment, however I felt the book was putting the cart before the horse. It was recommending 'gently' and continuously bringing oneself into the moment as a practice. In my experience I'd arrived there without any effort, the result of a deeper but as yet unknown cause.

I didn't have any better ideas however so eventually jumped in with both feet. Fast forward two years and I realized this really wasn't delivering. Not only had I not attained enlightenment, I wasn't even any more socially graceful. I observed that there were people around me who had never meditated a jot, but were far more at ease with themselves than I.

At this point I began to radically re-imagine how I was understanding this whole thing. I came to see that 'attaining enlightenment', at least in the way I'd conceived it, was an illusion. Life was actually perfect as it was with no need to change or improve anything. I had come to a place of existential rest.

I didn't stop meditating, but my reason for doing so changed. This in turn changed how I was approaching it. I was no longer meditating to *attain*, but rather because I found it an interesting pursuit. I moved from simply watching the breath, to turning my attention inwards and examining what consciousness is. This shift initially happened accidentally. Early one morning I fell asleep while meditating, but instead of losing consciousness, I became aware of myself *as* consciousness.

That was fifteen years ago, and I suppose it's what I've been playing with ever since. Along the way I've experienced all the things you read about: a sense of self dissolution and merging with an infinite ocean of love etc. I've also accessed meditative states to heal both psychological and physical illness.

Meditation has become very integrated for me now. Whilst there are times I devote myself exclusively to it, I am continuously aware of the field of consciousness in which all is arising. I would like to stress that this is due to understanding and not practice. I don't view meditation as being like a trip to the gym to strengthen cognitive muscles, rather I think of it as a vehicle for studying consciousness.

***

Amy

Pre-awakening: I had only started practicing a few weeks earlier, sitting at least once a day for 10-20 minutes, while my children played around me. It was the first time in my life I fully committed to regular and consistent meditation. Dedicated. I dedicated my whole self to it ... body, heart, mind, spirit. I was resolved.

Post-awakening: In the early days I did a lot of chanting. Chanting helped ground the energy. There were really strong 'power surges' and I didn't know what else to do, so I sat and chanted.

Eventually, there was a smoothing out of all the energy into something more fluid and continuous. It felt as though the body was in a walking meditation. Every breath was full and slow and deeply meditative. Every step was in sync with all of life happening around and through this body. My children still needed me to make lunches, play, clean ... and this was all done with so much more freedom and enjoyment. After two years of this I am once again chanting and meditating regularly. I found that the busy-ness of life forced a necessity for sitting quietly.

***

Marianne

Pre-awakening, I called myself a contemplative; I enjoyed silence and a deep contemplation of my inner world and life in general. But I was never much of a formal meditator. I certainly *tried* different sorts of meditation in formal settings, but I always found them rather boring. Guided meditations I found silly; I didn't want to imagine green fields with flowers or light. I wanted to know who I was and I wasn't going to find that out by imagining pretty things. The truth of who I was and why I suffered so much, was of far more interest. Inquiry and movement into depth has always been more my 'thing' than a formal meditation practice.

Post-awakening I knew I needed the help of a teacher in order to deepen into and understand the shift that had happened. The only local teacher who was 'enlightened' was a teacher of meditation. I didn't want to meditate, but I *did* want a teacher, so I thought I would commit to it and see what happened. There were times I asked the teacher why I was meditating, but I was told to "just keep meditating" ... so I did. I meditated intensively for two years, including many week-long silent retreats. Nothing happened and I learnt nothing. Nor did I deepen.

So where do I stand with meditation now? I find myself moved from time to time, to sit in deep silence with 'What Is' ... no separation ... just this ... always deeper and deeper. Sometimes this sitting is for a few minutes, sometimes it is for an hour or longer. There is no reason behind it; there is no 'I' that is trying to achieve something by meditating. There is simply a movement to sit.

***

Chapter 12 – Meditation

Jennifer

Meditation has been a huge part of my life and continues to be. For years the only thing that seemed to make sense was to sit in silence and attend meditation retreats with others.

For more than 20 years I practised both Tibetan Buddhist meditation and lots of visualizations, which included running energy and healing with energy.

The first meditation I did at the age of 19 was from a book called Spiritual Awareness by Sanaya Roman. The entire room dissolved into white light and it was alarming. I had a series of awakening or transpersonal experiences during that time.

Many years later a teacher recommended a practice: remembering who we are as God. Another awakened person I spent time with said to skip that step and simply be who you are. Although I am not sure how or even what I did, I attempted it in my next meditation. I began expanding and expanding. It seemed to spark the awakening experience that changed everything for me.

Then, within a period of a couple of years, I attended several Adyashanti retreats, several Tibetan Buddhist retreats and spent many weekends in meditation during workshops and programs. I sat with Gangaji, Mooji, attended a month-long, practice-based yoga teacher training and an Advaita Vedanta 'boot camp' both in India and spent time living and working in a remote Tibetan Buddhist Meditation Retreat center high in the mountains where we practiced together three times a day. The interesting thing is that I became terrified to sit alone because I felt the panic and terror of "knowing I did not exist as an individual self or separate ego".

Then for a time I dropped all meditation. It was part of a process of re-examining everything in my life to discern why I was doing it and whether or not it was helpful.

Currently, I meditate every day, although that could change tomorrow.

***

Elizabeth

Around the age of 15 I began secretly meditating on my own after everyone had gone to bed. I would get up, go to the window and open it, sit there and meditate. At that time I had only been exposed to Southern Baptist prayer which had its own virtues. I had never read

Buddhist texts and knew nothing (consciously) of Buddhism, and yet my meditations were straight-up Buddhist. When I was 19 my boyfriend took me to a New Age bookstore in which I found a Kundalini and yoga workbook. I started thumbing through it and discovered the exact meditation I'd been doing through my own inner guidance. It was quite specific and the details were the same as I had been practicing. To most this would be validation that I was on target, but I never needed validation. I knew it was valid from the beginning.

I've meditated ever since. I've taken silence programs both here in the US and in the Indian ashram, in which participants are silent for one or two weeks. I prefer silence, so working silence is ideal. It helps bring the meditative state into each movement, each breath. The working silence I participated in required that we keep our eyes directed at the ground at all times, not giving eye contact and not communicating with others, even with gesture. We worked in the kitchen, or with the saplings we were growing, or in the temple. It was always simple physical work, so our attention could remain within.

I started cycling when I was a teenager and found that it was also a meditation. Mountain biking was especially meditative for me. Each dangerous turn, each sharp rock, forced my concentration into the here and now. There was no space for moving into the past or future.

I've found that *pranayamas* (from the Yogic tradition - conscious breath work to bring about balance) are initially a great tool in meditation. Later, I think the need for a tool tends to drift away.

Sinking deeply into the depths of existence is the way to go for those of us who dwell in the ethers. But for others, moving up is the goal. After years of practice to transcend my energies, a teacher at a meditation retreat told me I'd already transcended ... and that my goal is to come back down into embodiment. So I stopped all *kriyas* and practices which brought the energy up, and allowed it to sink down, down. I have found that is the key for me. But everybody's different!

***

Erick

I learned TM (Transcendental Meditation®) at the age of 18 and have practiced every day since then. At the time I learned my motivation was for self-realization and world peace but I soon found that it felt so good to the body that it became as natural as breathing for me. When awakening dawned I continued out of habit, though there was less and less of a motivation since the seeking had stopped.

My post-awakening advisor questioned my continued practice, as if I were trying to achieve something more, but I told her that I did it because it kept my nervous system supple. I still practice to this day but the process has shifted from using a mantra and sutra techniques to simply sitting in silence of mind and letting the body and mind get a deep rest and cleansing.

Pre-awakening I used to get a sense of expanding my experience during meditation. Like I was adding to, or deepening my experience, but post-awakening there is nowhere to go and no place to expand to, so I just sit in silence and let the natural flow of mind settle down as the body rejuvenates. I credit a certain youthfulness that I maintain as I pass through my middle age to this practice. Other than that, there is no purpose to it.

I have heard of some who drop meditation after awakening. I heard of one respected teacher who took it up after awakening. I think it's a personal thing.

Every moment is meditation, in that I am in the place to which meditation points.

***

Andrew

Meditation is a step along the path. Some people say you don't need it but I think that is rubbish. You do need it, until you don't. It would be like being taught how to climb mountains, and the teachers tells you that you don't need to walk. Of course, when you are at the top you can stop walking but when you are on the way up you need to walk. If you want to stay at the top and enjoy the view for the rest of your life (and some people do this), then you can stop walking. However, if you want to get on with your life you need to walk down. After enlightenment, meditation can be an important practice to stop your mind from taking control again.

The only thing I can recommend here is the Zen drawings of ox herding. This gives a good summary of the process, and part of that is meditation.

The other thing I can recommend is to remember that the mind is not your enemy. Don't try to stop it or control it but simply be aware of what it does and how it does it. Your mind is trying to help you make sense of the world just like your sight. Don't try to stop seeing if the vision is not nice. Don't try to stop your mind if the thoughts are not nice. To me, meditation is simply being aware of the mind and not trying to control it.

***

Chapter 12 – Meditation

Grace

by
Jennifer

Bright white bird
against
deep gray sky.
No blue to be found.
She does not seem to notice.

***

Chapter 13

Religion, spirituality and God

Lisa

I was born into a Jewish family, but living in the then Soviet Union everything religious was completely absent both collectively and in our home. I didn't even know what a 'Jew' was until we emigrated to Sweden when I was eight, and as far as I can remember I had never heard of a 'God'.

In Sweden, I was put in a Jewish School, but our new Swedish and also Jewish friends celebrated Christmas, midsummer and all the other mainstream Christian holidays. It was all mixed up in a pot of 'hang out with friends and family, eat something nice, and kids get presents'.

My biggest spiritual influence was my NDE as a five year old. Some NDE-ers experience and describe 'God', but I didn't experience anything of the sort. Unfathomable unconditional love, beings of light, being one with everyone and everything, yes. But nothing resembling a concept of God. As a result, I have always been completely disinterested in any ritualistic religious concepts, and this didn't change after awakening. I still don't have a clue what people are talking about when they talk about 'God'. The only affinity I have for anything 'religious' is the teachings of Jesus. He seemed a wise, loving, most probably awake and enlightened person.

Still, if needed, I can discuss, relate to and use religious concepts and frameworks in connection with others. It all depends on the context. For me, spirituality and religion ultimately boil down to one very simple thing: if it's loving in any way, shape or form, it's meaningful, if not, it's a waste of time and energy.

***

Chapter 13 – Religion, spirituality and God

Stacy

Religion, with very few exceptions, is the codification of one person's awakening experience.

That person gets all excited and tells others. Most of the time some superstition arises about how it happened. Others try to duplicate it. Mostly, this is not likely. We don't control awakening. It shows up if and when it does and not a moment before that.

If anything, religion may make awakening impossible when we focus on rules and moral codes, rather than present moment awareness.

God is no longer a useful concept for me. It's just not. My mother always told me that God is the spirit of love. She told me the same thing about Santa Claus and the Easter Bunny. She is right.

Once seen through, I now must allow it all to be simply a mystery.

Spirituality is best defined by Sam Harris. He says something like this: that the purpose of spirituality is to recognise that the 'self' is illusory, and that this recognition brings both happiness and insight into the nature of consciousness. That works for me.

***

Andrew

I'm aware that the 'standard' line is that at best religion is a waste of time and can take you away from the path, or at worst will destroy your mind and make you a spiritual zombie. So perhaps those reading this book might be shocked, but I think religion is a beautiful thing. Really, it is.

Religion can give a deep and profound sense of peace, security and harmony. Religion can also help you find your spirituality and help you find your true God. The interesting thing is that just like anything beautiful in nature, if it isn't handled with care and respect it can become dangerous and even deadly.

Here's the really interesting thing from my perspective. If you read the original works you will find that Jesus never started a religion, or even gave the impression he wanted to start a religion. Yet he started the most influential religion of the western world. He was more like an enlightened sage who spoke to a few close people in terms they would each understand, which is why he spoke in parables. Much like Sri Nisargadatta Maharaj in more modern times. Maybe Islam has it correct and Jesus was simply a prophet of the one true and holy God. Jesus was merely pointing to the 'kingdom of heaven' and he said it was within you.

Many Buddhists proudly say they are not part of a religion because they do not have a central deity. However in almost every respect the Buddha actually did start a religion with rituals, rules and dogma. They certainly do worship the 'god of Nirvana'. The irony is so sweet.

Religion, spirituality, and God (by whatever name you prefer) are great paths and each has something positive about it, but there are also negatives about each. The trick is to find what it is that works for you, and then to let it go when it no longer serves a purpose.

***

Maureen

I was raised as an Anglican (sort of), and as an adult became deeply interested in Buddhism.

After awakening, everything shifted. I now feel that every religion, at its deepest, is pointing at the same thing. I'm happy to read and discuss from any religion, but only the deepest teachings, like the mystics, which are often suppressed in Western religions. The rest doesn't interest me at all.

***

Erick

One of the first things I noticed upon awakening to pure existence was the end of all spiritual longing. When the cup is full, it asks for no more. There was a sense of completeness, of being at home with myself in every moment. And there was a sense of directly knowing that which I had been seeking. Words could no longer captivate or inspire me the way they had before.

I naturally saw that the words of most spiritual teachers, particularly the founders of the great religions, were pointing towards this experience. Along with that I saw how the words had been misinterpreted and mistranslated over the centuries to the point where their deeper meanings were mostly obscured. This confusion of meanings makes sense since the experience of awakening defies description. Words can only point to it and never capture it.

For example, I was raised in a Christian tradition. I was taught about the teaching of life after death – we go to heaven or hell based on our acts. But looking at the words of Jesus, if you replace the word 'heaven' with 'awakening', his teachings make much more sense. "The kingdom of heaven lies within" could be "Awakening dwells within". This statement clearly indicates that salvation is here and now, not after death. Likewise throughout his teaching, Jesus was pointing us to being present with a loving God that dwells within this very time and place.

Another development after awakening was having less and less interest in reading spiritual or philosophical texts. The sense is that there is nothing that is not known in that arena, so reading the words of others is redundant. Along with this sense is the quick recognition of truth in the words of others who are awakened. I often use quotes and anecdotes I had learned before awakening to illustrate my perspective. For that reason, the study of spiritual traditions, particularly before awakening, is still quite valuable.

For the first few years after awakening I found great value in listening to the words of others who had been through the awakening process. I particularly liked the in-depth interviews by Rick Archer at *Buddha at the Gas Pump* (https://batgap.com/). Hearing the direct expressions of others helped confirm and clarify aspects of the experience. Awakening, when it dawns, does not fall into mind-based expectations, so there is a process of discovery, like when you move to a new country and have to learn the language and the landscape. It's good to have some friends who have been there to discuss your experience with.

I see religion as a pathway. A tool to use as the soul is developing. Once the bird hatches from the egg, the tools are not needed so much, but these philosophies can be used as channels for one's own teaching, should one be called to do that.

***

Ben

In my understanding, we aren't separate from God in any way. We are God, and God is us. All religions contain elements of insight and truth but the rituals and pageantry attached to the various faiths are purely of human making. Unquestioning belief takes away from understanding/knowing God. Fanatically deriving a sense of self from a particular religion is the source of religious violence. If someone from any religion approaches me unsolicited and preaches to me or tries to convert/save me, I tell them there are roughly 4200 religions in the world and that like them I have also discerned it is ridiculous to think that any of those 4199 other religions could possibly be the sole arbiter of moral and divine truth. I then explain I just happen to think that about one more religion too. The reactions to this are mixed!

***

Timothy

I believe that without religion the world in general would be in chaos. I think religion gives people a form of culture that focuses on the good things about life and promotes a peaceful society. I can see how this allows some people to relax into a sense of safety and so go beyond the average state of fight or flight, from which it may be possible to understand an enlightened perspective.

My definition of what many people call God is "a universal awareness of consciousness that is present everywhere, in everything that exists, which seems to unify with my intuition. God is a field of energy where everything exists in conscious unity." It is an All Existent Energy. I experience this as a calm and pleasant feeling, a love place. Because of this understanding of oneness in the universe l find I always gravitate towards what feels right.

I think the term 'spirituality' can be used similarly to the word 'religion' even if it doesn't necessarily promote a sense of unity among people. Spirituality isn't particularly about the culturing of a society. I've often observed it as a loosely individual approach that has varying definitions. The spiritual paths I've seen do include the sense that there is something beyond our everyday survival concerns, but unlike religion, they don't always refer to a specific path to bring this into awareness. That being said, post-awakening I find that spirituality is more useful for working through past conditioning and dealing with current issues, than religion.

***

Richard

It's interesting to consider how our religious views colour our mystical experiences. Having been raised inside a Christian culture (though not a fundamentalist one) there remains a touch of the Biblical Jehovah in the Mystical God for me. It's something I continue to examine.

As a teenager I rejected religious cosmology in favour of science. As a slightly older teenager, I came to find this empty of meaning and tried using philosophy to sneak God – minus some of his more genocidal instincts – back in. Then I had a series of mystical experiences which set the stage for the rest of my life.

I was originally drawn to Eastern philosophy to explain and explore these. Later I encountered the mystical gnostic texts, which helped me reconcile my relationship with the Christian religion. I feel very drawn to Christian myth, imagery and theology to this day, but as mysteries to be contemplated, not dogmas to expound.

Inwardly I feel like a very religious person, although you wouldn't observe that in my routine. I find church services as dreary as the rest of the population does, even the funky ones featuring guitars. Religion, in this setting, seems to be about trying to convince yourself something is true. For me religion is the opposite of that, a direct examination and experience of what is.

***

Kiran

Long before awakening, the religion of my birth had dropped out of me, but its message remained in me like a beacon. Connection with our prophet (an archetype of pure consciousness) never shattered. Even though the experience of awakening was of absolute oneness, in my lived experience the Godly images of prophets or saints, even those from other religions, remained as the object of my reverence.

Spiritual evolution and embodiment brought more and more oneness, and everything started to fall into the lap of deep inner silence. Every separation loosened, even the feeling of separation from God. Every form melted into the deepest inner silence and my journey towards an inner God seemed to come to an end.

My connection with God as source or finality without any form or quality was seeded within me as a little girl. I can still relate to the profound expressions about God given by Gurus of the Sikh religion. So in a sense religion did contribute to my journey, guiding me, evoking spirituality (living deeply within the soul) and keeping it alive throughout. Most of the time, I sense movements joining outer and inner as if it's all one movement, coming from one and going back into one. I never feel the absence of God; a doer from itself seems to be doing it all.

***

Michaela

Religion was not at the beginning of my search for truth. I saw it as a belief system and my mind (the one who was searching) would never be satisfied with a belief as the answer to the most important life question. The fact that there are many different religions with seemingly different beliefs made it even more obvious.

Philosophy with its analytical scientific approach seemed a far more correct navigation, but also here, I was left without the absolute certainty I was looking for. The greatest philosophers still differed in their conclusions, not to mention the scary fact that many of those great thinkers ended up in the madhouse (which was my nightmare at that time). So actually spirituality — that branch of it that does not grow beliefs, but strips them off in sincere self-inquiry, seemed to be the only way to my goal.

My journey was from head to heart. There I would find the essence of all religions — called God.

Since that simple revelation I see all labeling of the formless reality as more or less charming yet inaccurate attempts to describe the indescribable. And it is with great joy I contribute to such attempts myself!

***

Jennifer

Though I was raised by atheists without religion or spirituality, I was a deeply spiritual person. It started in my teens. Something in me had always been hungry for the deeper things in life.

Through a close friend, I found Naropa University's Transpersonal Psychology Program in my early 20s. Initially, I was skeptical about the Buddhist aspect of the school. Then I fell in love with the contemplative practices and dharma arts: dance and movement, Aikido, shamatha meditation, writing poetry and yoga. My heart opened wide to the maitri or gentle loving kindness teachings. Tibetan Buddhism was an integral part of my Bachelor's Degree education. The 'way of life teachings' were immensely helpful as I fumbled through my relationships

Chapter 13 – Religion, spirituality and God

while slowly recovering from the trauma of my early childhood. Twenty-five years later I am still committed to this Tibetan Buddhist path. It has taught me how to be with myself and others through the most difficult moments imaginable. I am deeply grateful for that lesson which I am still learning. I feel many of the teachings and practices in Tibetan Buddhism not only help to prepare a person for awakening but also help with the integration needed afterwards.

Hinduism taught me devotion and ecstasy. I didn't feel true devotion until the late age of thirty-something. I had always been way too proud to be in devotion to anyone or anything. It happened during a kirtan event. We were chanting to The Protector Mother Goddess, Durga. The experience was profoundly humbling and so filled with love. Yoga practices taught me to open my body so the Shakti could move more freely. Ecstatic chanting practices turned my whole being into pleasurable waves of electric grace almost every time. It was as if I could choose to connect with the current that was already present or not. I remember the first time I attempted to do a 40-day chanting and visualization practice with Ganesha. I did not have the faith that I could do anything for 40 days straight. That kind of discipline was not my strength especially by myself in my living room. I ended up making it through and then doing a second 40-day practice with Lakshmi. Then I did another 40-day practice with Parvati after that. It turned into a straight 120 days of practice! The experience was magical. My life was filled with beauty, abundance, love and grace. I felt a strength I had never known.

I have never fully committed to any one religion mainly because it is not my nature. There were times I wondered if it was a problem or an obstacle on my path. I have come to the conclusion that it has actually helped. By using my own discernment and wisdom, which has developed over many years, I feel I am led in the right direction at the right time to the right thing.

A deep love of The Divine and God had developed over the years but unfortunately after one of my awakening experiences my perspective on this changed drastically. Everything was now God, including me, so all of existence became extremely ordinary and deeply profound simultaneously. I could no longer access The Divine as a separate energy. It has been many years and sometimes I still miss the connection I used to have with my old experience or idea of God. The new way I experience God is in a deeply alive, wakeful, sensuous moment when I feel connected to all that is. It is magnificent and there is nothing personal about it.

***

At the crossroads

Photo by Michaela

A characteristic landscape of my native Moravia, Czech republic, where hundreds of crucifixes and small chapels line the roads.

Chapter 14

Relationships

Michaela

A very powerful subject. Relationship is perhaps our greatest teacher for becoming conscious and also one of our greatest triggers for becoming unconscious.

As messy as relationship can be in our everyday lives, in truth there is only one relating and that is love. It is a recognition of each other in oneness, whatever form that takes. Until we gain that perception and perspective we are searching for completeness outside ourselves; looking for affirmation and self-acceptance through the mirrors of relationship. In fact, we are always looking for an undiscovered part of love, which is ourselves.

The miracle happens when we open for giving. When we open for pure giving with no conditions involved, we open for love. Even the word indicates it: gift, present.

From one of my songs …

>Millions little me
>and millions little you
>playing game of life that's always new
>
>all singing their songs
>and dancing their dance
>dreaming their dreams becoming true.
>
>As lighting rays of sun
>together we are One
>like all the time before we even knew

> that Love is all we are
> and this is ever true
> all we do is being me and you.

***

Amy

Initially, my children woke me up. It was their unconditional love reflecting back at me that showed me the depth of my own self-hatred and allowed it to fall away.

This had a domino effect in which each belief was seen as made-up. Like a ball of yarn unravelling, it all quickly disappeared. I wasn't expecting that. It caught me by surprise.

At the time I thought I would just wander the Earth laughing and never speak again. But I was fortunate to have a mentor/teacher/friend at the time who guided me. She said, "Don't get hung up on language. Just talk." This was tremendously helpful.

But I also recognized the tremendous responsibility I was given to attend to my husband and two small children.

The first thing that was graced to me in my relationship with my husband, was seeing that I had been operating strictly from 'My Agenda'. It was like watching a movie history of all the times in our marriage that I had decided something 'for everyone': my husband, kids, and myself. The honesty of this recognition brought a wave of grief. I saw what was true. And it was heartbreaking to witness the selfishness of it.

Once it passed, all that was left was a purity of love. Without an agenda I suddenly KNEW my husband, almost as if for the first time. There was nothing blocking the way for a true intimacy with this person. What amazed me, was my ability to be so open and honest with him. In the midst of this, his physical attraction towards me was *intense*! He could *not* keep his hands off of me. We had the best sex of our lives during this time.

The only other major personal relationship that changed, was with my mother. Due to childhood trauma I had not spoken to her in five years. At some point, through the help of a therapist and a *lot* of writing, the frustration, anger, grief, and resentment left my body and I was able to experience love for her for the first time in my life. I did not call her right away. I was clear that even though I loved her and appreciated her beauty, she still would not be involved in my life. I did reach out to her and we are in contact on occasion. To be able to love her and simultaneously hold this boundary is something new. In the past, my life was so riddled with people-pleasing that I could never have done this.

In general, I have had a massive shift in how I relate to people. Instead of putting others on a pedestal, I was also able to see their flaws. People I looked up to, whether famous teachers, mentors or family members, all fell to one level. There was no higher authority than my 'own'. Coming from a history of people-pleasing, trauma and being squashed as a child, that part of awakening was the gift of balance. Previously I had lived my emotional and mental life from a place of poverty: "I'm not good enough", "No one really loves me". After awakening there was an opposite experience: "No ONE knows what's best for me." Currently, this is the most awkward experience for me to navigate. It's like living in a foreign land and I don't speak the language. But I love the culture, so I stay.

***

Lisa

Several important relationships in my life have had a 'spiritual' quality and have come up in past-life memories and experiences.

All my major partner relationships have begun on an intuitive basis, with a 'knowing' that we were meant to be together. With my current partner of 15 years (the father of my daughter), we hadn't even met in person when that happened. We connected on an Internet forum for spiritual and paranormal exploration, exchanged a couple of short messages, and when we met it was like coming home; like we'd already known each other for a very long time.

Some relationships in my life have been very difficult and traumatic, with an underpinning of having been 'antagonists' in other lives, times and places. The most difficult, and probably most interesting from an awakening and psychological point of view, has been a relationship with a member of my family of origin; a relationship that impacted me from a very early age. This family member's ego/personality was, and still is, that of a psychologically and emotionally abusive narcissist, and the relationship was very toxic and painful for me. Nevertheless, there's also been love in it and a very strong bonding. But for many years the positive aspects of our connection were deeply entangled and hidden within a mush of abuse, pain and resentment. In past life terms, I've 'remembered' this person as a Nazi guard in a Concentration camp where I was killed during WW2. This relationship has been my biggest challenge and in a sense also my biggest teacher in this life.

Over the years, my relationship with this person has changed several times, mirroring where I stood in my own journey.

Prior to awakening, after years of pain, trying to untangle all the unhealthy aspects of the relationship in therapy and trying different ways of dealing with the person and my feelings, I felt that in order to protect myself it was necessary to cut the person out of my life emotionally and psychologically, even if not physically.

But after awakening, the quality of the relationship changed. I no longer felt a need to 'protect myself', because there wasn't anyone or anything to protect anymore. I actually found this quite interesting. The result is that I can let the person come psychologically close to me again, and for instance, share thoughts and feelings if I choose to do so. When there are abusive remarks and behaviour, it now goes straight through me, doesn't 'stick' anywhere, and doesn't hurt or harm me in any way. I still don't like the way the person behaves and see it as destructive, but now I can choose to either keep the person at arms-length psychologically and emotionally, or not. It's all the same to me now. In a spiritual sense, I feel the purpose of this relationship has been to overcome the toxic aspects of it and reach a place of forgiveness and peace. I'm quite happy with the results so far.

As far as relationships in general, I'd say they've all become easier and smoother after awakening. I basically perceive the other person as 'me' and so I deal with them accordingly. There's no discomfort, or fear, or awe, or feeling less than or more than. I feel free and spontaneous and authentic when relating to others. On a superficial level there might be some fleeting feelings of discomfort or contraction, but I notice them and let them go. There is no more relationship drama. I can still feel that a person is behaving like a shithead, but now there's no separation between me and the shithead ... haha. I'm also not 'loving' towards everyone in the sense of being 'nice' or 'pleasant' as one might think an 'awakened' person should be. I find myself getting angry, telling people off, sometimes being more 'rude' or impatient than before awakening. But now there's a different quality to it because it doesn't come from a sense of separation. The place where separation was, is now filled with what I'd call love. So even if I tell someone off, I do it with love.

There's also a paradoxical feeling of being a lot closer to others now, but at the same time much further away. I suppose this is a part of what is meant by "being in the world but not of the world". I feel that we are basically all one, all the same, all this unbounded consciousness, this aliveness, this deeply mysterious beautiful being. But as long as most people consciously come from a completely different place, a sense of distance is unavoidable.

***

Ben

My first awakening experience was in 2004, my lasting experience in 2018. In that time I had a multitude of relationships that never lasted. I wasn't ready. I put too much emphasis on relationships being responsible for my happiness. As soon as I settled and finally, truly, embodied the understanding I had come to all those years before, my soulmate appeared when I wasn't even looking for her. Quite how perfectly we complement each other blows me away every single day and adds a deep source of joy to my life.

***

Marianne

I have been 'awake' twelve years. Relationship has changed greatly for me over that time.

With the continued falling away of the egoic 'selfing' and its memory and patterns of conditioned behaviour, there has also been a falling away of relationship. Without a separate 'me', there is also no separate 'other'. It may sound harsh but I cannot 'be in relationship'.

This has certainly been a difficult thing in my long-term relationship with my partner. I am empty. I am simply 'not there' to do all the psychological mirroring and meeting of needs that people do when they say they are 'having a relationship'. I think if it wasn't a long-term relationship with a long history, we would not have stayed together. Certainly my partner and I spoke a number of times over the years about whether we would continue or not, but we do enjoy spending time together, we enjoy bushwalking together, we enjoy the dogs, the garden, and we also take care of one another physically. And my partner *is* interested in spirituality so does understand the context for what is happening to some degree. There are also all the usual interactions of living with someone – the disagreements, the compromises, the miscommunications – but they all flow on through.

Recently, however, we got married. After three decades together it suddenly felt right to get married. We eloped and told everyone about it afterwards. In my vows I couldn't speak of an individual or special love, but I did speak of a love that is far bigger than both of us, and of which we are both a part. Love is no longer specific, and although I think there are times my partner would like it to be, she would never wish me to speak from other than authenticity.

As far as sex goes, I can take it or leave it. Sex used to be a big part of my life, but I rarely think about it now. There is no longer a 'me' that wants to 'feel connected' to someone else or 'have my needs met'. There is a sense of connectedness with all of Life in every moment. I look out the window at a tree and there is nothing 'better' than that complete fullness.

There has been much moving on from close friendships. At times this has been uncomfortable. With friendships I can no longer partake of egoic mirroring or collusion in drama. I am also unable to partake of idle conversation for very long. My intention has never been to cause others grief, but I know that my incapacity to continue as I was has definitely caused pain and confusion. At times I had hoped my silent presence might be enough, but others also perceived that as a threat and a problem. There is also no need to pursue 'new relationships'. I know this is confusing for people, as I am generally very open and friendly. The sequence of social niceties that presumably leads to closer relationships (go for a walk, meet for coffee, go out to dinner) doesn't interest me. And yet, yesterday afternoon, a dear friend I have known since high school visited us for the day. There was laughter, good food, reminiscing, walking in the garden, playing with the dogs ... it was delightful ... and there was no particular need to talk about spirituality or not talk about it. It just was what it was. Then she left; there is coming and then there is going.

Interestingly I now find family easier. I can delight in the smiles of a great nephew, I can care about my parents' health, and I can talk about my brother's latest overseas trip. It flows as it flows. Pre-awakening I did a lot of therapeutic work on my relationship with my family of origin. Post-awakening, although there were still issues to uncover, years upon years of angst and trauma dissolved without me realizing it. I recall having a cup of tea with someone who had caused me immense grief over the years, and as we chatted I could not find 'our history'; this person was now not other than 'myself'. I still wouldn't spend a great deal of time with this person, but the inner contraction had gone.

Chapter 14 – Relationships

***

Kiran

This word 'relationship' has slowly lost its mind-made meaning. Since relationship denotes two, the only real relationship is the innermost relationship with one's own Self.

At first, when awakening was experienced, and formless, conscious awareness had completely revealed itself as Pure Self, it felt as though I no longer knew anything of conditioning (relationship being part of that conditioning). However, it didn't last and eventually almost everything started to operate at the surface again in the same way.

There was a very deep and clear recognition at the time of awakening that the Relative world, the world of relationships, needed to be included into Oneness and not kept separately. It was seen that all relationships belonged to the separate self and that suffering came about from the creation of stories about those relationships. The separate self's first relation with itself was also the cause of suffering because it always needed things in a certain way based on its belief or conditioning. Very little was experienced directly as it was happening, because the loudness of conditioning always wanted things differently.

Now, there is nothing as 'relationship' which includes me, my biological children, family, spouse, friends and the rest of the world. They seem to be the part of ROM (Random Operating Memory) and perform their scenes without any resistance or attachment, as it is now part of One, included in One, and with Freedom in connectedness. The most important relationship is within, the relationship of Absolute and relative world within.

I realize this process has brought more aloneness by breaking the identification with the majority of relations and friends. However this aloneness doesn't cause much loneliness anymore because I feel grounded in the inner essence. At times, when I get identified with separating thoughts, I do experience related emotions and feelings, including loneliness. But I know it is an opportunity to include more.

At the moment I am visiting my husband's home city with a lot of relatives and it's so nice to notice that what they all do or not do in relation to my husband and I, seems to have no bearing; it is such a great taste of liberation.

***

Richard

Being more awake definitely improves my ability to relate to all people. That might sound trite and obvious, but I say it as I know that for some people awakening can bring a sense of disconnection. I was scared that this might happen to me, but I'm pleased to report that I have all the same friends as I did when I was fourteen. I'm only fifteen and a half now so we'll have to see how that turns out. Joking – I'm 37.

I've found it massively helpful to have friends with whom I can openly talk about awakening-related stuff – and then not do so with friends who aren't into it. Awakening has evoked a sense of life being fascinating, in all its mundanity, so I don't really mind the topic of conversation. I find most people respond well to having interest taken in them.

It's probably very helpful that I don't conceive of awakening as being a thing that people have. I therefore don't experience a great divide between myself and my family and friends.

As far as romantic relationships go … you're on your own.

***

Stacy

Re-late: relationships are about doing something again. After seeing there is no separate self, waking up and experiencing the oneness of it all, this is clearer than ever. There is only one of us here. We are playing a game of 'other'. Alan Watts spoke about this extensively.

The first thing is that the clearer I get, the fewer people can really relate to 'me', which makes sense because there is no me. There are so many allegories about this that I could quote, as throughout time people like us have had the same situation. It is a lived experience that 'they' are 'me'. But 'they' don't know that, and that's a challenge in communication and the seeming continuous expression of What Is that we call 'relationships'. This can be a muddy, murky area until this is lived. No self, no separation, no other. There is no one to blame.

My first impulse was to try to show 'them'; get them to see things the way they are seen now. Mostly that is pretty futile. If they wanted to know, they would be pursuing it. There is too much investment in believing the lie of separation. And fear. And expectations. There's a morass of thinking, supported by what you'd call our 'culture' or 'world' and most people never even think about it, much less come to questioning it! It must be assumed that this is perfection, since this is all there is. And yet, it is hard, at first, to let that sleeping dog lie. It seems there would be so much more peace if we *all* saw this truth of connection and oneness. War would stop, wouldn't it? But taking a closer look, there is no war.

One set of books calls this 'level confusion'. At one level, oneness, perfect peace. At another, the government spends more on war than anything else and bodies bleed and die. It can be confusing when identified with a self, but so clear when not. And there is virtually no explaining it – like this whole Awakening thing – words just don't do it!

Romantic, intimate relationships shifted.

A while after my clearest and longest sense of connection, I got into a relationship with someone who had no interest in these questions. I experienced what is called 'got it, lost it'. Got into believing we were separate and trying to bring her with me on this awakening, but no. At the same time, she connected well. She could viscerally experience being one with me without using the words and ideas I use about it. So I stayed with her for a few years. It was something. Some good sense of connection. However, since she did not want a lifelong relationship, I eventually weaned myself from it and spent the next five years mostly alone. I had 'lost it' some; although the awareness never really leaves. It's a permanent shift.

Five years later, a man from my teen years showed up declaring his undying love and proposing marriage with every other breath. He has even less awareness of any of this – awakening, The Work of Byron Katie. None. There's no one in him to share all of this with, to go into agreement with me about it. It's strange. To be honest, my thinking says that I would prefer a partner who is into all of this with me. But that's not what showed up, so I'm going with it. It seems to be exactly what I need - to give in and relate to those who don't have this awakening experience. Well, why not? That's most of these seemingly separate humans. But I have some inner work, inner questioning to do about all of this.

About every two to four weeks, he tells me he is leaving, going back to Texas. I just wait. It passes. He tells me he's not what I want. That's true. It's an odd relationship in this way. I have no idea how it will go, but here I am. He tells me that "nothing matters" to me - as if that's a bad thing? It's not, to me. It's true. I'm not that attached to who stays and who goes.

I'm taking this as a huge opportunity to be with what *does* matter to me - truth, connection, and my internal sense of being awake. We will see how that goes.

I admit I long for more camaraderie and maybe someday that will show up. It *sounds* good, right? But look at the paradox, the lesson. WHY would there be an 'I' who 'needs' these things? There isn't.

Loving is all there is.

Sounds corny. But it's true.

As for sex ...

When I tell someone that there is something better than sex and orgasm, I am met with complete disbelief. While it is true that I have had mind-blowing connected experiences during sex that were also a 'deep' (whatever that means) or 'intense' feeling of connectedness or awakening, sex is not at all the only way to get 'there'. Or more accurately, to become aware and awake to what is here and now.

I've spent my life seeking ways to feel this connectedness. For me, there are things that 'work' and things that 'don't work'. Things that 'work' include breathwork, sex, staring at moving water from a bridge, watching leaves move in the breeze, particularly those that have different colors front and back like a cottonwood, meditations that are 'pointers' or 'meta-meditation' that ask us to be aware in ways we normally are not (such as meeting everything in our awareness with the thought, "this is how God is showing up right now". No, I have no god belief. It just works for that meditation.) Some of these ask us to look for a 'self' or compare the difference between our imagination of a spoon and a spoon we are holding in our hand. Once you've had even one of these, what I call 'connected' experiences, you'll know what is meant here.

Tantric sex was popular in New Age and 'spiritual' circles for many years. Might still be for all I know. What was called 'tantra' was usually just a copy of a couple of teachers in the US who made up some rituals that had nothing to do with how tantra would be practiced in a country in Asia where there word 'tantra' came from. They co-opted some words, like 'puja' which is a fire ceremony originally, and turned it into some talking process done between partners in a circle that had nothing to do with the origin of the word. So, don't get me started on that, but it needed to be mentioned because it's out there. Ugh.

Sex has mattered less and less, even not at all, since awareness is here without it. It's still fun. It's still a pleasurable experience. Orgasm can range from the purely physical to mind-blowing connectedness. Only the partner I mentioned earlier seemed to 'join' 'me' in that awareness, to be aware when 'I' was in that state. My current partner doesn't know anything at all about this connectedness.

***

Chapter 14 – Relationships

Maureen

A therapist taught me that when we go through deep change, the people around us will try to pull us back into old patterns, because that's what they're used to. If we fall back, the change doesn't take hold. If we choose to stick with the change, then other people have three choices in how they react. They can:

1. Refuse to adapt. These relationships tend to fall away.
2. Adapt, and the relationships continue, in a healthier way.
3. Entrain. (I had to look this up. It means to get on the train with.) This happens when people like the change they see, and want to join in and do the work too.

This is a perfect description of what I've found, as I've done deep work, particularly post-awakening. Dysfunctional relationships determined to stay stuck simply fell away. Some people are happy to adapt to the changes in me, without any interest in the spiritual basis to the changes. And a few, delightfully, are deeply interested in a spiritual life and want to learn and grow with me.

I've never been hugely social, and am less so now, requiring a great deal of quiet. But I do enjoy connecting with people. Most people are not interested in spiritual discussions, so we talk about whatever people talk about, gardening or politics or the new baby in the family. It's lovely and casual and very human.

***

Timothy

At the time of the shift to enlightenment, I was estranged from my biological family due to their own challenges; I hadn't talked to them for over a year. As a single young adult, I moved around a lot during that period of my life. There weren't any Internet social networking sites or cell phones back then so I had lost touch with everyone I knew from my past. I was so focused on finding truth that I didn't have any new friends. My job at the time was washing dishes on weekends in the restaurant across the street from my inexpensive studio apartment. Being the quiet sort to begin with, I also didn't make any strong connections at work. Looking back, I realize I was blessed to have so much time to myself.

After enlightenment, I found that I didn't care whether I made friends or not. I wasn't opposed to being around others, I just wasn't motivated in that regard and knew I didn't need anyone to be happy within myself. Gradually, people did show up in my everyday life and I had some acquaintances towards whom I felt friendly.

After enlightenment my biological family did initiate a reconnection of sorts, so I told them what had happened to me. They thought I'd gone over the edge. My brother told me that my dad had said I was "all spaced out" and "lost", and that he was sad he couldn't do anything to help me. My dad never came to fully understand but he did finally listen to some of the things I told him and seemed to recognize a little of what I said. I think my words might even have helped him a bit with his own difficulties. Although we are still not particularly close, I now enjoy talking to various members of my family when they reach out.

I can say that I became more loving towards society in general. My 'me against the world' attitude evaporated and I naturally adjusted to the human experience with which I was left. Sexuality lost all importance, which was interesting because I was raised in the early years of the 1960s sexual revolution and sexuality was a big part of my previous identity. I was more interested in sharing love than in having sex. It was ironic though, that I was apparently suddenly more attractive to the women that I met. To gain a better understanding of how sexuality fit with my new awareness I studied Tantra at a school that taught sex as ritual. I completed their three-year course and found it very informative and quite useful for navigating this area of life when needed. This learning was also very balancing for my physical body and for knowing how to use such energies in positive and life-affirming ways. It's helped me stay youthful in my attitudes and intimate relationships.

Pre-enlightenment, I always said I'd never get married and that I didn't want children. Afterwards I let go of the fear that fuelled such a commitment. In my mid-30s I met someone I could imagine being with for a long time, someone on a path of seeking truth. She wanted a child, so I agreed but only if we got married. We planned to travel the world with our little spirit baby and I knew I could only protect my new family in a foreign country if I was her legal husband and the father listed on our child's birth certificate. These were just pieces of paper to me, but necessary ones, I felt, to keep my family safe. Unfortunately, this ultimately brought up old childhood conditioning for her that she couldn't work through. My wife's difficulties had me baffled, as nothing I tried seemed to help, which brought up similar old conditioning for me, but unlike her, I

Chapter 14 – Relationships

was able to resolve it. After years of attempting to remedy this discord, she told me one day she didn't think she had ever loved me, she didn't know why she married me, and she wanted me to leave. I couldn't stay where I wasn't wanted, so we divorced amicably. Our son was nine at the time and I made sure to live within walking distance of their home until he was old enough to take public transportation to visit me. I saw him as often as he wanted me to, until he was 19. He's since chosen not to stay in touch, unfortunately, so I haven't talked to him for five years. He's a lot like I was at his age, though, so I know he'll be fine.

After my marriage ended, I swore I'd never have another intimate relationship and that I'd just live alone from then on. Of course, it wasn't long before the universe presented just the opposite and a woman appeared in my life who is also enlightened. We've been together for 16 years, living in our own little field of love and companionship. We've never had an argument and we've always worked through life's challenges together. It's definitely a most beautiful relationship for which I'm so very grateful. I helped raise her two daughters from a previous relationship. They're all grown up and on their own now but unlike my son they choose to stay in touch.

I never feel lonely and sometimes wonder if I would miss anyone if I went away to a remote land. I don't really want to test that though, as it's nice to feel I belong. It's especially wonderful to be around someone who has found truth, works on their own challenges, is always friendly to me, and knows what love is.

As a result of living in my heart, other relationships always feel casual. But there are also people who, so to speak, make me shine. I very much like to be near them and I can even have a brief feeling that I miss them when they're not around. Essentially, I don't have the dramatics of mentally labelling relationships, and the 'this means this' rollercoaster ride that most people engage with when it comes to being social.

To me, friendship is the most important relationship, and its apparent modus operandi is simply 'being friendly'. Without this act of being friendly, our species would never have survived. Helping a stranger is a good example of the friendliness that our very existence relies upon. I don't think about this much, I just live it.

In general, children seem to connect with me quicker than they do with most people. I've had some instances where autistic children and Down syndrome adults have opened up and excitedly approached me. I suspect that they can sense my magnetic field and can feel that it's gentler, more stable, or more available than others. I'm not purposely doing anything to make that happen, it just is. I've always been able to 'talk to the animals' but that also improved a bit post-enlightenment.

***

Jennifer

When I was in graduate school in The San Francisco Bay Area, I had a lovely friend who was such a gift to me. I considered him farther along on his journey than I was. We talked for hours and hours about what it was like to see and live from this awakened perspective. He practiced a lot with dissolving the self, as well as being with reality as it is. He often had great wisdom to share and made me feel heard and understood in ways that no one else did, largely because they hadn't lived it yet. We went to see Adya together a few times which was sweet to share. I am grateful to him. It was so helpful to have one person who understood and shared his wisdom with me

I also had a partner who was a former Buddhist monk at Gampo Abbey where Pema Chodron lives and teaches. During his time there, he learned a lot about himself and the awakening process that he shared with me while we were together. We shared a similar pain that can arise from seeing through the illusion of existence; it was a deep sadness that can come as a result of this knowing. He encouraged me to find the strength and courage to be with the incredibly painful, traumatic experiences that were surfacing to be healed. When we made love, his energy moving through my body washed these blockages up and out of my system. Sometimes I cried or my whole body shook uncontrollably. Other times it was too much and I shut down emotionally and energetically. It was a beautiful thing to be in that world of wakefulness and presence together when we were open and made love. Though our relationship had plenty of challenges, it would have been difficult to have been with someone who wasn't awake.

***

Erick

I think much less about relationships. That is probably because I don't need to base my happiness on them. I find that I can be more direct and loving with everyone – a dear family member or a complete stranger. When the love flows the listening is very close and the gaps between personalities closes tight. Misunderstandings are fewer, as are oversights and mistakes.

That doesn't mean everything is perfect. I still have to watch out for my weak areas and try to give a little more attention there, but overall, relationships are getting better. Long-time adversaries are now close working partners. Relationships that were once somewhat co-dependent have either moved onto a more balanced track or have faded away. Strong relationships have grown deeper.

Awakening is not a panacea for relationships, but it is the oil in the gears that allows the machine to run cool and smooth.

There is an alone-ness that developed in knowing that we are all one in consciousness, yet we are also fictions of that single consciousness. As such, there is no one to know or to be known by another. It took me a while to get used to that. At first I sought out others who were awake. That was not a very fruitful endeavour, though I met some marvellous folks. Over time the longing subsided as the inner oneness grew to include all of the moving world. Now I live in the most exquisite collective aloneness.

**

Kathy

Friendships:

Initially upon awakening, I felt it was extremely important to surround myself with awakened people. That has changed over time. It's become clear that even if awake, people have their personalities and preferences. We may not get along or may not have much in common on the personality level, even though we share a common thread and understanding.

Some people I had called friends before awakening are no longer in my life, because it became clear that the relationships were constructed on unhealthy beliefs and ideas. Once these were seen through, those relationships naturally fell away. Then there are some friendships that continue. These are based on a love of the essence of these friends. I am fine supporting them in times of need and celebrating their successes with them, all the while realizing there exists a deeper version of us beyond words, beliefs and labels. While on one level nothing is real, we are still in this human form and their story and feelings are very real. Just as with awake friends, I offer them my presence and love. That said, there is a preference to have friends that are awake with shared interests.

Family:

Etched in my mind for at least 20 years were the words of Ram Dass, "If you think you are enlightened, go spend a week with your family". I was very convinced that if I were awake, all the family pain would disappear and I would become Teflon, where nothing would stick other than love. Yet I was surprised to see that it's not that simple. While I could move on that did not mean others involved in a past story would.

My core childhood wound was abandonment. My mother sent me to live with my father as a pre-teen and denied my existence to those in her world. While I have found peace around this after my world shattered upon awakening, it became clear that until she could find forgiveness and acceptance for herself, our relationship could only exist if we maintained an unhealthy dynamic that no longer served me. It took me a couple of years after awakening to see this. I realized nothing I could do would help her heal from her own wounds or guilt, the constant insults, lack of acceptance of who I was, amongst other unhealthy dynamics, just did not work anymore. While there was a profound sense of freedom and peace in this realization, it was accompanied by a sadness that I can still feel today.

With my father, even though there were childhood issues, there was always love and acceptance. After awakening, it's been even easier to love him.

Romantic Relationships:

It was the ending of a romantic relationship with an awake person that ultimately pushed me over the edge and helped me awaken. As with all my significant relationships, it too ended in abandonment. Each past relationship was an invitation to go into that core wound and by going truly and fully into it, the pain dissolved along with the stories and accompanying beliefs.

Since then, there has been little interest in finding romantic love, but I am pretty sure that is because my old beliefs of how that should look are gone. And there no longer exists a gaping hole looking to be filled. A few people have shown up as potential partners, and it became quickly clear that they were looking for relationship that would be intertwined with unhealthy patterns. That no longer interests me. Right now, I am open to a romantic relationship if it feels right and am fine without one as well.

***

Creating Story

by
Maureen

The universal oneness
great energy in the sky
godness
whatever the hell we want to call it/us
creates
bubbles up
in a great joy of creation
We the oneness playwright creates the set
the scripts
the roles
we step on stage as actors
When our feet touch the stage
we forget who we are
we believe we are the roles
Romeo, Juliet, the old nurse
playing out great dramas tragedies comedies
In these roles, we create
we write books movies poems
children play dress up, dance figures in the sand
we play
we create
because we forget
but not quite
We are story creating story

***

Chapter 15

Mind, cognition and memory

Marianne

After I 'awoke', even though the mind was very quiet during the two-year honeymoon period, I actually hadn't seen *through* the mind. I had seen what I *am*, I knew my true identity, but I hadn't deeply understood and explored what I was *not*. But at that time it seemed irrelevant to look further. All was very quiet and peaceful. There was only the entirety without argument.

But at some point the honeymoon period ended. I never lost the 'awakening' – the vastness of my true nature was always the background of all and could not be unseen – but the mind kicked in again from time to time, cluttering the foreground. As a result, I suffered. In this suffering, it was difficult to discern between the residue of trauma from my past and the rote churning of mind 'stuff'. I found that spiritual teachers tended to ignore or negate the former (I actually found none who had any wisdom to offer on the matter of trauma), and therapists tended to ignore or negate the latter. I had to make my own path.

I begrudgingly re-engaged in therapeutic work and once again looked at past trauma but now from the perspective of awakening. This was immensely valuable. But the monkey mind was still there to some extent, insisting on getting my attention. The advice of teachers to ignore the mind and surrender didn't fit with me. I tried that countless times. I had to know and experience exactly what the mind was and how it functioned. And so I inquired.

I saw that the brain was just like any other bodily 'organ'; it had a task. Just like the heart pumped blood, the brain pumped thoughts. It was basically a self-preservation mechanism for the organism. Undoubtedly the mind's job in ages past was to continually scan the environment making sure that the body was safe and fed: What is this? Can I trust it? What are they doing? That mastodon looks angry. Later this task was appropriated by the egoic self. The mind pitted this ego self against the world and others (duality), always watching out for what was good for 'me' and what was not. The 'emotions' let the mind know if I was safe (felt good and loved) or if I was in danger (felt angry, sad or defensive). The mind was a very good tool for doing sums, negotiating traffic, reading and following instruction manuals, but it was hopeless at the 'ego' job assigned to it. Not surprisingly it was a task doomed to failure; duality can never be won. There would always be one more thing/person to fight or defend against. Suffering on and on.

In addition it became clear that I retained an underlying assumption that the mind had just a little validity and could be used to make at least *some* valid judgements about my life. I realized that this commentary from my mind, particularly about my 'spiritual progress' or lack thereof, was based on an underlying certainty that my mind (identified as 'me') was basically of profound goodwill and could therefore be trusted to a degree. There was a core assumption that my mind was 'looking out for me' and *always* had my best interests at heart. But in believing that, I stumbled. The mind is indeed doing the best job it can, and that job is 100% well-intentioned and protective; the mind is not 'bad'. But within its limited operating framework it does not know, and indeed *cannot* ever know **who I truly *am***. So if the mind can never know my true nature, how then can even one sentence of the mind's commentary about spirituality, 'me', or almost anything else for that matter, *ever* have validity? The mind can *never* be the expert, organizer, watchman, champion, judge or jury of that which is beyond it. It is impossible. All the mind's commentary can only ever be about a dualistic world.

So how is life lived now? I live very much in the present moment. Just this. There is the direct experience of what is in front of me: seeing, hearing, touching. I actually find it very hard to 'think' now. It no longer comes easily. Most thoughts were about a 'me', and there isn't one. Even as I write this, it is difficult to remember and to reflect and then put my experience into words. But I can think clearly in a functional way: when I have to build a drainage channel so stormwater can flow, when I have to balance finances. Life has been shown to be a mystery. I don't know what is going on and I don't need to. Nor do I have any need to argue the point, create lines across reality or have opinions. THIS is it.

I do 'struggle' from time to time with understanding people and talking with them. I have forgotten to some extent what it is to live in duality and in memory. There are times people might say things like, "Wasn't the heat last week awful!" and I scramble inside to find a response. I don't really remember a 'last week' in the way that they do and I made no judgement about it at the time. But I know they're simply wishing to make a connection with me, so I usually mumble something in agreement and move on.

But there is no perfection here. I am well aware that the mind is very good at upping the ante and coming up with dire scenarios to take my attention.

***

Sarah

On all levels – from who I am to who bought the toilet paper last – those great tsunami waves of forgetfulness have come and gone, sometimes for long stretches of time, and sometimes for a few days.

And then my system seems to adjust, and memory and cognition improve.

There were long stretches of time when words made no sense, sentences were gibberish, and it felt as though I couldn't function 'normally' without causing concern.

But eventually an adjustment of my entire system took place, and there was a sense of having caught up.

There have been many, many waves of this. It usually occurs now when the prior realizations are sinking more deeply into my being, changing this nervous system, creating new neural pathways. There is an opening into Totality and fullness and liveliness now, rather than the fallings away and the great Emptiness of the earlier awakenings. And so sometimes there is a flood of stimuli of this body/mind stream and system, and I am not 'firing on all cylinders' for a while.

Then again … there is a natural adjustment that occurs. In time, this body/mind catches up. So I've found I lean into these waves of total uselessness, and somehow, what needs to get done, gets done.

***

Chapter 15 – Mind, cognition and memory

Erick

Immediately after awakening I noticed that time had compressed. It seemed like events in the recent past were not distant in time but were still as clear as if they had just happened. It was as if the gentle fog that gathers between now and past events, making them fade as the years pass, was gone and the past was now crystal clear. Over time I got accustomed to the changed perception and it is no longer strange.

Other than that, the clarity of perception of both the 'external' world and the world of my thoughts continues to grow. Unity deepens. Communication with others is just seen as an extension of the internal communication of thoughts. The reality of the world is no greater, or lesser than that of the flow of intelligence we call thoughts.

Naturally relationships become more balanced – they are seen clearly from deeper and deeper levels of unity. When there is no 'other' then love and empathy can flow. This extends into family. There is peace and co-creating among us. Even though the skeletons of the old patterns are still in place, they have little flesh and serve more as channels for communicating. I dream of everyone awakening.

Self-referential thoughts are fairly simple – I observe myself as another funny little animal running around on this sweet little planet, just like our friends in the trees and burrows. I maintain my place here just as a bird keeps its nest. When my time comes to go I'll go.

Emotions stay in the positive range generally, but 'positive' can also mean energetically creative and industrious.

***

Maureen

Mind? Cognition? Memory? They all turned to mush. Slowly, they're emerging in a new way. My mind seems to function totally differently now.

Memory is either not there – things seem to drop away and simply not matter – or is more precise. I have to stop, allow a little time for the memory to ... emerge? download? reform? Then it can be astoundingly accurate. Or not there at all.

Cognition is sharper, but used more sparingly. My cognitive brain is a tool I can use when I need it, and put down when I don't. Before, I was thinking thinking thinking all the time. Now I can turn it on or off, as I need it or don't. (There are still times when I wind up into thinking thinking thinking. But it always settles back into silence).

I know less and less. It's marvellous to be comfortable with not knowing, to not need endless answers. It opens up a world of curiosity.

The changes are not finished yet, I suspect. A deeper calm? More direct focus when I need it? Less memory? More precise memory? I don't know. Every day is an adventure.

***

Kiran

Before awakening, the memory disc contained a lot of conscious and unconscious data. This brought much hurt, pain and misery. After awakening there were many changes. Memory lost its capacity to hold beliefs and participate in them. Mind, which had worked hand-in-hand with memory, changed course towards the moment; being in the moment has greatly reduced the use of memory and mind. I now live more from an awake and alert place; responses come from a restfulness and compassion instead of from the unconscious and automatic responses of ego.

As these changes were happening, there was a lot of confusion in the mind. Mind and intellect had been accustomed to dividing and labelling everything according to the happiness or unhappiness of the ego entity. When understanding and perception through the mind (and its identification with a separate self) was relinquished, everything became so much more experiential, direct and simple.

The relationship of awareness with mind, memory and cognition continues to change. Further purity (absence of separate self) allows most thought forms to rise and fall without any change to the restfulness and silence. This has affected almost everything that happens on the surface level. The responses that arise, bypass the ego/mind conglomerate, and do not involve memory and the conditioned/dualistic mind. Moments are experienced directly and communications and interactions are more direct, unprotected and not in line with societal dos-and-don'ts. The gentle softness of the innermost silence brings a very different quality of truth to interactions and communication. If identification does arise there is discomfort.

These paragraphs are however a very summarized and compacted description of what has happened; the issue of mind is not simple. There is a sense of a continual transformation within that guides and helps to establish attention more and more in formlessness. This mode of attention is open and allowing, and less and less narrow. Because mind creates a subject/object relationship and can only understand reality in this way, there is also much less objectification. Additionally, mind trusts only knowing and form, while truth resides in formlessness. I am not yet at the point where every form and perception is immediately and silently experienced As Is ie. complete abidance in No-Self, No-Form, as a ground of potentiality. It is a work in progress, but the sticky ground of mind is disappearing at a rapid pace and No-Self is expanding.

This profound continuous shift was highlighted after a recent spiritual experience I had while holidaying in India (although on the whole even spiritual experiences occur less now). While sitting on a bench, talking to my husband, I started sinking into unknown depths. People walking around me, including my husband, were all just forms like moving robots and had no influence on these greater depths. I am now feeling and living more from that place. This became even more apparent when we returned from holiday and stayed with my son and his children. I'm recognizing more often and profoundly that there was never anyone journeying, even though it was perceived as such.

Mind and its perceptions are misrepresentations. Even the innermost movements within silence can be perceived by the speculating mind and labelled as an idea or a thought. When the mind becomes free of this speculating habit, it reaches its own true nature/silence. Abiding in that innermost silence, it feels fully transcended; just mind resting in the core without a sound. Complete absence of will, with full openness towards manifestation, without a trace of resistance. All senses including mind remain available to be used as required by life but with no ego-based agenda. Mind in full surrender.

***

Elizabeth

I have always had a terrible memory. Awareness of awakening has come and gone since childbirth, so it's hard to tell what happened 'post' awakening. It's always been very difficult to 'keep' anything, but it is most definitely worse now. I've even gone to doctors about my memory loss. No one has any suggestions.

Many years ago, there were times I would drive along a highly familiar route to school, the grocery store or to my parents' house, and then suddenly I would look around and have NO idea where I was! I'd keep driving and keep open, looking at the landscape, hoping I would recognize something – anything! Usually, right before my turnoff, intuition would guide me strongly and I would know what to do, even though I still didn't recognize where I was. Then my memory would slowly return as I continued to drive. I attended an Adyashanti retreat during this time and members of the audience stood up, telling him of the exact same experience! He ended up deeming it one of the main themes of the retreat!

As for thinking processes ... I always check in before making a decision.

I've become more emboldened in my communications, as fear of disapproval is greatly lightened these days. It's certainly not gone, but it is less. Things in the inner realm are so loose. Body is but a shell and mind is an empty space within body. So ... I don't really know what is important anymore. Many things I thought were important at certain times have slipped away into this void. But I still have my hang-ups, like most people.

***

Lisa

Immediately after the transition into awakening my mind went absolutely silent. It was a huge change. Until I got used to the new sensation (a couple of weeks later) I went about my day listening to and enjoying this tremendous *silence*. Prior to that, thoughts had constantly poured out of my mind like blood, or maybe more like pus oozing out of an open wound. And that was what it felt like – it was painful. All thoughts, almost without exception, made me suffer. They were thoughts of fear, sometimes of horror, of worry about the future or of obsessing about an event in the past. They were thoughts of being less than others, of being worthless, or of being better than others in some shape or form – of being exceptional, special, remarkable.

These thoughts were like two different sides of the same coin: Being special on one side and being worthless on the other. Worrying about the future on one side and obsessing about the past on the other. Want, need and longing for what I didn't have on one side, and resentment, disgust, hate and rejection of what I didn't want on the other. And I believed them all. I thought they were a reflection of reality: a painful reality

Chapter 15 – Mind, cognition and memory

of lack, of fear, of loneliness, of unfulfilled desires, of envy, of hate, of resistance and suffering.

After the transition, the whole coin suddenly disappeared altogether and there was *silence* instead. It was and still is a tremendous relief. All those thoughts meant absolutely nothing, they were all meaningless, but if someone had said something like that to me before the transition, I would have thought they were crazy. I thought my thoughts were a part of *me*. Well, it turned out they weren't.

Now, my mind is a tool, like a hand. If I need to think about some specific issue, I do. Mainly, it's about the practicalities of life: which train to take, how to fill in a form. Otherwise, there's *silence*. I love this silence. It's peaceful.

I don't 'think about' things the way I used to. If I experience beauty, there's no thought that says, "This is beautiful". There is beauty. If there is pain, there is pain but no thoughts about it. The experience of life is much more raw and direct without the filter of thoughts. When thoughts arise, as they still do at times, I no longer automatically believe them or feel that they are part of 'me'.

Memory has changed as well. After the transition, it was as though all the files with memories stored in folders on the hard drive of my mind were cleaned of attached viruses of pain, longing or resentment. The memories were still there and I could still remember what I had felt at the time, but I could no longer feel those emotions in the now. Before, I used to suck on a memory like a sweet and feel the taste of past pain, anger, joy, or fear. The memories could be used as a pastime, or to conjure up a feeling about a particular person or event. After the transition, everything that had been painful and difficult in the past was 'forgiven'. Or rather, it was seen that there had never really been anything to forgive in the first place; nobody had done anything to 'me' because the 'me' was no longer there. This made it possible to start relating to people from what was actually happening in the now, not from what had transpired yesterday or twenty years ago.

In connection to this 'cleansing' of memories, there was a realization that the only true reality in all that had transpired in the past, and all that would happen in the future, was love. If there was no love, nothing had actually happened at all. This is a bit difficult to explain and verbalize and it doesn't mean that I deny or bypass my own or others' pain and suffering, but still, that was what was realized. Now, when someone says something mean to me or does something hurtful, I can actually feel that there's a 'glitch' in the flow of events, because just then, there was nothing happening. And there is no memory of any 'hurt' stored even if the facts of the event are remembered. Next time I meet the person I can literally relate to them anew. This is a really cool feeling.

***

Stacy

One of the Inquiry processes that has been involved in my awakening is all about questioning my untrue thinking. I've been catapulted into blissful Awareness simply through asking, "Is it true?" and the follow-up questions and Turn Arounds of The Work of Byron Katie, through little-known IAM meditations and through Liberation Unleashed pointers.

I'm Teflon to stressful and untrue thinking in areas where I've done this work, although other unquestioned thinking can still grab me sometimes.

Memory? I've never had a great memory. It's kind of a blessing that helps keep me in the present.

This is all a work in progress.

***

Amy

After awakening, memory has been hilarious. Nothing my mind had 'trapped' held as much importance as I had believed.

I had to get accustomed to not having access to the databank of information that I had stored in case my children or husband needed something. Even though my children are still fed and cared for, at times I can also forget. For instance the other morning my daughter sighed, "Mommy, when are you gonna make breakfast?" I had no idea I hadn't made breakfast, and it was already 9:30 am. The difference is that before waking from the dream, I would have abused myself, mentally and emotionally for the whole day, months, maybe even years – I would have held onto it: "What a terrible mother I am to forget to feed my children … blah, blah, blah …" Now, it just makes for an entertaining and funny story. As soon as I knew I needed to make food, I made food. Problem solved. No thinking. No abusing myself. Just action. This is just one of millions of examples from the last couple years.

My mentor said to me early on, when I got stuck one day and was wandering through my mind palace searching for help with a problem: "Stop going to the head as if it has a solution for you. You're trying to go back to find help, but there's no one there. No one can help you there anymore."

I found this helpful because I immediately recognized this as a habit, and once she pointed to it, it never happened again. There's no solution there. And I laughed so hard. What a relief! ... and so beautiful.

I am also surprised by what I am able to remember. I find that many times I am not conscious that certain things have been 'filed away'. This happens in class for example. I won't remember knowing the information we have learned, but suddenly, when I need it, for instance, during a test, it appears at the front of my mind. It's like the files are easily accessible to my new operating system, with no thought or effort on my part. When I was the person 'Amy' I spent a lot of time trying really hard to memorize things and hold onto those things that seemed important.

***

Timothy

For about a year after enlightenment, my brain-mind was so silent that I had difficulty forming complete sentences. Words would come out two or three at a time as if I was being very thoughtful and cautious about what I was saying. I didn't feel or appear to be struggling with speaking per se, and I wasn't worried about it, but it did seem unusual. I've since heard that this isn't a common occurrence.

After that first year, I became more verbal and started sounding like everyone else again, although there's no longer an automatic internal voice. I don't think in my head unless I want to; my brain-mind is quiet unless I have a problem to solve. Sometimes ideas as words do 'appear' but it's like they're coming from somewhere else. Now and then thoughts come as if I'm picking up on what someone else is thinking which, occasionally, proves to be true.

I've also found that my short-term memory is fleeting, so I tend to use various methods to help me better remember things. I make to-do lists. Recurring events are easier to remember but I keep a pocket calendar for random engagements, mostly because I don't want to have to wait to get rescheduled if I miss an appointment. By keeping an itinerary and maintaining and updating my to-do lists, the only thing I have to remember is to check my records daily.

I don't have many thoughts about myself but when I do they're mostly glimpses of my past, which I don't often review. For example, one time I remembered that I'd been to Paris, which was only triggered when I heard a story from someone else about their recent trip to London. I hadn't thought of my Paris memory for decades, and it surprised me a little that I'd forgotten I'd been there. I don't seem to carry my memories around like I once did, probably because I no longer identify with them.

Where I think I've excelled regarding cognition is that my intuition is stronger, although that may be more a function of the heart-mind. I feel that my heart, as well as my brain, has a mind, and that they intuitively work together. My heart does most of the mind work now, which is why it seems that I don't think much in my brain, or behind my eyes. When I need to recall, or research some information, my attention goes to my brain, which I call 'up periscope'. Otherwise, I rest in my heart.

***

Richard

I don't think my day to day experience of memory has changed. What is different is that I am able to 'open up' memory in a much more vivid way, through meditation. I can induce more intense memories. Awakening also brings a different perspective on memories, allowing me to relive childhood events but with an awareness of transcendent consciousness that was absent the first time round. This has massive implications for healing.

Bar a brief spell near the beginning, I've always stayed away from the anti-mind forms of spirituality, which posit the mind as an enemy to be subdued and overcome. People talk about the mind becoming silent through awakening. I experience that, but it's inconsequential to me. The mind, like all phenomenon, arises in silence, so if I'm not identified with it then it's not more disruptive than having the radio on. Sometimes the radio can be annoying and I turn it off, but I don't identify my sense of self with the DJ.

Cognition is totally different for me. Awakening allowed me to see how we identify with patterns of thought which then construct and constrict our worldview. Through studying consciousness directly, I was able to step into a place prior to thought, the place which holds thought. This allows me to step out of my default worldview and into another. I've mentioned the implications of this for communication in another chapter. The effect on cognition is equally important. I would contend that many issues in this world are too complex to be understood from only one perspective. The ability to see perspectives as arising in

Chapter 15 – Mind, cognition and memory

something deeper and to move between them has allowed me to form a greater appreciation of many issues.

An example is the famous story of the blind men feeling different parts of an elephant and all concluding it is something entirely different. Either a thick trunk like thing (the leg) or a thick or thin rope (the tail and trunk) etc. They then proceed to fight over who is right. This arises out of the human tendency to lock into our ideas. Consciousness allows us to loosen this attachment and move around the elephant, feeling different parts.

***

What's Awakening Really Like?

Pedestrian Tunnel under the Freeway

Photo by Marianne

Chapter 16

Emotions

Ben

Pre-awakening I used to hold onto negative emotions as if they were somehow a comfort as well as a burden. That desire to hold on to them has now gone. I still get angry, but less and less frequently. The main difference is that the anger is very short-lived and I don't seek to justify or defend it.

In most cases a negative emotional reaction in a particular situation highlights that there is some pre-awakening habitual pain that I haven't yet looked at. So I use it to be brutally honest with myself. I'm lucky to have an incredible partner. She is very calm, non-judgemental and wise, and will listen as I try and get to the root cause of an unconscious reaction. She bounces ideas off me, asks probing questions and inevitably when we discover the cause, she holds the space for me to react to that raw pain. After that it dissipates and it's very rare that the same thing will make me angry again. If it does, rinse and repeat until it doesn't. I would go so far as to say that the relief and joy of finding the hidden demon and inviting it out of the darkness, brings an element of joy; the next time I face the same situation I recognize the lack of pain in the place where pain once was.

My sense of inner peace deepens every day; even though this continues to happen I find it incredible. I experience more positive emotions, not with more intensity but rather more frequency. The space that has been created by clearing out negative emotions has to be filled with something, and positive is what is left.

***

Michaela

Before the realization, I had a hard time understanding my emotions, my feelings ... understanding *myself*. From time to time I took one of those small psychological tests to tell me who I was and what emotions I had. They seemed to know me better than I knew myself! How silly that seems to me now...

Today I would actually make a distinction between feelings and emotions. Feelings represent the sensitivity of one's soul — the capacity to sense love and beauty. This capacity definitely deepened with awakening. I am moved by life's beauty in a way I did not know before; I see it everywhere.

Emotions I take as any kind of movement that thoughts, when believed and reacted to, bring with their content. They are linked to the programs of our psyche, which see everything in the world from the perspective of polarity; as having two sides ... good or bad. I dare to say, that when I am 'at home' within myself, I have no emotions, only feelings.

But emotions are definitely not gone, they appear in all their variety. I cannot deny them, so I rather enjoy them. After all, these are also gifts of life. The best example for me is in music, when expressing all kinds of emotions deepens the image and reveals a profound world of beauty.

Yes, anger can show up, as well as other so called negative emotions. If I do not want to act them out or dwell in that state, I simply remember the known truth of self. Reminding myself and generating compassion within, is a very quick cure for any unpleasant emotions.

***

Richard

I'm pleased to report that I still experience the full range of human emotions, all the way from elation to despair; from passionate love to an anger that is capable of descending into rage.

The difference is that I also have an awareness of the greater field of consciousness in which these emotions are rising up and falling away again. Whilst I certainly can get pulled into them, I can also step back and allow them to play out. They always present a gateway, an entry point into a deeper understanding of self. Elation, for example, may alert me to what I feel attached to; whilst anger informs me of what I fear.

I mentioned 'anger descending into rage'. Some may feel that's quite strong—too strong! A bit unhinged even! I used the word 'rage' quite deliberately, as I feel there can be an (entirely understandable) tendency in spiritual circles to want to rise above such feelings. I've come to do the opposite, I think the more interesting spiritual challenge is to feel and express as many of our more uncomfortable emotional aspects as we can. I obviously don't mean in the form of going round screaming at people, but rather as a kind of meditative practice. Making a virtue out of feeling as much as possible can counteract our all too easily embraced tendency to not fully acknowledge our shadow.

***

Lisa

My emotions have definitely become less pronounced. They feel superficial and dissipate quickly; there might be an emotion but then it's gone. I don't see them as part of 'me' anymore, just like I don't see thoughts as 'me'.

Sometimes I notice how a feeling or a thought draws me away from the present. When I see that, and consciously get back to the present, the feeling usually dissipates. In the present, there is mostly peace, which rather than an emotion, is more of a state of being. Same goes for love. It's not a feeling or an emotion either. But some feelings do float by on the surface of my being now and then. Sometimes they can be quite powerful. The other day, I got so angry I choked up and couldn't breathe properly! But it's still superficial and it's not 'me'. It's like a current or a wave or a bubble on the surface of a deep ocean.

***

Sarah

Earlier in the unfoldment of awakening there appeared to be fewer emotions. But really, I was less reactive. As awakening continues to deepen and mature, and the continuous direct sense that what I am is infinitely spacious, there is room for everything to come and go as it will. I'd say I feel my emotions more fully now because there is not a filter of exclusive identity. It's pure experiencing. I am not the emotions, and when they are experienced there's no story that is triggered that might set my mind spinning. It's quiet. And emotions come and go quickly without my grasping at them or pushing them away. There is this moment, and the next, and the next. My humanity in all its complexity and multiplicity is experienced within the simplicity and emptiness of what I ultimately am.

So my heart has cracked open wider in that I feel emotions very deeply, and they rise and fall like a wave. Since they aren't as sticky as they once were, when emotions arise they're regarded as precious; a delightful bounty of sensation and heat and vibration and humanity that is experienced momentarily. And then they dissolve back into the sea of vast emptiness from where they came.

I do notice I can feel the emotions of the collective more acutely. Some days I wake up in the morning with a heaviness, a surge of emotions. When I check the news, there may be an event that's happened that is emotional for hundreds or maybe even thousands of people. I've become more adept at knowing what's 'mine' and what is 'the collective'. Of course at the ultimate level it's all one thing, which is why it's felt, but there are layers to distinction. I can tell when I'm feeling a collective grief, for instance, rather than experiencing an old pain from my own life coming forward. So I let this wide wave of collective emotionality wash through me as I ground in my body, and it passes.

I've become a more feeling, intuitive instrument, but this is viewed as less of a problem than it once was. States are always changing. There is an openness now that allows for this.

***

Kiran

Prior to awakening, I was unconsciously driven by emotions such as agitation and enjoyment.

Awakening brought the recognition of how emotions drive life only when coming from the false egoic entity.

Calm stillness and silence have replaced emotions, both on a personal and collective level. Life after awakening is not devoid of humanity, but rather, is mostly aware of everything *in* humanity. Clarity that is devoid of emotional toil, is now possible.

While experience and behavior are now informed by deeper wisdom and an aligned oneness, there are still uncomfortable moments and flashes based on old patterns. But most of the time, the duality of the conditioning of the egoic sense of self, has no effect. Open spaciousness has created space for things to happen as they should versus being intentionally driven by me.

This doesn't imply that there is a lack of compassion. Although there is an individual form, it is still whole, connected and part of a much larger spectrum; its movements arise naturally from love and compassion and not from the hardness of resistance, conflict or shallow-level emotional love.

***

Stacy

Ah, emotions. For me, emotions used to be very strong and seemed to be justified and involuntary. No longer. I am far calmer than I've ever been.

It is annoying when others see some expression from me and take it *way* more seriously and strongly than I do because of their own filters and perspective - particularly my boyfriend! He often sees me as 'angry', when I was barely troubled at all. Nothing I say convinces him that it wasn't much. Then again, ACIM (*A Course in Miracles*) warns us that there is no difference in our upsets. They are all equally disturbing to our peace of mind. So, maybe my boyfriend's reactions help me to recall that.

Along the way to the understandings I now have, I was lucky to study with Phil Laut who had some very helpful explanations of emotions. Also Byron Katie, who had some eye-opening things to say about them. They are definitions, so I will simply list them:

Love: Love is not an emotion. Love is who we are when everything illusory drops away.

Fear: Fear is the only other state of being. All emotions can be traced to a fear.

Anger: Anger is "the attempt to do something, contaminated by the illusion that we are presently helpless." Phil Laut.

Sadness: Sadness is "a temper tantrum against reality or 'what is'." Byron Katie.

Depression: Depression is "anger turned inwards". Sigmund Freud.

If y'all want to throw out other emotions, maybe I can recall a helpful context for those!

Another thing about emotions is that I used to try to fix or control something outside of myself to handle them. I also completely misinterpreted the hard knot in my gut when I experienced them. Now I know that means I am lying to myself. Lies are contractions. Truth is an expansive feeling.

So now, instead of trying to go outside to get rid of that gut-punched feeling, I go inside. I typically use The Work of Byron Katie, The Sedona Method, BreathWork or simply 'releasing'. It's easy if I'm open to seeing what is true. Sometimes I have to ask myself whether I really want to know the truth. That opens the door.

Of course, don't ask my boyfriend whether I've mastered this. I have not!

***

Jennifer

Emotions and my capacity to feel them got much bigger. I felt both the deepest despair, shame and hopelessness (that I didn't even know existed), as well as the greatest peace, bliss and pleasure. I also felt others' emotions more, whether they were in the same room or thousands of miles away.

The waking-up process has brought past pain and trauma to the surface to be experienced and healed while simultaneously making room for me to feel more of the ecstasy. One of the reasons this was so surprising was because I had done so much psychological healing work over the previous 20 years. Thanks to Adyashanti's guidance, my practice has been to find the 'yes' to whatever is arising, however difficult or delightful it may be.

***

Marianne

In my childhood I learnt that my emotions were bad. Even so-called 'positive' emotions, were squashed. It seemed that being 'too happy', or 'too excited', was just as bad as being 'too angry' or 'too upset'. It was crazy-making and I never learnt to self-regulate.

As I began to suffer, I saw my emotions basically as 'me'. I was, quite naturally, completely identified with them. I saw myself as a fearful and anxious person. I saw them as some sort of indicator of how I was doing in life. I tried to get rid of painful emotions or work them through in therapy. The goal was to 'feel good'; to have more positive emotions. This is probably quite a simplistic description, but for brevity, true enough.

Later, through therapy, I began to tolerate the more painful emotions;

Chapter 16 – Emotions

move into them, understand them. I thought of emotions as a music of sorts; Beethoven's music would have been utterly boring without the *Sturm und Drang* alongside the joy. Still, the immense ups and downs ruled my life. I moved frequently between ecstasy and suicidality, with not much in between.

I also suffered intense bouts of depression. At one stage, I came across some written material which described depression, not as an emotion as such, but rather as a "movement of awareness". It was described as a pressure which we can actively 'follow' down and within ourselves ... ultimately to 'bottom out' and come to a point of stability. It made utter sense to me that depression wasn't 'bad', but rather an escape valve for the human organism when we are overwhelmed by the world at large and have lost touch with a deeper sense of self. It gave me a context through which I stopped fighting myself. I learnt to follow the depression and I learnt that I only became depressed when I had lost touch with a deep ground. Ultimately, this material was a godsend to me and in no small way, I believe, tilled the soil for awakening.

With awakening, the emotions as they had been, quite literally stopped overnight. I never felt depressed again. In many ways, this was one of the things that my partner found hardest. She too had seen my emotions as somehow 'me'. She had fallen in love with a volatile, sensitive, artistic person. Without them, who was this strange woman? And why was she so easy-going and even? My family also continued to assume a pattern of behavior from me that wasn't there any more. Marianne didn't 'get upset' any more. What?

Certainly, during the 'honeymoon period' I had very few movements that could have been termed an 'emotion'. There was only a profound and calm stillness. When conditioning reasserted itself, this was accompanied by emotions. Emotions were the indicator of conditioning; that I was identified with a particular aspect of the 'small self' that decided reality should go MY way. But now, from the perspective of awakening, I really didn't take these emotions very seriously. The grabbing on of identification that allowed them to escalate wasn't there. They moved through like clouds, or if they lingered I looked a little deeper into whether they could simply be surrendered or needed a little more delving. Certainly, after awakening I did two years of further therapy, which I have mentioned in other parts of this book.

In my daily life now, there are very few emotions. They do flash from time to time, but just move on through. I do get angry; often there is a sense of 'using' anger. Anger is understood by others in ways that a calm voice isn't. If I'm in a position in which I need to say to someone, "No, that's not okay!" I am aware that a tone of anger, assertiveness and forcefulness is sometimes necessary. I feel that with my entire being, although am not identified.

What is here now is a ground of open spaciousness. That ground is our natural state. It is Life. Within that there is certainly an ebb and flow of sorts, but that ebb and flow is not of a 'me'. There is a jolt of fear when I lose my balance, there are tears when I see the plight of the world or of other beings, there is an awe at witnessing pretty much everything. Some days I feel full of energy and activity, other days quiet and contemplative.

Additionally, our natural state, our being-ness, is not an empty stainless-steel oblivion. In this human form it seems to have very distinct qualities: clarity, love, compassion, strength, stillness. These are not emotions. They are the very essence of what we *are*. We *are* love. We *are* compassion. But not in any way that the 'egoic self' might imagine them.

***

Erick

I used to get into emotional loops where I could not find the resolution to a sense of incompleteness and I would project that out onto my surroundings: friends, family etc. With awakening, my emotions settled into a more conscious affair, with the source and course of any arising negative emotions being much more clear and manageable.

Now my emotions still run the full range – from love to fear, from joy to sorrow – but they pass through me like ocean waves rather than taking me over and ruling the moment. I recently had a few days of very intense emotions with great loss in multiple areas of my life. In fully acknowledging the pain and sorrow, I remained free and infinite while still being sad and stressed. It's funny that they could co-exist. The bliss of awakening exists on a deeper level than the daily emotions. It remains while the mind and heart go through their dance.

Someone seeing me from the outside would not necessarily think that I am different from anyone else in my reactions to situations. Responses are still very personal and based on my past conditioning. The inner reality does not have to express perfect calmness through every event, and it certainly does not mean never having 'negative' emotions. Awakening is more of an additional dimension added to experience, one that affects the experience but does not take it over. It's hard to explain in words. Emotions come but they do not overtake pure, vast awareness. Essentially, emotions are the same but free from their binding effect. They cannot overtake to the point of causing suffering.

Love is a much easier emotion to have. Love can come at any moment, in fact, simply resting in awareness, I can find myself loving people and things that I would have previously found difficult or tedious. Joy is also ready at the drop of a pin. Just stop focusing on actions and joy flows right in.

***

Timothy

I'll start by saying that my definition of emotion is: energy in motion which can be perceived within the body.

With regard to how my emotions have changed, I usually don't 'feel' anything in particular. I'm just generally aware of a permanent, loving, happiness that underlies everything.

I don't even experience love like I used to. To say, "I love you" to someone doesn't make sense anymore. Love isn't something I can 'do'. Instead, love is somewhere that I live, and that somewhere is everywhere: inside and out. I gratefully share this spaciousness with friendly people who are also living in this love place.

Although this may sound quite boring, I definitely still have moments of joyous appreciation, such as big belly laughs in spontaneous reaction to my present experiences. They're usually triggered by the intellect, like when I have an unusual mental shift from hearing a joke with a totally unexpected punch line. Another example of this experience of appreciation is that I deeply enjoy being out in Nature.

On the other hand, I can also have tearful emotions that well up when I witness others' suffering, but I no longer fight or judge these feelings so they quickly fade. These emotions are mostly from acknowledging another's sorrow or pain based on similar past experiences. I often think of them as 'tears of recognition'.

At times, although less often as I get older, a deep rooted mental conditioning tries to re-present itself to me. When that happens, I don't feel a desire to attach. I just see it as something I need to shine some light on and recognize more fully, in order to dissolve any interference this recollection may bring to my sense of peacefulness.

Prior to enlightenment, I used to label and perpetuate my feelings of hurt, but now they just come and go without much thought. I never get depressed about anything, but sometimes I do feel a bit lethargic even though I'm not feeding into those feelings, just observing them.

In regards to the stronger negative emotions of anger and hate, they are gone. They never come, not even in the face of other people's negativity. I know that such emotions are usually a result of fear, and I don't fear anything, not even death. I'm not saying I don't get startled, or scared, or that I don't have adrenaline rushes, I just don't fear such experiences. The movement of all these energies are just that, movements of energy perceived within my body.

***

Chapter 16 – Emotions

Love Letter to the Moon

by
Jennifer

Kiss my hair like you kiss the palms
that blow in the salt breeze at the edge of the sea
Make my eyes and skin glow from the inside
like the powdery white sand at midnight
Pull me close to you and then when it's time …
let me go in trust just like the tide
Bathe me in your light through black cloud nights
when I forget who we are
Silently call to me when I have forgotten how to listen
and only when I have remembered
Dance deep with me like you do the waves
Playing sparkle songs on their surface
I will be here

***

Chapter 17

Motivation

Amy

Prior to awakening I ran largely on agendas. I had them all over me, all over you and all over those closest to me. One day, *poof* they all dropped. I was no longer powered by the things I desired. This did not lead to an immediate lack of motivation; in fact one might say that in the beginning of awakened life, I was very motivated. I played with my children, cleaned house, and even made the decision (with my husband) to go back to school and pursue a degree. All was well.....

But slowly, slowly and very subtly, I felt a shift inside; over the course of a couple of years I became less and less interested in doing ... anything. I questioned whether I was in some kind of depression; I felt low, dark, stuck. Looking back I felt like Artex in *The Never Ending Story*; stuck in the mud and slowly seeping further and further down into the swamps of sadness. Many days I sat on the couch not engaging in any *real* way with my life, my husband or my children. I knew something was 'off' but did not have enough experience with spiritual matters to know what to do about it. I kept waiting for Life to show up and live me again. Then, as Life has a way of doing, something 'seemingly' random happened: I was connected with someone who introduced me to a new meditation.

Any sadness, darkness or lack of motivation was replaced with Stillness. Connection. Light. The bottom fell out. My husband told me that I seemed brighter and he was happy for the change!

I now have a deeper understanding. For a regular practice, I sit twice a day and do yoga several times a week. This helps to continue to clear the body of the subtle, stuck and contracted places in my nervous system and allows for energy to flow through the Whole. Motivation now is

Chapter 17 – Motivation

simple. Do what's Here. My children ask to play cards … yes, if I'm not doing something else. And if I'm busy, I am able to set a clear boundary full of love. I communicate with them in a way that they feel honored and heard, whereas before I was shutting them down.

Now I don't experience a sense of motivation; I just experience being lived. Every moment.

***

Ben

I have been unmotivated recently. Upon examination I was unable to find a single motivation that did not tie into building an egoic sense of self in some way. I feel capable of anything but simultaneously have no drive or need to do anything; 'need' being the operative word. This is hard to reconcile after a life of being assured by friends, family, school and society that striving for things is absolutely necessary, and may even be the purpose of life. Now it appears to me that awakened motivation must be spontaneous, born out of the situation as it arises in the moment.

***

Michaela

Is it motivation, when I have a strong desire to celebrate beauty and love? And is it motivation that often urges me to react to injustice?

Rather than motivation, I feel it is acting spontaneously in response to what comes my way. Doing what needs or wants to be done.

***

Marianne

I have had long periods of no motivation. Gradually there was less and less of an 'I' who might care about motivation or lack of it; the 'I' dropped and dropped away.

What is it that might 'motivate' me to put together a book? What is it that might 'motivate' me to pick up a camera? It's a movement that comes from Life itself; it's not from the mind. That movement always feels 'right' and whole and alive and unencumbered; it's an unmistakable sense. And it's also a trust as that movement is followed through. There is no 'I' in the way that might say, "Well *I* made other plans this year. Sorry!" To follow *that* voice would be at my peril.

Such movements come in a moment: "Oh, I will put together a book! Oh that's interesting!"

***

Timothy

I found that motivation dropped off for a while. My old reasons for doing things changed. A lot of my activity was to improve or add to who I thought I was. That was suddenly not needed any more. I also no longer cared what anyone thought of me; as long as they weren't carrying pitch forks and torches! Eventually, I began following my heart and I'd watch for what I tended to lean towards. If I leaned far enough, I'd have to take a step to keep my balance.

***

Kiran

Reflecting on motivation I realize that everything is becoming increasingly quiet, both within and without. There is no resistance to what comes in and no wanting to do anything either. At the same time what needs to be done, simply gets done without any personal involvement.

Occasionally I do get involved in ideas thrown my way by my mind or by my husband, but somehow everything falls off easily and effortlessly, leaving room for what is.

I have been noticing all this for quite some time. I seem to live from such stillness and silence that there is no need to seek anything at all, not even motivation. Quietude has become my solo deepest friend. Life seems to be happening by itself and with such grace and equanimity, that there is no need to see any kind of light at the end of the tunnel. Life is a doer of its own and supports itself, without needing a 'me' to support it in any endeavor. It is pleasantly surprising yet deeply fulfilling and self-nurturing. It's like the heart beating and the breath happening without any motivation yet expressing life in the physical body.

***

Chapter 17 – Motivation

Maureen

Motivation fell away. It crashed to the ground and splintered to bits. I wrote for children; with awakening, the urge to write and the joy in creating story completely dried up. I was told a new motivation would come. I waited, and waited, and waited.

New forms of creativity rose up for play, but nothing significant. Motivation to be active in the world? Nothing.

What arose was something else. I wouldn't call it motivation – more like clarity. A sense of the right next thing to do. An errand, designing a new garden bed, taking a nap. Nothing substantial – I live a deeply quiet life, which I love.

Doing something physical in the world doesn't seem to be required of me right now. My life has become more about being. Be a light. Be a presence. Be loving and joyful. Let that radiate.

***

Stacy

Motivation? Meaningless. What would that be for? If I were to say any sentence about 'motivation':

I need some motivation.

I'm motivated to … (fill in the blank) …

I've got to get my motivation back.

I would notice a gut-crushing tension in my stomach, solar plexus, or heart.

To quote Byron Katie, "If it hurts, you're lying."

***

Lisa

What motivates me to write these words? It's not the 'little man/woman' in my head. It's not a thought. It's not a feeling. The answer is … I actually don't have a clue! I guess I could call it an energetic drive of some sort. It's a force; maybe life itself. This is what mainly motivates me nowadays.

Sometimes I know exactly what I'm supposed to do in a certain situation, and it's not a question of whether I 'want' to do it or not. It might be something happening in my personal life, like when a friend died of cancer recently, or in the public domain, like a refugee crisis or the pandemic. I know what 'my part' is in these events and that I'm supposed to do the best I can in these particular circumstances. This part might not be easy and it might even have undesirable results for me 'personally'. This is in opposition to what is commonly proclaimed in spiritual circles; that everything becomes nice and cosy and love and bliss after awakening.

What drives me is a deep sense that this force is telling the truth. But it might be an uncomfortable truth, or a truth other people don't want to know or see so that they attack the messenger. Look at what happened to Jesus! Not that I equate myself with Jesus in any grandiose sense. In this context we are all Jesus. In an everyday sense, whatever I do I need to be true to myself first and foremost, and act accordingly. And it's not the 'ego' self I need to be true to, but the other, 'real' self, this life force.

With this book, for instance, it's clear to me that my part here is to participate and share in the best way I can, whether I personally want to or not! Sometimes the force recedes and rests and doesn't drive me in any particular direction, and then I do ordinary everyday stuff. Make dinner, wash the dishes, vacuum the floor, walk the dog.

***

Jennifer

Because there was so much that inspired me in life and so much I wanted to do, I often struggled with what to actually take action on. So it was strange, when after awakening, I lost my motivation. From this new perspective, it seemed as if nothing needed to be changed, fixed, achieved, healed, experienced … If everything was perfect as it was, what was the point? This new insight cut through it all. What had been driving me for decades was the desire to be better or make things better in order to feel better. Now, in moments, it had simply fallen away. This made decision-making challenging. It was like life would happen through me and much of the time that looked like sitting and being still. For years, the only real initiative I took to put something into action was to attend meditation retreats or to spend time with people who were awake.

Now many years later, I fall in and out of a drive to create things: a school, a dance piece, a poem or a shrine. Sometimes the force is very strong like a big wave that has a life of its own. Other times it feels like a gentle effortless happening closer to a soft rain which nudges me into action.

***

Chapter 17 – Motivation

A sloth

Photo taken by Kathy
in Costa Rica.

Chapter 18

Body and health

Kathy

It was body issues that put me on the path, and I see now that my body has actually been my greatest guide and teacher, as well as my greatest obstacle. It continues to be my biggest challenge and there is a tendency to want to bypass it or transcend it when it is not feeling well.

It was a combination of a genetic defect of my connective tissue and a car accident that took me from healthy and athletic to incapacitated. Memories of this period are full of bitter sweetness. There was so much growth and soul-searching that accompanied the constant and quite severe pain. The right people magically showed up and so many others fell away, which did not feel as magical. Flat on my back and feeling quite alone and lost, my soul-searching led me to my first glimpse of awakening. This glimpse triggered a deep yearning for spirituality, causing the trajectory of my spiritual life and career to change course.

Twenty-five years later, after awakening, it quickly became clear my body issues were not going to magically disappear. To my surprise, new issues arose instead which was confusing. Within six months my usually high-energy self, could barely work or even function. My energy dropped dramatically, and I gained about 35 lbs while only eating organic greens and berries. It felt as if my body was failing. I was told I could have died if I did not seek help. It turns out my pituitary had started to fail. For some reason it was full of spinal fluid. My blood chemistry revealed that 24 things were very low, including my cortisol, which was dangerously low. While it took two years to sort all that out by replacing and balancing the things my pituitary no longer produced, other body issues seemed to pile up, most related to my connective tissue issue.

Today I have much more energy and face other challenges and future surgeries. I have learned that my body is a precious instrument that needs to be tended to and cared for. Transcending it is not the answer, nor can issues always be corrected by positive or magical thinking, or even awakening

***

Timothy

After enlightenment my awareness of my body became more astute; I could better detect subtle changes in my overall constitution. I began to look for natural ways to stay at a consistent energy level. Nutrition and medicinal herbs became a hobby for me and I've been healthy most of my life. When I see a doctor for a check-up they're usually surprised that I'm not on any medications. That's apparently unusual especially being a man in my sixties with a family history that doesn't predict that. I get colds and the flu occasionally, and I still carry an inhaler in case of an asthma attack, but other than injuries, I haven't needed any extreme healthcare services.

Overall, my body is just where all my awarenesses join together.

***

Lisa

My perception of the body changed after awakening. There was no feeling of someone being 'in' the body anymore. For a while, it felt like the body was in me; that the consciousness was bigger and encompassed the body in some way. Now, that feeling seems to be waning and there is simply a body. One day that body will die, but it won't be me who dies. Sometimes the body has aches and pains and gets sick. It's not pleasant but it's not 'me' who is sick, so there's no suffering, only sickness and pain. Nevertheless, I take very good care of the body to try to prevent sickness and pain as much as possible.

I used to poison the body with smoking, which I now see as a symbol for all the poison that was entrenched in my psyche and my mind. When I worked through the poisonous content of the psyche, I had no need to manifest it by literally poisoning myself again and again from morning to night. Smoking is a very neurotic behaviour.

Now, I see the body as a tool to be used in this physical existence, and you need to take good care of your tools to be able to use them in the best possible way.

***

Stacy

Body, body, body.

You know, I used to hope that some of my chronic pain and autoimmune issues would go away or that I'd be detached enough to do the right diet or take the right supplements or whatever it took for this to recede. But I have not, and it has not, and I don't actually know whether it would help if I did all of that stuff. Maybe.

However, as I was learning and practicing The Work of Byron Katie, there was a meeting in a meditation space that had pictures of enlightened teachers and books by enlightened teachers all over the small, pillowed room. One of the frequent students at these inquiry circles came often to do The Work on her bodily pains. At those times, our teacher was fond of pointing to some picture on the wall or some book, saying, "This one … (famous enlightened person) couldn't get out of the bed for weeks at a time because they were so weak from … (whatever disease they had), and this one … (another famous enlightened person) could barely speak for coughing and this one … (yep - famous, yep - enlightened) could not walk for the last 20 years of their life."

Those examples went on and on and on. Gandhi was one. The man couldn't get out of his bed he was so weak from fasting. There's a reason someone parodied that he was a "super-calloused fragile mystic cursed with halitosis". He was ill. And he was doing his activist work. And he was awake.

I've lived with dull to sharp chronic pain in all of my ligaments, tendons and joints since I was about five years old. Oh, it was better back then, but my entire life, any repetitive motion, such as exercise, swimming, cutting things with a knife and sleeping wrong, then blessed me with excruciating pain in the area that I had twisted, moved wrong, or tried to move and use as normal people do.

Well, none of that is me. I just keep doing what I do, taking care not to strain or cause myself more pain. It didn't change at all, yet. And sure, I imagine I have more to question. No self is just the first step. Seeing through right/wrong and other items (see the Ten Fetters) are yet to be concluded for 'me'. Okay, fine.

Recently, it came to my attention that maybe all of it is the result of acute mold sensitivity. I know I am 'allergic' to fungus and mold. But I did not know that beyond my bi-yearly sneezing attacks, it can affect joints and the gut and other areas of the body. That's probably what I have and what I must deal with or live with.

Yes, I read articles, go to health care professionals and do what I can. Hot Dead Sea salt baths help a lot. Sometimes some things help.

But it's no use making a big story out of it or playing 'poor me' in any way. I just keep going, inquiring, and doing the next thing.

***

Marianne

I always wondered about the body and its relationship to spirituality. Stories about out-of-body experiences and astral travelling had me thinking that spirituality was a journey beyond the body; perhaps even an escape from the body and its suffering!

And prior to awakening I was probably quite divorced from the body. I wasn't IN the body; I don't think most people are. Most people are following a story in their heads.

But gradually I realized that the spiritual journey is a journey *into* the body. One of my teachers used to say, "You can't know *who* you are if you don't know *where* you are." I think that's true. This now-ness is nowhere other than *here* and prior to awakening the body is the key to that. For me that journey into the body included somatic psychotherapy, grounding in the *hara* and being consciously present to the body in meditation and everyday life. That now-ness, that presence is what we are. We do come to realize that we aren't the body, but not in the way the mind might imagine it. Everything is our body and that includes the body!

About five years post-awakening I had a major health crisis. Without realizing it, the egoic self had subtly started to appropriate the awakening as its own; I had started to push myself to be some sort of perfect awakened being. I felt I could finally be a dutiful daughter, an always-smiling partner, an infinitely compassionate friend, a conscientious worker. I disregarded my deeper knowing and I disregarded the body. Things started to feel a little 'off', but I also disregarded that. I developed vertigo while travelling but continued to push myself relentlessly on. Walking became difficult. I felt dreadfully ill. I ended up in the stroke ward of a hospital, but they didn't know what was wrong. Eventually I was diagnosed with Mal de Debarquement Syndrome, a condition I still live with. For six months I barely got out of bed. I felt as though I was dying.

It was a wake-up call; the body will not be denied. I went to a naturopath and addressed all aspects of my physical health. I wanted my body to be in the best health possible. I made dietary changes, lifestyle changes and I slowed down. I went back to therapy and addressed issues from my past that hadn't yet been seen from an awakened perspective, most particularly my need for 'mothering' and also my tendency to push myself towards an ideal of perfection.

Now I take better care of the body and listen to it; it is a very finely-tuned sensing organ. But I also take better care of everything. Not in any perfect way. In the preciousness of what this all is, this is the only thing that makes sense. But I still have aches and pains like everyone else. And I still eat chocolate cake occasionally even though I know the body will grumble later on.

***

Richard

People who are inclined towards the spiritual often have a complex relationship with their bodies, one that is both better and worse than that of other people. Plato described the body as "a tomb where the soul comes to die", which just about sums it up. Spirituality is about moving away from the body and wider material world and accessing a non-material transcendent realm. Paradoxically however, this escape from the flesh can provide a space that allows ultimately for a much greater sense of bodily integration.

This is pretty much my story. I had a very awkward and uncomfortable relationship with my body throughout my teenage years. Half-jokingly, I sometimes say this convinced me reincarnation is true, as no events in my life really accounted for those feelings. After my interest in awakening began, I started to cultivate a relationship with my body. This was important to me, hence why I was drawn to the martial arts as a spiritual vehicle. Initially it was something of a contrived process, I forced my mind into my body, but the former harboured no great love for the latter. Ultimately I had to allow for the emergence of a lot of stored pain around body-shaming.

I also had something of a paradigm shift around appearance. Spiritual practice allowed me to directly perceive beauty and attractiveness as arising in the deep-self, with the body merely reflecting that beauty. This was foundational in changing the way I perceived other people's bodies, and ultimately my own. It took the pressure off my body having to be a certain way.

***

Kiran

It feels as though the body has been bestowed as a blessing, because it is through this body and its various senses, that consciousness has all kinds of experiences and also evolves. Although the body is impermanent in nature, it houses the eternal essence and also withstands the effects of this journey.

The body adjusts itself to suit the individual part of totality that is housed within. For instance, when consciousness was trapped in strong and fixed perceptions, the body was also hard and strong in order to accommodate that kind of 'resident'. As consciousness liberated and became open and soft, the body readjusted itself to suit that softness; it became gentler too. The body continues to adjust and readjust itself as the journey of refinement into subtlety continues. So, awakening has made significant changes to this body. I don't function anymore the way I used to; this is not perceived as a limitation but rather a natural weeding out of unnecessary influences.

I also realized that a different sort of change in the body results from the aging process. In subtle and sensitive ways, the body needs to be respected, heard and cared for. The deepest inner-ness somehow guides my attention to its subtle requirements: where realignment is needed, and when I need to be restfully present in it and for how long. I have also experienced inner guidance to exercise in a specific way.

This aware and revised respect for the body comes from someone who once attempted to commit suicide and end this body; it is such a clear difference from ignorance to now. To me, awakening opens consciousness and that includes the physical, mental and emotional levels.

I have also observed how very intelligent this body is. Once opened, it constantly processes all kinds of stimuli by itself: inner and outer, personal and collective, psychic and emotional. My body had stored a lot of data from past events and this seems to have melted during this journey. There has been healing in many ways including of clinically diagnosed diseases.

This healing has made the body so naked; more sensitive for better intake of stimuli and a capacity to process them intelligently and quickly. Because the body is so open, soft, gentle and so natural, it has much more sensitivity towards the different energies and movements that flow within.

***

Maureen

I don't know how awakening has affected my body. I suspect the awakening process is very hard on it, but there's no way to tease apart the effects of awakening, menopause, and other health issues.

I am not physically cured, much as I wish that would happen. I do feel an underlying wellness, even when I am not well; a bubbling energy, as if change is happening at an energetic level, and has not yet manifested in physical form.

I love this body, much more than I ever did. It allows me to exist on earth, to be in human form, and that is a delight. The human body is amazing.

***

Erick

Health has been steadily good. I have lots of energy and I thrive on being busy. I can pick up and run a mile pretty much any time and I love to bound up the stairs two at a time, even at work. I'm in my early 60s now and I'm pretty much the way I was when I was 30. The deep rest and inner cleansing of daily meditation is also a major factor in my vitality. This is my experience, and I know others experience very different things with the body after awakening.

Shortly after the initial awakening I felt waves of bliss in my body. I observed that this bliss was the natural state of the cells of the body and that the limited self-concept that had previously ruled my awareness had been suppressing the natural joy that the cells wanted to express. I also observed that this deeply-rooted joy was exactly the nourishment that the cells thrive upon. In the Vedic texts this nourishment is described as 'soma'. When the soul feels that universal freedom, the cells and physiological systems soak that up and it allows them to express their own nature most fully.

Philosophically, the body is as real as the infinite Existence that we all are ... and it is as illusory as a passing thought. It is an expression of Eternity, like a gentle wave upon the vast ocean. It is as important as the entire universe and as trivial as a grain of sand. It is pure energy and pure consciousness ... a channel for Universal Awareness to experience itself in its infinitely creative forms. It is a pure expression of love, growing to encompass ever more of the world in its loving gaze. It is our interface with the natural laws of existence.

***

A story

by
Marianne

A few years ago I travelled with a traditional Aboriginal man on the land. He was always able to find his way, even if we were in unfamiliar surroundings.

As we rode in the car, he always sat quietly, grounded deeply in his body. With his body he listened to the spirits of the places where we were and then gently pointed out the directions: "Take that trail, go over that hill, drive past that bush." The land was not separate from him and his 'map' an internal one.

At one stage I met with him in the city. I asked him if he was also able to find his way amidst the buildings, signs, cars and roads. He grinned back at me, waving his hands in front of him and said, "Too many tracks here." He then sat back, pondering and quietly taking in the people around him. After a short while he looked at me, shook his head, and indicating his body with a wave of his hands and then pointing to the region of the hara, said, "Not connected. They can't feel where they are going."

***

Chapter 19

Sleep

Erick

Sleep is a great topic. According to my teacher, Maharishi Mahesh Yogi, the truest test for awakening is if you 'witness' sleep. That means having unbroken silent awareness as the body and mind go through the phases of sleep. For me, I noticed that upon waking in the morning, I had not really slept but had simply shifted from one mode of awareness to another – like moving from one dream to another. The dreamer remained the same. It's not that I was lying awake all night, rather, the thread of my being continued as the body and mind slept.

The effect was actually noticed some months prior to my clear and sudden recognition of eternal Existence as the common element of all experience at every moment. It has continued much the same ever since.

Other than the change in the character of sleep described above, I have pretty much the same sleep as before awakening except that I dream much less and seldom have lucid dreams. I also almost never have dreams that leave a feeling that lingers through the day. It seems like the mental housecleaning that dreams effect is being done during the waking experience and there is less need to process subconscious feelings during sleep. I also seldom have anxious nights or difficulty falling or staying asleep.

***

Kiran

As I mentioned in other responses, I was raised in a Sikh environment.

Early in my life, waking up at 3:30 am was one of the important tenets of Sikh religion and this became my way of life regardless of the demands of the day (work or family). After more than 10 years of this early rising, I developed many physical difficulties such as migraines brought on by interrupted sleep (medically evaluated). Yet, my fired-up longing and seeking wouldn't permit me to stop the practice.

Initially what had developed as a pattern of practice, later became my love. I still love to wake up very early to enjoy the deepest innermost stillness: my real, very connected and pure interaction. One noticeable consequence of this, is that I am not concerned about sleep – when or how much I sleep. I sleep 4, 6 or 8 hours. It's all good and doesn't pose any challenge now as I am retired and can nap in the afternoons if need be. Sleep, its lack or excess, doesn't concern me anymore.

***

Richard

I don't have difficulty with sleep, but sleep itself is central to my concept of spirituality.

I came to view the sleep state as the Ground of Being, the field of consciousness which we unconsciously sink into at night, but can also enter consciously through meditation. In my meditative practice that's essentially what I'm doing: falling asleep and being wide awake at the same time. I suspect this probably could help with insomnia, but as I haven't had it, I don't know.

Most of the transformative experiences I've undergone have arisen in the middle of the night as I come out of deep sleep. I imagine this is for the reason I've stated above. If sleep is the Ground of Being, to become conscious within it is to touch the transcendent. Depending on the depth, this can be immensely transformative or utterly terrifying or perhaps both.

***

Michaela

There were actually some periods in my life, when falling asleep was a really traumatic experience. I could see the parallel of sleep and death clearly and would become paralysed by the fear of letting go of 'control'. The mind was scared to death to dissolve into nothingness. It was very

Chapter 19 – Sleep

unpleasant, especially when I was exhausted and desperately needed to sleep but didn't allow myself to.

Obviously all this dropped away after the realization; experiencing that this non-personal state of nothingness is in fact our home (as a state of pure being) and there is absolutely nothing to fear. On the contrary, it is peace itself.

***

Amy

Sleep, oh sleep ... wherefore art thou sleep?

Bonnie Greenwell has a video in which she discusses kundalini and how it affects our whole system, including sleep. It helped clarify my misunderstanding of my lack of sleep.

It has taken the old personality longer to adjust to this new lack of sleep. As a mother of two small children, at first I resisted getting less sleep. However, one day, there was a small shift in my personality's argument and instead of resisting, I just relaxed into less sleep – accepted this new reality on a deep level. Now, I get even less sleep! But I am able to meet it with humor and ease.

***

Stacy

Sleep? I've never had any trouble sleeping. Possibly due to hypoglycemia. I sleep. I nap. I power nap. I wake up when my cat wants food. If someone calls me in the middle of the night, I am fortunate to wake up, have a coherent conversation, have no trouble falling back asleep and am able to remember the conversation in the morning.

***

Elizabeth

I often wake around 3:30am and stay up for a while.

As a teenager, when I was going through one of my major transitions in terms of becoming aligned with spirit, I would awake at 3:30am and feel compelled to go outside and look up at the stars. The Pleiades were always directly overhead. I felt a strong connection to that cluster of stars and the energy they emitted. I would stand outside our house in the dark, looking up, until I felt it was time to go back in.

Even many years later, I wake at this time. I try to sit with spine erect. Sometimes I meditate. Sometimes I spend the time reading or on social media. It seems to be a time of uploading for me.

Another special time is the ambrosial time, a bit later on in the morning. Connecting with the earth energies at this time is particularly nice. To me, it's the sweetest time of the 24 hours.

***

Lisa

I sleep and dream as usual, but after awakening there is a stronger sense of presence which is there both in sleep and the waking state, and feels more real than either one of them.

***

Timothy

I became enlightened while my body was asleep. I was dreaming and I didn't like what I was dreaming about, so I started changing it. I'd never been able to do that before, and I knew I was making alterations that were impossible in 'real' life. The second I realized I was asleep and dreaming, I lit up with light and floated silently without any thoughts until my body awoke sometime later. I've stayed in that mode ever since.

For the first decade or so after this happened, I averaged two to four hours of dreamless sleep a night. If I had a physically active day I slept up to six hours. Then I fell into a cycle of about five to six hours a night but not slept consecutively; I'd wake up in the middle for an hour or two, and then go back to bed. Science says the average person uses 20% of their daily energy thinking. I believe that since I was hardly thinking at all, I didn't need as much sleep.

Now I'm in my 60s I only sleep about four hours a night, and nod off in my chair for a few minutes to an hour in the afternoon or early evening. In the last few years I've started to dream occasionally, but the dreams lack any sense that they're real. It's more like I'm picking up on someone else's dream. Sometimes there's a message in the dream but so far they're innocuous.

When I sleep, I can instantly be fully awake if something doesn't feel right. Once, I sat bolt upright with my vision locked onto the window fan. Within a few seconds, it burst into flames and I knew exactly what to do. I jumped up and opened the window further and pushed it out. A few more seconds and the drapes would have caught on fire. Another time I woke suddenly when a wall hanging caught on fire. Two tall thin candles were in separate holders on the altar but they were too close to each other. One burned quicker than the other and caused the taller one to soften and bend towards the wall. I went from lying down to standing, by pushing off the bed with one arm, not even bending at the waste. I haven't done that before or since. On the way up I grabbed a small blanket off the bed with my free hand and tore the wall hanging down. I immediately used it to put out the fire seconds before it damaged anything. Neither time was there any unusual sound to alert me; I just knew to wake up. So, on some level I'm not really asleep, only my body is asleep. I lie in bed 'awake to myself', ignorant of time, without any thoughts and in a deep restful state. Every day my body wakes and I delight that I'm still here.

***

Marianne

I have never been a good sleeper and have suffered from insomnia since my early 20s.

Prior to awakening, when I was suffering greatly, sleep was very disturbed and difficult. My dreams were wild with memories and anxiety. I frequently dreamt of being swamped by a tsunami, of drowning, of eating glass, of being tortured. There were times my dreams gave me deep insights into my psychological processes and helped me to remember events in my life I had repressed. I carefully wrote each dream in my diary, looking for meaning and for resolution. There were also times of lucid dreaming, when, for instance, I could willingly stop a tsunami and choose to fly above it. I read in books that lucid dreaming was somehow 'special' so I lived in hope that I was progressing spiritually in some way.

Post-awakening this has changed. I never lucid dream any more (it seems irrelevant) and my dreams overall are very mild and about innocuous everyday activities. Looking for meaning anywhere else other than in the simple living of this moment does not occur to me.

Particularly for the first few years after awakening I had difficulty getting to sleep. There was a lot of energy in the system; it was as though the body was charged with an electrical current that I could not turn off. I used a number of herbal remedies at this time and also sleeping pills if I had important engagements the next day.

Over time, I have become more accustomed to the energy; it now feels normal. Still, there are times I don't sleep well. There are also times it can feel so *good* to be alive that I wake very early, eager to get into the day. A few days in a row of this, however, and I am tired.

In addition it is worth mentioning that frequently there is the sense, that although I am sleeping, that which I truly am is always 'awake'. This started quite subtly approximately eight years after awakening. I would wake up in the morning and realize that awareness had remained throughout the night.

***

Chapter 19 – Sleep

Rovnodennost/Equinox

Photo by Michaela

Beloved sun captured on that symbolic magical day, when daytime and night-time are of equal duration all over the planet and the sun's ecliptic longitude is zero.

It is a magical reflection of the inner truth, where from 'zero' – the nothingness of our core being – everything is now seen as equal, as One.

Chapter 20

Humor

Sarah

My sense of humor has deepened and expanded and matured since awakening. It's been an interesting ride with it, since awakening occurred when I was working as a stand-up comic.

When I awakened to myself as Awareness, I laughed and laughed and laughed. The absurdity of it – the great cosmic joke – was that I had ever taken myself to be this contracted bundle of thinking, memories, and grasping, when I am actually something so vast and spacious! I fell on the floor in the meeting room at a Zen Center where I was on retreat, and laughed for what seemed to be an hour.

I was a stand-up comedian and actor and I quit it all. There was no more draw towards it. I didn't know at the time, but what was happening was a draining away of the false 'me', and that 'me' had been a performer for a very long time.

I became very earnest and I didn't find the same things funny anymore. My life became about helping people in an explicitly defined 'helper' role that society could understand.

And then ... and then ... there was a calling to get back on stage. And soon, came the deeper shift: I realized that not only was I Awareness, but I was everything everywhere. It's all One Thing. Unity. More laughter! The hilarious thing to me as I laughed and laughed and laughed was that I ever thought I was separate! Oh the ridiculousness of it all!

There were more shifts as 'me' in all its facets has continued to dissolve. Those have been quieter. And with those shifts, my humor in the world as a professional has been returning more and more.

Chapter 20 – Humor

I began to find being human – which includes not just me but all of us – divinely ridiculous. And so my sharpness, my fierceness, began to return.

There is a deep compassion for all beings.

Compassion, I've found, has many faces. It felt like a young, naive compassion to be nice all the time and help people. Now I may get on stage and seem outraged about something and poke fun at human foibles – but it's coming from a fierce love for all of us. There is a pull to celebrate as well as expose our human messiness with laughter. In doing so, we can relax with the inclusion of it all. Because with the later awakening shifts, nothing is excluded. Dirty jokes mingle with divine realization and it's all one big Totality.

I've been surprised that my humor can penetrate, shake up, or confront an audience with an underlying sense of care and love. I am constantly surprised at the freedom I feel to say and do on stage what my 'spiritual ego' would have deemed 'un-spiritual' some years back.

I feel so very ordinary. I am just a woman up there telling jokes about being alive. I speak for being human now, not just for being 'Sarah'. How I write jokes now has changed.

Material often comes from deeper themes like identity, or how we grasp, or how we are connected by being the One Thing. But unless I sink deeply into my ordinary shared humanity, using communication styles they are used to, the audience won't listen.

But the jokes often come from something deeper.

One day, after the later awakening shifts, I ordered a salad at a restaurant and when it arrived it had jicama on it. I looked at it and cognitively knew that I had never liked jicama. I had stories about jicama: it was yucky, it tricked me because it looked like an apple but was flavorless, it was a nuisance at the salad bar, etc. But that day, as I gazed down at it, none of that was there. There was presence, and emptiness pervaded all – an absence of assessments and preconceived notions. After all, I was the jicama and that was clear.

So I took a bite and WOW! Crunch and crispness; I was present with this experience of biting into jicama. It was a radical moment – one of many that were becoming standard now – of pure experiencing without the filters of mind. My friend looked at me oddly, as she knew how I felt about this root vegetable. Then I paused a moment and turned to her and said: "Don't get me wrong. I still don't f***ing like jicama."

And so a five minute bit about jicama was born, that I use in my act. The on-stage bit doesn't share the details of the experience I actually had.

I employ comedic devices like exaggeration and puffed up 'anger' at the audacity and confidence of jicama when it's really just a sad apple, but to me it's rooted in something deeper that was evident in that experience at the restaurant.

When I perform this bit, people laugh at how ridiculous it is. But it's ridiculous that we humans get worked up about a lot of things. We have expectations of life and get bent out of shape when it's not to our liking. The joke is about that. It's about relaxing our grip.

So I'd say my sense of humor disappeared and then reappeared several times before a maturing began to occur where everything is included. Dirty jokes, political jokes, existential jokes – bring 'em on! It all gets to be expressed, and when the core of these jokes is rooted in emptiness or love, then who cares about the words I'm actually saying. Well, some people might care. But that's OK. Everything is included.

***

Erick

I used to need more 'play time'. Now I am always playing inside. Stress dissolves so quickly that the inner joy is always accessible.

***

Richard

Humour was a big part of my pre-awakening teenage life. I was lucky to have some very funny friends (one went on to write a book of observational humour) and I would often finish the school day with my jaw aching from laughing.

However, I clearly remember walking to the bus, complete with sore jaw, and thinking that I wasn't happy. This troubled me, as society informed me that laughter was one of the things that was supposed to make me happy. Charlie Chaplin himself had said so! What then was wrong with me, I wondered. If I didn't find happiness in humour, could I find it anywhere?

Looking at life through a mystical lens obviously helped answer this. True happiness of the nature I was seeking isn't to be found in laughter or any other thing we do, but in our transcendent self. I do recall there were at least a couple of years in the beginning of spiritual journeying when I really didn't laugh much. Perhaps it was good to step away from

Chapter 20 – Humor

it and break away from trying to find happiness there, but probably I was taking things too far.

Eventually my humour did return. I remember a specific incident when my dog did something hilarious (I won't recount it, because you really had to be there) and it broke me. I couldn't stop laughing. My mother commented that she hadn't seen me really laugh in a long time. And so it re-emerged from there.

Humour again became a big part of my life. To this day I still regularly go to the pub with the same school friends and strain my jaw. But all this now rests on a foundation of happiness … rather than looking for that foundation from within it.

As for how awakening affects humour; I find that the more in touch I am with my deeper self, the more of a sense of spaciousness I have for creativity and spontaneity to emerge. Humour is very much the art of misdirection, of flowing into the place no one is expecting. So yes, awakening helps with this. Another factor is that I feel it brings an intention to humour. As a teenager my jokes probably arose out of a desire to have people like me. From a more awakened/whole place humour carries the intention of bringing everyone into an appreciation of the beauty of both themselves and life itself. I'm not claiming to always get that right; sometimes I'm just a jerk.

***

Kiran

The most hilarious thing that comes to mind is when I was feeling, "Now I am finally *getting somewhere*." Every time I felt that I was getting somewhere, I found out that I couldn't and wouldn't get anywhere until I came to know that "I am … nowhere".

This was of course post-awakening. Before awakening I was faced mostly with pain. The awakening experience itself was of a grounding, quieting and stilling kind, and far from any humor or laughter.

***

Lisa

The 'me' was and is the biggest joke of all. I put all of my adult life into this 'me': shielding it, protecting it from hurt and harm, 'developing' it to make it wiser, more mature, more spiritual, more 'ego-less' (haha!) or less afraid, less anxious, less insecure. I 'worked with myself' in therapy and in spiritual practice to give it a happier and better life and to protect it from pain and suffering. All that work, all that energy, all that commitment, all that action and drama ... and then that same 'me' went 'poof'! The pot of gold at the end of the rainbow was actually its final undoing! To me, that was a big joke and absolutely hilarious.

One of my favourite memes at the moment is of a powerful contemporary political leader who is portrayed sitting in the robes of a Buddhist monk with spiritual paraphernalia all around, saying, "People love me because I have transcended my ego. I transcend egos better than anyone else. You'll never meet anyone who has transcended their ego better than me!" I love it. A good joke and a reminder not to become spiritually self-important.

***

Timothy

My sense of humor improved after enlightenment but I can't seem to do it on purpose. I've written a few song parodies, and years ago I was hired to open at a comedy club for 12 shows. Sometimes I see things as funny but I can't let on in front of other people because they'll probably misunderstand. For instance, I think it's funny that people judge other people for being judgmental.

***

Michaela

I consider humor a beautiful gift and a great privilege of humanity. Humor makes it possible to unite in a relaxed detached perspective in presence, while seeing the joyful fun of a situation. It always felt very natural to communicate with humor and I was at ease being 'witty' and entertaining my friends.

After awakening I deeply realized that humor has to reflect love, and has to be kind and ethical. I suddenly saw that there is often a non-loving aspect hiding behind the mask of 'just humor' and so I disengaged from any kind of satire. I am now rather sensitive to it and no longer consider anything that belittles a person and their way of being, as humorous.

Chapter 20 – Humor

It is actually a great practice, to stabilize in an open-hearted place, always keeping in mind that everyone is our brother or sister.

***

Stacy

I've had almost nothing come to mind about humor - only my peals of laughter which I wrote about in the chapter on death.

I suppose one thing is that I can easily find things funny that others are very serious about. Sometimes they get offended. Oh well. *A Course in Miracles* says the world was created in a "tiny, mad moment when the son of God forgot to laugh." So there. It's all pretty ridiculous, isn't it?

***

Maureen

I laugh a lot. Everything's funnier, especially seeing the nothingness of drama. When all the mind-spinning I've been caught up in dissolves, laughter bubbles up in joy and relief. Laughter seems to be the response to shock. When something falls away, laughter bursts out - this is so much fun!

***

Ben

From a certain angle almost anything can be funny. Awakening has given me a lot more of that angle from which to view life. Especially in the 'bad' moments.

***

Marianne

My sense of humor is much the same as it was prior to awakening. I love to laugh and be funny. I also enjoy spontaneous silliness, particularly at home with my partner. Together we laugh a lot.

Pre-awakening, when I initially met people, I would probably have been seen as serious and reserved. Post-awakening that has changed. At one point I realized that people often turned to look at me, smile, or even say hello as though they knew me. One day I asked my partner, "Are you aware that people keep looking at me and then smiling? It's really odd. I wonder why they're doing that?" And my partner said, "You're walking around with a smile on your face." I hadn't realized, because it was so natural. What was inside was seamless with what was outside. Life is a simple joy of walking around, of being alive, of people, of insects, of grass, of This ... and it bubbles out. How can you not smile at the simple fact that the sky is blue?

***

Andrew

No change here. People still only laugh at me when I'm being serious.

***

Chapter 20 – Humor

> # A joke
>
> by
> Sarah
> (As told in her Divine Mess Show
> and other live performances.)
>
> "I guess I'm a Buddhist.
> I say 'I guess' because the further I go on the Buddhist path,
> the less I feel like a Buddhist.
> Which means the Buddhism is working!
> I don't exist!"
>
> ***

Chapter 21

Creativity

Erick

My post-awakening world has been one of great energy and creativity. In fact, I see a direct link between my creative activities in the years prior to awakening and the awakening itself.

I was learning the violin at the ripe old age of 45 and since I had never tried to acquire a skill of such magnitude and refinement, I was not sure I could do it. But after about a year of diligent practice it started to sound like music and I knew that I was onto something. I thought at the time, "If I can develop this subtle skill, then why not apply the same principles to my spiritual practice?"

About a year later awakening fell in upon me and the thread of creativity has blossomed even more. My music is a strong and growing part of my life. I write my 'knowing' into stories that will resonate with the Truth inside everyone, but which are wrapped in everyday themes. I find that any mission I want to accomplish is easily done with steady attention and a positive attitude. The resources are always at hand for the work that must be done. Every moment is a creative act and there are no limits. Recently I was given a cello and am learning that quickly. I also taught myself sound and video editing. In the past few years I have learned to navigate the worlds of mechanical engineering and manufacturing management. Things blossom naturally when given the space to grow.

If I were to ever engage in spiritual teaching I would use creativity as my medium – applying the creative process to spiritual discernment.

***

Chapter 21 – Creativity

Lisa

I've always loved both reading and writing. Language has been my path of creativity, both before and after awakening.

The further along the road of spiritual transformation I've travelled, the more my taste in books has changed. At a certain point I was no longer able to read fiction and could only read biography and facts. I still feel that way. Fiction, no matter how profound, beautiful or insightful, feels meaningless to me because it's made up. It's not real, not true. I don't have time for made-up stories when reality itself is so infinitely vast that I can never hope to grasp it all within my lifetime.

For many years, I wanted to write and share some of what I'd learned along the road in order to help and inspire others. But I was unable to write. I was still too full of egoic junk and felt that whatever I would write, would come out all wrong. It would be full of self-pity, resentment, or blame. Deep down I wanted to share stories from the point of view of true reality, not meaningless and unreal ego-stories.

After awakening, I finally felt it was time to share, so I've recently published a book in Swedish with the title *Born to Love - the Near-death Experience and the Meaning of life*. It includes both my own and others' stories and insights of spiritual transformation from the perspective of the NDE.

When I was a teenager, I used to write poetry. Decades later after awakening, it's interesting to look at some of those poems. Some of them express my spiritual longing in a powerful way that I wasn't aware of at the time. I wrote the poem below when I was 16, more than 30 years before awakening. I did not know what I actually longed for or what I was really writing about. In a lot of ways, this poem depicts exactly what happened many years later. Freeing yourself and setting others free are two sides of the same coin. I instinctively and deeply felt that I couldn't really hear, see or touch my own true self or anyone else, as long as I was asleep.

> Behind a wall of mirror glass
> you are no more than a shadow.
> Pain in your laughter,
> screaming, an echo of silence.
> Your calling falls without sound on my ears
> reaching, I cannot touch you.
> If only I could break through that mirror,
> if only.
> A million pieces,
> thousands and thousands of splinters.

And I will blast every border,
beyond both the Gods and the Devils
will I be transforming,
again and again and again
through the fire.
And I will return again,
and I will set you
free.

***

Marianne

As a child and teenager I was never very creative. My body was rigid and braced and I had no clue what freedom of expression or creativity might mean. And yet, somehow I yearned to create. I copied the style of others' paintings, filled journal upon journal with descriptions of my day and I played music. I also wrote stilted little poems about a strange longing for 'home':

If I were strong,
of mind
of body.
I would build a home for me
That no one else could see.

It would be solid
And impenetrable.
I'm not me now
But perhaps one day I can rebuild as I want
And then I can truly be me.
(age 11-12)

As I grew into adulthood I started to suffer. In therapy I met that child I had been and the intensity of emotional pain was extreme. Although my outer life disintegrated, the inner floodgates opened and a period of wild creative expression broke through. It was both acutely painful and wonderfully liberating. I took large sheets of paper, placed them on the floor and squeezed out tube after tube of paint. I ran my hands through the wetness, scratching and wailing. I twisted the paper into the shapes of little girls who needed to be held; I cried as I saw myself in their form. It was messy and it was glorious. And it was ME.

Over time I realized the potency of the creative impulse; it was a bridge between my inner and outer worlds. I learnt to listen more deeply and subtly and slowly. My use of colour and patterning became more assured. Edges became more defined. The paintings became large, bold and powerful; people were left speechless and in that I took a secret joy.

But I'd never really wanted to be an artist. It was writing and speaking and words that were most difficult for me and as such, my greatest calling. And so, in the same manner as my painting, I began to allow my inner voice to speak through my words. I played with metaphor and made mistakes. I was curious, playful and bold. I delved into the freedom of poetry.

When I 'awoke' to my True Nature, the creative impulse abruptly stopped. There was no longer any need to bridge inner and outer; it was all the same. For some time this was very disconcerting.

I now know myself as not separate from Creation itself. Every moment, every movement, every leaf, every gesture, every word, IS Creation. Life is the ultimate creative act and I am not separate from that.

After a time, however, I picked up a camera. Perhaps photography is creative in a way. I simply feel a great and increasing joy in capturing the beauty of a moment, the silence of a moment, the preciousness of a moment, and through macro photography in particular, a vision of a world that lies unseen and yet is just here, perfect and beautiful to the tiniest detail. And I know that in sharing my photos, there is a communication of that vision and that immediacy, and I enjoy that immensely.

Macro photo of a tiny Shaggy Jumping Spider.

And there are still moments when Life moves me to write a poem. But now there is no angst; no tension to resolve.

As a postscript I will add that in my working life I was a professional orchestral musician and I also wrote a music book for children. However, I never felt music to be inherently creative in the same way that art or writing was for me. I was certainly able to 'put myself' into the music but I was always limited by the composer's notes on the page, the conductor, my fellow musicians and the style. As a musician I always saw myself more as a translator.

***

Kiran

From my earliest years I had a desire to be creative: as a teenager by styling my long hair and as a married woman by dressing beautifully. Creativity was embedded in all the insignificant and significant things that I did. I enjoyed the arts and creativity. I created many items from stained glass, including large-sized windows. I also had a brief fling with clay modelling; everything was either given to friends and relatives, or used to adorn the walls of my home.

Eventually I realized that my *real* impulse was to write. I wanted to write biographies, but never felt equipped with the right language requirements. Furthermore, I never felt mentally focused and articulate enough to create thoughts in written form.

I did write in my daily journal as this helped me with my inner work. Journaling became my daily habit and it continues today. In the past 12 years, more than 65 poems have been produced (from a deeper perspective) and they flow spontaneously in three languages. All poems reflect this journey (if it can be called a journey).

> That, ONE, showed up yet once again, of its own free will
> cleaned up the whole house of all its clutter in a split moment
> left this fragrant jar of LOVE open deep in the middle of the house
> bringing fragrance of pure emotion into every corner
> leaving two precious drops of tears in two eyes
> Heart racing and pounding with unfamiliar touch
> Every pore desired this self-invited guest to be the permanent host.

Chapter 21 – Creativity

Recently, I had a few pangs to express the deeper feelings by painting again, but this amounted to nothing. I could focus on only one thing; this inner unfolding.

Now, creativity is not separate and is not guided by a 'me'. Its unfolding is as it is, just as unknown as the rest. I've come to understand that earlier on, creativity was a misplaced sense. The true impulse *is* creative; discovering that which needed to be discovered artistically and masterfully.

***

Stacy

Creativity? Hmm. I was born to very creative parents. Daddy was always futzing with some new toy or Radio Shack thing with my brothers. He played a little boogie woogie on the piano. Mother taught piano for many years. She designed our bedrooms and other rooms in our home. The bedroom I shared with my sister became a lovely creamy green gazebo with white lattice around the ceiling

Me? Nothing like that. I wrote a little poetry back then. I sing a little. I record what's around me with my phone camera. That's about it. There are times when things around me glow with beauty.

But neither before nor after whatever awakening I've done, have I really related much to 'creativity'.

***

Maureen

I've been through radical changes in how I express myself creatively.

I used to write novels for children; that has fallen away entirely. Poetry emerged, particularly in the first six months after awakening. Photography has become an ongoing focus, with a change in how I see light, and notice detail. I feel the rightness of a photo at the back of my tongue and down my throat. The right colours together trigger a feeling of singing through my body.

Reflections on Ice.

I have a sense of more creativity emerging, but not yet, not yet.

***

Richard

Awakening has vastly increased my capacity for creativity. The reason for this is straightforward. The deep state of consciousness that I seek to slip into is the source of creativity. Dissolving into it allows for a freedom and spontaneity to arise.

That's probably a sufficient and practical answer. If I wanted to go beyond it, exactly what creativity is and how it comes about are very open questions for me. Some of it does appear explicable.

Sinking into consciousness allows me to 'zoom out' and see how disparate thoughts in my mind may be related. I think a lot of

Chapter 21 – Creativity

creativity is not so much creating something new, but seeing new relationships between existing things. (There's a theological argument that says only God is truly creative, we just rearrange stuff.) For example, depending on how you look at it, *Star Wars* was either a ground-breaking original film or just a Western, Samurai and air combat film stuck together and done in space.

At other times however, things come through consciousness that amaze me. As one example, I wrote the following poem after a lucid dream in which I heard music I'd swear I'd never heard before:

Music in Mind
Have you ever been
To a concert
In a dream?

It's incredible!

Consciousness takes stage
With Melody to amaze

All original score
Or covers ne'er heard before

Spontaneously composed
Instruments present but transposed

The only thing abhorred…
There's no way to record!

***

Ben

I spend time every day doing creative things. My job is writing music, which by default is for selling, but I have also written novels, poetry, a TV show, created a board game and am in the process of writing a movie just because it's fun. It is also possible in a broader sense that I, as an aspect of consciousness, may have created the Universe too but I will probably leave that speculation off my resume … I wouldn't want to get blamed for how it's panning out at the moment. A small poem then:

What is the meaning of life?
What is: the meaning of life.

***

Timothy

As a child I liked to draw and in my school years I took every art class I could. I experimented with sculpture, painting, and charcoal drawing. When I was eleven I wrote a short story for one of my sixth grade classes. It was like an episode of Twilight Zone and it was chosen to be published in the school paper. I started writing poetry when I was 14 and that morphed into song lyrics and music composition. I learned to sing while I played guitar and for a couple of years majored in vocal music in college. Around 15 I started my first business, raising hand-tamed hamsters. I wasn't old enough to get a job, so I traded these pets to the local Five & Dime variety store for credits. Entrepreneurship became another creative part of my life as I was always looking to make my hobbies and interests pay for themselves. Sometimes they even made a profit.

Creativity has always been a part of my life, but after enlightenment it expanded. I learned about wild medicinal plants and studied alchemy, both of which I used to create healing remedies. I also learned how astrology was used to help make these products. Later this became a cottage business, a teaching practice, and I've written two books on the subject.

Several creative avenues also opened up. My music performance abilities blossomed as I had suddenly lost all fear of being on stage – or fear of anything else for that matter. I also focused on writing songs and recorded three CDs in a professional studio.

I created a music magazine in Chicago which was successful for a few years. I learned how to use the computers at the library which allowed me to desktop publish without any need for business loans. It helped musicians make the transition from playing at home to being in front of audiences. It was free to the public (no cover price) and funded by advertising. It sparked the creation of a mini-Buddha field where solo musicians could find a safe place to present their music, increasing the number of venues hosting open mics from about a dozen to over a hundred within about a year. This lead to city-wide talent contests and helped some schools of music to gain prominence. From all of this I learned how to create websites when the Internet was in its infancy. I lived off the proceeds of that business for several years.

Chapter 21 – Creativity

I came to make items for sale at craft shows: uniquely intricate gemstone jewellery, leather pouches, and carved vinyl signature stamps. My jewellery made its way into a few shops and sold for hundreds of dollars.

I know this all sounds like a resume, but what I'm trying to say is that for me, enlightenment made all these activities easy. It gave me a seemingly limitless supply of energy and amplified my ability to create anything I wanted to do. I'm still writing and communicating to people who want to learn some of the things I know. I perform occasionally and I've been considering a new direction for my song writing.

***

Stacy (age 13-14)

I know not now.
I stumble through unknowingness
But not unknowingly.
I seek - and comes -
not knowingness, but remembrance of me.
In ultimate remembrance
there is knowingness.
Then knowingness is unimportant.
Only Being.

***

Georgette (age 16)

A song
Everywhere I turn I see him.
My beloved is the sky.
In all of Nature I see his face and look into his eyes.
My love, I am returning.
To once again be with you.
You wave your magic mirror of visions and of dreams.
Before my eyes, many lives.
Forever towards the ocean, he whispers in the wind.
I see my soul reflected in each sunrise born again.
My love, I am returning. To once again be with you.

***

Chapter 22

Work and money

Timothy

I don't worry about money and I don't have any desire for it. Ideas about how to acquire it seem to happen when I need the income. It's usually enough to get by, and sometimes I have a little left over to go on an adventure or purchase a new gadget. The energy to take action on an idea is abundantly available, so much so, it doesn't feel like work. Overall, it's a good balance between survival and having time to enjoy my life.

***

Jennifer

If everyone and everything is God, why would they need any help? I completely lost interest in my work. I had been working as a transpersonal counselor, spirituality teacher and intuitive healer for more than ten years. I simply saw no purpose for any of it. It felt completely meaningless. This happened with most things in my life. They all seemed to be built on the foundation of achieving something. I could clearly see there was nowhere to get to and nothing to get. Although I was half way through, I lost interest in completing my PhD in East West Psychology. I also lost interest in continuing with my beloved sacred world dance and unplanned international solo travel, both of which had been passions I designed my life around for decades. Even my close relationships felt pointless.

The implications of what I now knew genuinely scared a part of me. Was I truly going to let EVERYTHING go? One of the hardest parts about what I was experiencing was that very few people understood, so I eventually stopped trying to explain it.

***

Erick

I am more deeply engaged in work than ever ... yet I am unattached to outcomes. My love for family and co-workers drives me to be very active. I also enjoy challenges, both physical and mental. Particularly with wealth and work, I can see the divine play unfolding. I play my part but I am just an actor reading his lines.

I used to worry about failure and loss, but I now feel infinite wealth so there is no need. I define infinite wealth as always having what you need when you need it. We are all infinitely wealthy but for most people the belief that there is lack is strong enough to prevent them from looking around and finding what they need right in front of them.

Finances have become much more stable, though not instantly. One interesting anecdote: during the Great Recession of 2008-2009 both my house and business were threatened with foreclosure. While my mind wanted to allow that misfortune to drag me into self-condemnation, I couldn't go to that place emotionally ... because I could find no self to blame.

As I move toward retirement age I see the support system rising up to meet my needs. While I am working very hard to create that support, no effort is expended. I am coasting downhill to the mountain top.

***

Ben

I never cared about money much beyond a roof and food. And I never had any money! Every month, from university to last year, I lived hand to mouth trying to survive. I was constantly worried about rent.

After awakening I still don't care much for money, but suddenly find myself with access to lots of it. And it's fun. It opens up experiences I can't have without it. But the biggest gift of having money now is not having the stress of worrying whether I have enough money to survive. That mindset had become so normal that only when that burden was gone did I realize how heavily it had weighed on me over the years. I'm grateful it's been lifted.

***

Chapter 22 – Work and money

Stacy

I tend not to have money … and there always seems to be enough. But I do have past due debts and student loans in deferment.

I have studied money in the context of an awakened perspective. Key things I learned:

> There is always enough, no matter what my mind says.
> Success is a side-effect of clarity.
> It's never money we actually want. We don't even want the things it seems to buy. We want the story and the feelings that go along with that story of comfort and a pleasant life.

The main thing I learned is to relax and notice there is already a pleasant and comfortable life. Get that 'goal' first, the inner peace, and then see what arises to do next.

Speaking of next, we only ever know the next step. Take one step and the entire landscape changes, maybe subtly, maybe in a big way. But one step and everything shifts, like turning a kaleidoscope. So much for 'goals' eh?

Whatever arises to do next – that's my work.

***

Lisa

When it comes to work and money, there's no big difference for me between before and after awakening. Like many NDE-ers, I've never been interested in money, other than having enough to lead a reasonably comfortable and safe life.

Before I had a family, I lived for decades in a 25-square-meter one-room apartment and was perfectly fine with it. Other than when I was really young, I've never worked solely for money, but rather for helping others and for the love of the work. But I've also been pretty pragmatic and taken the opportunities that presented themselves, like buying property for a price that tripled within two years.

For a time though, I was in a very difficult situation economically, work-wise and health-wise. This was a patch in my journey when I hit a practical, psychological and spiritual rock bottom (mentioned in the chapter on teachers). At this time, my work situation fell apart and I was also under threat of being hit with a substantial debt. Eventually this situation cleared and my family and I have had a comparatively small but steady income ever since.

Compared with others around us and the median income in Europe, we are living under the 'poverty line', but I feel like we're living a luxurious life. We have a wonderful big-enough apartment, our daughter has a beautiful room of her own and all the toys and other stuff she wants, we have all the electronic equipment and gadgets we need, and also the opportunity to travel when we really want to (although not necessarily wherever and whenever). We have subsidized health care, social care and free education. Our home is very nice, even if I buy mostly second hand furnishings. And we have the opportunity to put our time and effort into what really matters - love, creativity, helping others. Within our modest circumstances, we've even been able to help and house refugees and give to charities. What else does one need in life? We even have savings and property that's still worth some money (but who knows for how long in the corona crisis days). So, what 'poverty'? I always laugh when people who make a lot more than me complain how tough their economic situation is. And there are plenty here who do.

Money to me is like air and food. You need some to live, but only enough, not in excess. And if I would need to work mainly for money to be able to get that basic level of income, I would, but mostly I've been able to do what I want to do and what I love, and have what I need as well.

***

Marianne

Before awakening I was very matter-of-fact with money, and after awakening I am very matter-of-fact with money. No difference. None at all. To me it has always made sense to save for a rainy day, to invest and spend money wisely. And it comes naturally to me to do so. For me money isn't 'good' or 'bad' or a 'problem'. Money is just money.

From the time I was about 14, I earned my own money; I gave music lessons to local children. That capacity to teach music, has always stood me in good stead. I was also a professional musician and earned a substantial amount of money for a time. When my life fell apart and I suffered greatly, my partner earned money. Since then I have worked at all sorts of jobs: a concert organizer at a university, a care worker for people with a joint mental health/terminal diagnosis, a mental health advocate for those in psychiatric hospitals, an artist (selling my paintings), conservation work, mentoring and royalties from books.

I like to live comfortably, but I'm not particularly materialistic. I live very simply. I buy second-hand clothes, I don't care for fancy cars or fancy holidays. I eat good nutritious food, but rarely eat out. I do a lot of work around the house myself, am very handy with concrete and wood and grow lots of vegetables. My idea of having a good time is to go for a walk in the bush with a camera in my hand.

I do give money to animal welfare, but beyond that prefer to offer my time. I am quite okay about giving my time for various causes or interests that I feel strongly about: conservation, wildlife, and the running of this Facebook group for instance.

With my mentoring work I charge money. It is not a lot, but I think it is important. It is sometimes suggested that spiritual mentors or teachers should not receive money because what they are offering is freely available for everyone ie. it is our true nature, our natural state. I feel this misses the point. There has to be an exchange for my *time*. And there has to be a valuing of what is received: the wisdom and insight gained from many years living in this terrain. Additionally, in this present day and age, there is no support from an ashram or a school. (Of course I always take people's circumstances into account.)

***

Richard

I wish I was one of those people who made a million bucks in their twenties, then came to question the ultimate value of materialism from a place of opulence. Unfortunately I became interested in spirituality at school, which scuppered my financial aspirations.

It's interesting to reflect on this, as I probably haven't thought about it in twenty years. I actually think, in spite of quaint expressions to the contrary, the very nature of the schooling system conveys the centrality of money as the thing that brings meaning. We were focussed on passing exams, to get to a better place to pass more exams to ultimately get a higher paying job. It was clear the point was in no way to gain a meaningful understanding of subjects we were studying, indeed some teachers were candid enough to say so. Things like relationships and hobbies were all to take a backseat to this all-important endeavour, which ultimately equalled more money.

Every child was assigned a number between one and seven, which reflected their mental capacity and therefore their worth. It didn't take a genius to spot the pretty strong correlation between the number and the economic status of the child's family. People might *say* money isn't everything, but our whole environment screams the opposite.

I certainly bought into that idea and had a nice little career in computers planned out for myself. I even imagined what type of car I might drive, which is funny because I couldn't care less about cars. I suppose I thought it would make girls interested in me, which I did care about.

I recall coming to question this around the same time my questions over identity were forming. I read some Greek philosophy, about Diogenies living in his barrel for example, which helped me along the way. I remember talking with a friend, who was explaining all the money he was going to make as a lawyer, and thinking, "But if we both lay in a field looking at the blue sky on a sunny day, it wouldn't make any difference how much money we had; the experience would be the same for both of us."

Then awakening experiences happened and life came alive and presented so many things to be interested in. I always earned just enough money to get by. I made a conscious choice to prioritize things other than material success, which I certainly don't regret. Perhaps if I had my time over I'd be a little more pragmatic. I'm not sure. Nah, I wouldn't be!

At the time of writing I feel I haven't yet fully integrated money with spirituality. They exist in slightly separate fields for me; I haven't found a way of being with money that I'm entirely comfortable with. I suppose this is to be expected, as we're really talking about the integration of spirit and matter, which is no small thing!

I tend to work in areas not related to my real interest, as I'm aware that bringing money into the equation can change the results. Would I be able to resist the psychological pressure to be someone and act in a certain way, if my livelihood was on the line? It's my hope that in the future I can come to a place of greater resolution. If you're reading this ten years from now perhaps check to see if I ever did!

***

Kiran

After a childhood of shortages, I planned to attain a designation, become a professional and build a great career so I could live comfortably.

Chapter 22 – Work and money

This 'I' worked tirelessly to accomplish that task. Things went according to plan, but when it came to the reality of my life, nothing worked as planned. The impulse of seeking was raging and compelled me to leave a great career well before any of my financial/work goals were accomplished.

I quit my job and abandoned my other aspirations to follow this inner pursuit completely.

Everything has worked out so well, that 20 years later, I have never experienced any feelings of 'less than' in this area. I have always felt 'looked after' and have lived in much comfort. I don't know if this happened as a result of this trust or any other reason, but this has been my experience.

If I look into future I see the same trust. It says "The one who looked after you all these years, will always look after you". This expression of deep inner trust and oneness feels complete and in union with everything. Who knows what the next moment is going to reveal, yet there is trust in the unfolding of life as it is and there is no worry or thought around money.

***

What's Awakening Really Like?

On the highway

Photo by Stacy

Chapter 23

Global challenges

Elizabeth

The 'I' still wishes to change the world. She identifies herself as a teacher and wishes to set injustices right. She sees the Earth being destroyed and wants to speak out, so people will realize how each small action makes a difference. She sees a pandemic and wishes to educate people to wear masks and social distance.

For a short period the 'I' attempted to 'let go' of this persona and just 'let things be'. This didn't work out too well; I felt as if I were imploding all the time. I'm fairly certain this is something that eventually falls away and isn't 'done' as such, just like so many other things on the path. I finally came to the realization that the personality has its own agenda, and if it is to be useful, so much the better! There will always be the underlying Self which sees all of this and knows all is well.

I often flip-flop in my outlook. Sometimes I watch out from the depths, where everything is as it should be, and sometimes (more often) I identify with the personality who is shocked and dismayed at the state of things here on the planet at this time. I have wondered off and on if there 'should' be more of a perceived marriage of what I see as my persona and the ultimate self, but in the grand scheme of things, it simply doesn't seem to matter. My feeling is that the more we rest in the Infinite, the more personality loosens.

It isn't as if these issues will become meaningless or apathy will set in. It's more that a deeper, more centered compassion will be there … And it will reach out with its appropriate responses to each worldly dilemma. However, I'm only in this space when I take the time to ground.

Does the 'I' get distraught and distracted by the horrors of the world at this point in history? Yes. On an almost daily basis. Is there something more, watching and Being? Yes. Always.

***

Erick

A few years ago I noticed that there were almost no dead bugs on my car windshield in June. I noticed that I was not plagued by mosquitos at dusk in the garden. That's when the degree of environmental imbalance began to hit home. A few years year later the news of the great insect decline hit. My response is a deep sadness, feeling more alone than words can express. All of the years that I took all of these precious beings for granted (even if they posed a bit of annoyance, they were just doing their thing as part of the whole) and now humanity's collective selfishness has created a situation on this planet that I had never imagined.

I understand that we are simply doing our thing as human animals on the limited surface of this planet. I know that we have great intelligence as a species, but I question if we have the tools to take full responsibility for the results of our exploding population. Successful species ebb and grow. We are witnessing a rare moment in time.

On the other hand, consciousness, in its infinite creativity, is molding a future quite unique from the past and we are witness to a great transition. Though the loss of life on earth is very sad, there is no loss in Pure Consciousness. It is ever and eternally whole. The best cure for the collapse of life is for all to awaken and to dive deep into the natural wholeness, radiating that back out into the projected world.

***

Lisa

My feeling is that the present condition of the human species on a collective level is very warped, and the results are in many ways disastrous. Not only do we wage wars, form dictatorships, ruthlessly exploit the earth and other human beings, and inflict immeasurable suffering on ourselves, one another and on our fellow beings the animals. Now, with our extremely destructive and self-destructive behaviour, we are on the verge of destroying the prerequisites for life

Chapter 23 – Global challenges

on this beautiful planet. At least part of all this destruction, I believe, is due to the illusion of separation and ego. As a species we are anthropocentric, ethnocentric and egocentric.

As I reflect on my lived experience, the paradoxes come in. I have a double sense that everything is immensely important, no matter how small, while at the same time it is completely unimportant because ultimately all is peace, all is love, and all is well. Every blade of grass is a work of art, a unique piece of life and part of the whole, which is lovable and beautiful beyond measure, and every bit of suffering and destruction inflicted on every part of creation is felt deeply throughout the heart of all existence. When we hurt something or someone, we hurt ourselves, and when we hurt ourselves, we hurt all of existence, because it is all one. So I feel deep compassion for what I perceive as suffering 'outside' of me and within my capacity, try to help in any way I can. Recently I've been volunteering to help refugees and I've housed a few. Sometimes I can be fierce when taking a stand.

So I do have 'opinions' of sorts, and I do help alleviate pain and suffering as much as possible. But at the same time, I recognize all form as ultimately an illusion, ephemeral and perishable, and I have an unshakable sense there is a fundamental unchanging, peaceful, loving, eternal core within it all. So even though I participate in life to the fullest while here in this form, nowadays I also feel peace even in the face of great upheaval, challenges, pain and suffering. At some point every form, all that's not eternal, is going to perish, and that is okay and as it should be. What is eternal can never be harmed. It always was, always is, and will always remain.

I live in Sweden and from the point of view of humaneness and compassion, it was extremely painful for me to see the path chosen by my country during the coronavirus crisis. Love and compassion had no place in decision-making and thousands of people's lives and health were sacrificed in the name of the herd, the strongest and the healthiest. My part and my calling was to express the pain, anger and disappointment with this path, and I was actively involved in protesting and sharing my 'personal' point of view. At the same time I could also rest in the peace and acceptance that is beyond 'wrong' or 'right', beyond opinions and turmoil, and know that all is well.

Ultimately, when it comes to challenges, for me it boils down to a very simple question: Is what is happening an expression of love? Or is the underpinning and the foundation of what is happening something else? The answer decides my course of action. Of course there is the perspective (expressed for example in *A Course in Miracles*), that everything that is real is Love, everywhere and always, and everything else is an illusion. From an awakened point of view this is true, but as long as I'm physically alive in this world, even if not 'of the world' there is also my human part to play.

***

Kiran

It is a very tricky topic especially if spoken from oneness or non-identification. There was a time I gave a lot of attention to all these social issues, especially social inequalities. Now, although collective issues have multiplied in the outside world, my active interest in getting involved, has greatly diminished. It has almost become a non-issue, which may not feel right to many readers.

At the same time, there is a heartfelt support of those who are playing active roles in these areas. I feel creation itself is the greatest and only activist, as it works in multi- dimensional ways. The only thing we as human beings can do is to support it, firstly by awakening and secondly by embodying that awakening; that would be the real healing of this earth and its environment in every way. The cleaning and reorientation that comes from that, will itself look after the bleakness being sensed in the world. Only when humanity lives from unconditional love as an embodied way of living will everything be perfectly looked after. Then the personal agenda that is the root cause of most disasters will greatly diminish, re-establishing the health of creation in every way.

To me, density at the individual level contributes to painful results at all levels. This brings up great compassion of heart and right action takes place as needed. Although I do feel the stresses and pains related to these challenges, I stay personally conscious and gently active. The peace, silence and restfulness that is experienced sustains the trust that all is included and all is okay As It Is.

***

Stacy

Global Challenges – it's the same as anything we perceive from our seemingly separate level as a 'problem'. It isn't one.

So, knowing that it's all completely perfect, whatever arises, arises. Maybe I send money to Greenpeace. Maybe I don't. Knowing there is no decision, no decision maker, while I may tell the 'story' that some 'I' made some 'decision', that's a lie.

Same as the global challenge of politics and nations and national leaders. No way can the whole be seen from my perspective. Back when the Bushes were president, I tended to say that the boomerang effect would be good. It was. We got Obama. Global 'challenges' also fit this model. There is a horrific fire in California or Australia. COVID-19. Death and rebirth. How can we say this is 'bad' or 'good'? It is certainly 'natural', even if humans are involved. We are part of nature.

I realize this may sound glib or trite, but I assure you it is not. And only being in that more global perspective can show this. Words cannot. Thinking cannot.

***

Maureen

I find myself reacting from different levels of understanding, close in and then with broader views, like rings on a bull's-eye. Whether it's a pandemic, a climate disaster or a personal health problem, I can spin up into panic and oh my god oh my god oh my god. When I catch my breath and take a step back, I watch the patterns, find some clarity on why, and see a way to help. If I keep stepping back into the broadest view, I recognize that everything is consciousness. This is how consciousness dances, through beauty and joy and horrible disasters – this is how it plays out.

I find it difficult to reconcile, to hold this distant view and a close, deep compassion at the same time. There's an awkwardness to it, and such unkindness in talking about it to anyone fully caught in the story. *Yes, you will die, but it's okay because this is all consciousness dancing* is not helpful in a crisis.

Yet we need to be able to step back, to see with awareness, and not be entirely reactive. Both are important: being able to step back and remember, and to step forward with compassion. Perhaps this is how we embody being consciousness in human form.

***

Ben

The aspects of 'Unity', things that in our perception connect us to everyone and everything else in this world, are known as 'Good'. When we feel connected we experience 'Positive/Preferable' emotions. The opposite is also true. The aspects of 'Division', things that apparently separate us from each other and the world around us, are traditionally called 'Bad'. Feeling this lack of connection brings about 'Negative/Undesired' emotions. Although in truth we can never be connected or separated, as connection would suggest there was more than one part to the system and separation would suggest that somehow this Oneness could be split apart, we can still perceive things this way and our perception can affect how we act in the world.

Aspects of Unity include love, friendship, compassion, forgiveness, generosity, acceptance, tolerance, patience and selflessness. When as humans we apply these aspects to our lives and the lives around us, we feel connection, and thus the preferable emotions like happiness and peace. Aspects of Division include fear, war, terrorism, conflict, blame, selfishness, self-righteousness, greed, racism, sexism, homophobia, hierarchy and extremism or intolerance of any kind. When these things come into our lives they increase the perception of separation and thus our experience of the undesirable emotions like sadness and anger.

For humans, self-aware aspects of a conscious universe, it is easy to see a true separation where only a theoretical one exists. That the viewer and the viewed are somehow fundamentally different and apart from each other is the persisting illusion. The unawakened society we live in solidifies and perpetuates this misunderstanding in us from the earliest age. Consequently, we forget over and over that we are 'connected' to everything around us by the default of actually *being* it, so we need constant reminders and assurances that this is the case. However, until we awaken we feel some degree of separation all the time, which means we feel some degree of pain and fear all of the time. Acting through those emotions that belong to Division, means we inadvertently continue to create Division and more separation even when our intention is to Unify.

Take racism. It is easy for most to see that racism is wrong. But if self-righteousness comes in, an individual might put themselves 'above' a racist for having greater 'wisdom'/being a 'better' person and immediately perpetuate the basic behavior of Division in a different form! They just choose ideology instead of skin color as that which separates them from a racist, hate the difference and so create more

Division. This is how we end up with anti-fascists who, without any sense of irony, believe freedom of speech should only be allowed for those who agree with them politically or people espousing the ideal of 'equality' whilst in reality trying to suppress the groups they feel have suppressed them!

Modern society is full of people who have defined themselves by their cause, convinced that if they can just preach/protest/complain enough they will make the world a better place when at a deeper level they are in fact causing just as many problems as they are solving. The -isms and the -phobias of our world are the symptoms of Division, not the cause of it. Solve the issue of Division and the symptoms will be much easier to treat.

Within this backdrop, I asked myself a couple of questions when considering the major global issues.

1. Whilst in this human body, do I believe the illusion of connection is preferable to the illusion of separation in terms of how it makes me feel? Yes.

2. Do I believe any aspect of Unity can ever be brought about using any aspect of Division to do so? Can peace be brought about by fighting for it, can love be created through fear, or happiness through selfishness? No.

So then I prefer Unity but I cannot fight for it otherwise I will create its opposite. Yet I also cannot ignore it. I cannot get angry with people for creating more and more Division otherwise I will be creating more of it myself. To create heaven on earth the illusion of Division has to end. So before I try to solve any problems, I first need to make sure I don't create any new ones. If each individual was dedicated to not bringing any new division into the world, regardless of how righteous their cause might feel, that would be a step forward.

I don't believe you necessarily need to act globally to help solve global issues. Instead do all anyone can do: live the truth as best you understand it. To increase understanding is the key to all of it, but that can only be done by example not by forcing it on people or legislating for it. I try to live kindly and compassionately, and forgive the ignorant and hateful. Not because it's moral or righteous or spiritually superior, but because it's the truth. Ironically, if everyone understood they were already connected, and gave up their causes at the same time we'd instantly have world peace! So perhaps we can do one thing: educate people to give up fighting … for anything. As always, it comes back to this: let go.

***

Richard

This is the question that has perhaps come to occupy me the most, not so much how I relate to global challenges, but how does awakening relate to them.

The starting point has to be that awakening brings a sense of identity outside of the world. If I have the sense that I am ultimately safe, then I feel a freedom to engage with either personal or global problems/challenges absent the anxiety they can provoke.

Following on from that, this sense of stepping back out of the world has given me the perspective to acknowledge that I don't know what this world is. I don't know if it's a material world or ultimately a dream, I don't know if disincarnate spirits attempt to influence it for good or ill, I don't know if our problems arise from nefarious conspiracies or are a natural consequence of the structures we set up. Awakening gives me the spaciousness to hold all these views without being wedded to a particular one.

This is also true when it comes to particular global issues. The biggest problem I find, is that when we are not rooted in the full depth of our being, we form an identity around our opinions. It then becomes impossible to really dialogue with anyone of an opposing view; it feels threatening to our very sense of self. Opening up the potential for dialogue is what spirituality most brings to global challenges.

This isn't to say I don't have strong opinions. I do. On politics, economics, global warming, all sorts of issues. These opinions are often at odds with people I meet in spiritual groups. I'd like to think I'm not dogmatic with them though and can see how other people have rationally formed their opinions as well.

***

Andrew

"All the world's a stage, and all the men and women merely players: they have their exits and their entrances; and one man in his time plays many parts, his acts being seven ages." William Shakespeare.

Looking at the world from within the play, it is a mess and there are many challenges ahead as there have been for centuries or millennia. It is easy to be caught up in the play, and also exciting so the challenges appear real and daunting. That's fine and I get caught up as well.

However looking at it as the play it is, gives a different perspective. There have always been challenges just different ones at different times. It makes the play exciting. There have also been many predictions of doom and just as many of a new global awakening. That's all part of the play.

People will go on a roller coaster for the thrill and excitement and the apparent danger; when you get on you know it is safe but you feel the danger to get the adrenalin rush. The world is a bit like that. It is full of contradictions and dangers, but it is safe in an ultimate sense beyond the perceptions of the body. The play is mesmerizing and I laugh and I cry and I shout out "Look behind you!", but I also know it is a play.

***

Michaela

Global challenges … and yet, as with any challenge, we can only respond as an individual.

The awakened perspective knows there is no real separation, nor any superiority of one life form over another. This quite naturally brings compassion, responsibility and caring for this beautiful earth and its beings. At the same time, there is no real panic or fear for any outcome, as there is complete trust in the intelligence beyond the processes happening, based on deep knowing, that all is perfectly orchestrated and cared for. There is acceptance and peace, as well as a vision and energy to contribute to an improvement for the well-being of this world. Personally I involve myself in protecting animals. It feels as though it is my duty to speak for the mistreated and misused fellow beings that have no voice to defend their rights.

I see the actual turbulence in the world as a great opportunity; all that is hidden and suppressed can come to the surface to become visible and understood. We know from the individual journey towards peace, that the cleaning process can be very painful, and now it seems to be happening on the collective scale, where the human species are on a crucial crossroad. We are challenged not to lose ourselves in the dramas, to stay sane in the middle of misinformation, conspiracies and the growing number of conflicts, and to bring the light and peace we know in our lives, into this world.

***

Timothy

When I consider global challenges I like to research and come to an understanding of the issues from a more intellectual viewpoint. I educate myself just in case there is some positive remedy that I can initiate or insight I can contribute. I make a concerted effort to gain some wisdom so I can personally accept what is happening as a more responsible being. Then I allow my heart-felt existence to add to the positive feelings that are, in my opinion, magically beneficial to 'the greater good', so to speak. Hopefully this way I'll be more inclined to realize a time when I can take action.

During the pandemic I used this same approach. I educated myself and reviewed all the conflicting arguments without taking a political or emotional stance. I studied the science, checked the sources and compiled the best answers based on common sense. I also checked-in with those who commit their lives to protecting the public and helping people with their personal health concerns. I added in my own observations and drew the best conclusions for the current situation while staying open to new information.

Another example is climate change. It has always intrigued me since I learned in grade school that the glaciers once covered half of the North American continent. Then about 12,000 years ago they began to melt and recede. In our comparatively short human lives the weather seemed to stabilize for a while but that melting never really stopped. I've since learned that over millennia the climate has gone through many cycles.

I read hundreds of scientific publications and found that the climate is still slowly changing similarly to when it began 12,000 years ago. It's a more rapid change in the last 200 to 1000 years but it's not all caused by us. I do however think we should begin preparing for climate changes and stop adding to the greenhouse gas volume.

I'm happy that people have more awareness about pollution. The coronavirus pandemic highlighted just how much pollution humans create on a daily basis when we were restricted to staying home and factory production was greatly reduced. The skies and the waters cleared and many animals came out of hiding.

***

Chapter 23 – Global challenges

Marianne

Political instability, environmental destruction, economic collapse, global pandemic. They're what we might term global challenges, but in reality they're humanity's challenges.

What I see with awakening is Oneness. No separation. There is no separate self. What I see when I am walking in the bush and notice a small delicate mushroom, is Oneness. It is not a Oneness that comes from an addition process ... the merging of a 'me' with a mushroom, the merging of inner and outer, physical and spiritual, human and not-human. No. There is only one thing. Already always one. The mushrooms know it, the birds know it.

Only humanity is at odds with this and as such, with itself. Only humanity has banished itself from Truth, nature and the natural state by believing the stories of the mind and separating itself out. Only humanity is at odds with its environment, breeding and living beyond the capacity of this planet to sustain us. But we continue blithely on ... me me me. I want my overseas holiday! I want the latest television! I want a big family! I want the latest car! Humanity is never content. Never at home. We look for the Garden of Eden everywhere. We want it back! Not realizing that it is already here. Not realizing that it has never gone anywhere.

Humanity is not the entirety, but on the whole humanity believes it *is* the entirety. Kingpin. Top dog. There is humanity and then there are all those other things that we can use and abuse to suit ourselves and our whims. Swat that mosquito, eat that chicken, spray those weeds with poison. It seems that the fate of our planet hangs in the hands of humanity. I believe, and it *is* a belief, that the Intelligence of whatever 'this' is, will step in at some point. Perhaps there are balances in place which we have no clue about. Perhaps this Intelligence is stepping in right now, saying "enough is enough" ... again, I don't know ...

Awakening probably IS the answer. It sounds simplistic but it's not. Until we know ourselves as a Lifing that is not separate from the Lifing of a bird or a fungus, I think we're doomed as a species. We aren't exempt from Life.

And yet I still feel overwhelming positive. There is only NOW ... and in that now-ness there is nothing 'wrong' and nothing happening. Yes as a species we may die, but in the rock crevices a tiny spider will continue on, a cockroach will make its way along the earth, an amazing fungus will rise from the flames. And there too go I.

I do know that I have to live according to what I have seen. The earth needs that simplicity, that gentleness, that clarity, that sincerity, that honesty. It needs a vision of Truth and Oneness. It needs us to walk ever-so-lightly. And who knows how that gentle seeing will affect the whole …

***

Kathy

After my first glimpse into awakening, although I had little interest in politics or world affairs, I did have an overwhelming personal calling to live a life of service. I realized that many of the world's problems could be resolved by investing in access to education; I found myself helping at-risk children in Central America access education.

Then, just before my awakening, a president was elected for my country who was non-presidential in every way and that struck me to my core. It was hard to accept that someone with such terrible values and morals was about to become one of the most powerful men in the world. Then the awakening happened. My perspective on the situation shifted. It became clear to me that this man was here for us. Unbeknownst to him, he was here to help us wake up … just by being who he was. There was a knowing that he may end up pushing us so far that we might all unite. Interestingly, he no longer bothered me; I believe he represents our individual and collective shadow side which needs to emerge so that we can face it as a nation.

Shortly after this, Nicaragua, my home country for over 12 years, spiralled into a political crisis. What started as peaceful protesting, turned into a shocking mass killing of young students by the government. Instead of backing down, both political parties joined forces and marched as one, donning blue and white, the national colors. It was chilling and heart wrenching. It was personal for me and touched me to my innermost depths. I recall listening to the government news, almost fascinated by the completely different reality they projected, than the one portrayed by the underground (social media).

With the global pandemic, the same man was still in office in my country of origin. It's so clear to me that it was here for us to wake up, to realize our interconnectedness and interdependence, to unmask our issues, and ideally find collective solutions. Yet, it is also clear, that this may be one of many wake-up calls.

I don't know how any of these situations will end, but I am now very clear that these are opportunities or invitations on individual and collective levels to wake up. Neither of the polarized sides is better than the other; I can see how both are looking through strong egoic filters. While my tendencies are more left, I see strong egoic leftists in a similar light to those extremists on the right. At times I find myself yearning to find ways to bring the two sides together, but find it daunting.

In summary, I am now more interested than ever in political and world affairs but from a very different perspective.

***

Drawing

by
Silvia

When I started to draw
the only thing I knew
was that I wanted to express
what I felt and know I am.
If I were to give it a title it would be 'I'.
I can't say more than this,
except that the continents and countries
are purposely wrong in place, size and shape.
Somebody asked me if the 'I' is the woman in the center ...
no, obviously the 'I' is not just her.

Chapter 24

Death

Jennifer

Death has really come to the foreground for me since awakening.

I had experienced my father's death to stomach cancer at age 19 which is also the time my spiritual path began. In my 20s, because of my father's death, when friends or friends' parents died, I had a strange sense of being comfortable with it all, even finding beauty and intimacy in what happened for people around death. Strangely, prior to awakening, I mostly felt free to live in ways which others perceived as me risking my life. I did things like camp alone, sleep in my car on long road trips, travel solo to developing countries with deadly illnesses or dangerously high crime rates, and heal my skin cancer intuitively.

In recent years, my fear of death has been much more present. A week after my awakening experience in Ubud, Bali, I got Dengue Fever and I remember lying in my hotel bed feeling I could be dying. It wasn't because of the pain or fear; it felt like an awareness. A few days later my platelets dropped to dangerously low levels which meant my chances of internally bleeding and dying were greatly increased. Rather than being hospitalized, I got on a plane and flew back to Boulder, Colorado to recover. I was later told by an intuitive healer that fevers are common after awakening experiences because the body is burning up all that is no longer true or real. About 6 months later, again I was alone in my hotel room, this time in Rishikesh, India, and got extremely sick. I couldn't eat for a week. When I returned to the US a few months later, I had a series of health problems from mysterious extreme pain, to fatigue, to cognitive challenges, to vertigo which years later was diagnosed as a chronic illness. These experiences brought up the fear of death again.

I had a friend die recently and it somehow felt different. Although it felt deeply sad, it felt less monumental. A few months later while I was in meditation, he came to me and asked me to share some things with the people he loves. I did.

My next encounter with death was when my partner's body began shutting down and he had to be helicoptered to ICU. We thought he was going to die. Slowly his functioning came back and a week later he was released from the hospital. We were both forever changed by the experience.

During Covid-19 I was in solo quarantine and death was never more present in my daily life. Having traveled the world for more than 20 years without any serious problems, now in the five years since that magical experience in Bali, all this has happened. So perhaps death feels much less far away … or there is much less between my experience of self and death. My sense is that this is a fear that has risen to the surface of my conscious mind in order to be healed.

I also have the knowingness that to die is the epitome of liberation. It is the ultimate freedom from any and all limitations. I can feel that truth. I am in the fifth week of a Bardo, Death and Dying course with Andrew Holocek. He says if we can die before we die we will be truly free.

***

Michaela

I remember frequently reflecting on death even as a very young child. I lived the first years of my life with my elderly grandparents and every night I was scared they would pass away in their sleep. I also reflected on the end of my own existence. I imagined it as a terrifying black endless nothingness. Death seemed to be the only absolute certainty we have in our lives and I often wondered: What is the point of it all? Why this cruel game? The fear of death was certainly a catalyst in my search for something that might triumph over that black scary ghost.

It was during my first deep dive into the absolute that the frightening image of death dissolved. I saw that all is well as it is and that Life can be absolutely trusted, regardless of how it plays with form. This awakening experience itself was actually a near-death experience, as it was the death of the mind-made identity and an experience of pure being. The overwhelming peace that was present then brought an insight: that life has no opposite, just like love. To manifest as existence it simply needs the inseparable birth and death phenomena on every level of its creation.

Chapter 24 – Death

We would not be able to experience existence without this process of permanent change.

Since that realization, I am at peace with what is. That does not mean I am not vulnerable and have no emotions. I will not deny that it is hard to say goodbye to loved ones. It is sad and can be heartbreaking, but it is accepted as a natural part of human existence.

***

Maureen

Dancing
birth and death
inhaling
exhaling
energy to matter
matter to energy
this is our dance

Fear of death is gone, most of the time. There's still fear of the process of dying, of the many ways human bodies fail. But death? It's a doorway, not an end. A beautiful return.

Grieving and loss shifted. When someone dies, while I grieve for my loss, I don't grieve for theirs, as I can feel their energy dancing in release and joy.

Talking about any of this is awkward. It feels confrontational to many people, and for someone who is grieving, it's painful. Joy is not welcome, not yet.

Death
his energy rises
dancing
light

he is released

we are bereft
not seeing
his joy.

***

Silvia

Seeing I am 'The All' and its Source, radically changed my relationship with death.

Recently my father 'died' and I experienced sadness, of course, for not being able to appreciate his physical person in my everyday life anymore, but what I mostly felt was peace. The fear of death as a big unknown question mark was erased from my mind.

Yet I recognize that very old traumatic experiences around survival are still registered in my body. When triggered, they fire messages of fear into the system. Their intensity is very challenging and I can fall into the trap of believing them.

***

Marianne

I have reflected on death my entire life. It was the one big thing that we could all be assured of, and it was the one big thing that nobody seemed to want to talk about. As child I recall feeling myself as alive in this one little body and marveling at that. How did it come to be? How would it be after that little body died?

When, in my early 20s I started to suffer, I thought often of suicide. I wanted to die. I wanted an escape. I tried to imagine my non-existence over and over. But for all my thoughts of killing myself, the reality was that I actually wanted to find a way to truly LIVE. I made a pact with myself not to suicide. If I continually gave myself an 'out', I knew I would never find a way to truly be 'in' … to truly *live*.

When I awoke, it was so clear to me that the 'awakeness' that we are, was never born and would never die. But it was also clear that any mind-constructed notions of a 'Marianne' separate from that, would not continue. There were times I lay in bed at night stroking my partner's cheek, knowing without a doubt that we are all part of a vast all-encompassing Love, and yet wondering where the softness of her cheek would be in a hundred years, or a thousand. There was such a beauty here, but also a tragedy. It was all included.

A couple of months ago, after a friend had a mild heart attack, I was once again contemplating death. I was picking vegetables in the garden when suddenly the veil between living and dying became completely transparent; it was still there but vapor-thin. It was seen as an illusion. It was not a mental thing; it was an actual seeing of reality.

This living/dying wondrous Mystery is beyond our capacity to know. There is no other than this Oneness, this Love. This. Over and over, in Truth, we are thrust upon this Nowness; it is a miracle in which we disappear and are saved. It is so good to be alive.

***

Timothy

Upon enlightenment I immediately knew I'd never die. I realized that 'all that is' is eternally present and so, being one with that, am I.

I am also reminded of a video I saw from someone who is a Death Doula. He said, "Death is perfectly safe."

***

Lisa

My life has been defined by a NDE (near-death experience) as a five-year old. I consider this experience the most important of my life and the beginning of awakening. Every step I took from then on was basically a seeking and yearning for that 'place', and an attempt to integrate, understand and put to use what I had experienced.

The NDE started with a complete surrender and letting go of myself, my body and my life as I was swept away by a wave in the ocean. Awakening as an adult many years later, turned out to be the same thing – a complete surrender and letting go, but this time, rather than into death, into life. When we truly surrender to life, we experience something very similar to death, although for me, my NDE was much more powerful than all the spiritual experiences (including the transition/awakening) I've experienced in this physical life.

What I knew in death was the most profound peace, unfathomable freedom and a wondrous unconditional love that knew no bounds and permeated all of existence and non-existence. I experienced the mystical light that most NDE-ers speak of: the light of true Life. In death, I knew myself completely. Death was so beautiful, words fail.

In this physical life, the awakening I've experienced so far, is but a shadow of what I knew in my NDE. But they are nevertheless related.

Awakening is also peace, freedom, knowing who we truly are, love, light, life. It is surrendering and letting go. The only difference for me after awakening is that I am a lot more accepting of, or in a sense indifferent to, physical pain and physical death than I was before. But this doesn't mean I don't feel loss or sorrow or compassion – I do – even a lot deeper than before. But I no longer suffer. It is all Being.

The way I see it, there is basically no difference between life and death. They are two sides of the same coin. Physical life includes the physical world, disembodied life doesn't. When we die physically, we let go of and lose the physical side of life, but keep on being. This is impossible to explain or comprehend intellectually, and even express properly, but it is very possible to know, to experience, to sense, and to realize.

Western society mainly considers death a taboo and most people are phobic when it comes to death. It is very rare to come across someone who has deeply realized, accepted and integrated the fact that we will all die physically one day, and that we will lose everything and everyone we love. Different spiritual traditions offer teachings for contemplating death, which I feel is a wise approach. If we as a society could take death to heart and diminish the massive fear that exists on a collective level, it would help us to take big steps towards revering and preserving life.

On an individual level, accepting death without being afraid of it is immensely liberating and beneficial. With death as our friend to be embraced and valued, instead of an enemy to be loathed and feared, we see so much more clearly what is important: How we want to treat ourselves and others. What and who we love, and how we can express that love. What is less important, what has meaning and what is meaningless. Diminishing fear of death diminishes fear of life, of living to the fullest. Embracing death helps us to embrace life and loving and living it fully. When we stop being afraid of death, we realize there is actually nothing in existence to be afraid of.

***

Kathy

When my grandmother, who raised me, was transitioning, there were several moments when she was lucid and glowing. She told me her parents were coming soon. She saw herself die (an hour ago she said). She pointed to the ceiling with a smile. Those moments were so special and unforgettable, and helped ease any discomfort I had about death.

Chapter 24 – Death

During one of the first awakenings I experienced the timeless realm and it was seen with so much clarity that 'I' was never born so could never die. That said, there is a discomfort about the body aging and concern about it being able to get around, but there seems to be little issue about leaving the body.

***

Elizabeth

Though a lot of folks in this realm tend to pooh-pooh attachment, or deny it, I've made a conscious choice to become attached to form – and to mourn its loss. After living in the ashram (way back in 2005), I returned with a resolve to fully enter every human experience.

I always think of Ramana Maharshi, crying with the local farmers when one of their cows died.

But I get that we pick sorrow. It is our choice whether we laugh or cry. Not sure why I still choose one over the other at times. It's all so … loose now.

***

Kiran

I always felt myself to be a little different around death. When I was in my teens, my grandfather passed away. When he was alive, he was the only person who told me bedtime stories at night, and even though I was very close to him, I was the only person in the family who didn't cry or mourn. I witnessed the deaths of many other people, including close relations, but never felt loss, pain or hurt, even when my young sister-in-law died at the age of 29. However moving beyond birth and death was still my belief during the years of seeking.

A few months before awakening in July 2012, I witnessed a dog (not mine) being put to sleep and I saw death in a very different way. It was strange and deeply touching. A realization arose that there is only one death and that is the death of the 'me': that aspect of mind that takes duration in the body as 'me'. Somehow the death of Lucas (the dog) showed me a very real side to it and the following poem bubbled up:

Tasting Death
(July 8, 2012)
O great one, your touch, so pure, so real, O good one
So nothing, yet so piercing neither liquid nor solid
Pulling me, sucking me into your deep vacuum
Tempts me, lures me to melt in your realm
With open wide arms, with loving welcoming heart
With head on your feet surrendering all to that
I long to be with you slipping into your arms more and more
They call you death, O beautiful one,
the taste of life in you I adore.

As a result of that experience, my deepest inner perspective changed. It was as if the ventilator plug was pulled out of the surviving body-mind conglomerate. It was just a matter of time before the process was completed. It was the beginning of the awakening.

Now I feel no concern regarding this physical death; it is not even a question anymore. The eternal nature of my reality has been recognized deeply. Form is born and it will definitely perish. I was, before this body was born, and I will remain after this body falls. I do see the timeless life force living through this body tasting its own creation in each moment as it appears. With the realization of my eternal Self, connectedness or oneness is experienced, so there is no separate anything that dies. The arising and falling, or birth and death, are all within.

***

Andrew

Every night I go to sleep and 'lose myself' and the next morning I wake up refreshed. I've had surgery where scientists would tell me I was unconscious, and I had no memory of any events during that time.

Every day I 'die' to myself. I have lost my identity as 'myself' so what possible hold could death have over me? It is just part of the cycle of life. As I like to say … There is only one condition known to humankind that is guaranteed to be terminal, and that is life. One goes with the other in a glorious cycle. Enjoy the part of the cycle you are in, and neither want the next nor fear it.

***

Chapter 24 – Death

Stacy

Death is a favorite shift for me! In the one-time meditation workshop of April 2007, mentioned elsewhere in the book, we did a meditation of zooming in on death. I learned that there is a sect of Buddhist monks whose practice is to meditate on all the ways one could die.

Our pointer was to focus on the precise moment of death – not one second before when it seems you can turn back, not one second after when it's all done, but the precise moment. We looked to see what was there.

Everyone in the workshop experienced some form or 'release' or 'letting go' or 'relief'.

This was recorded. Me? I laughed hysterically for several minutes. It seemed hilarious, like the biggest joke ever that anyone could die or that there was anyone *to* die.

So, death hasn't happened, yet, but the sense is that it will not matter one bit. This tends to be a little difficult when others are processing death. To stay truthful is a challenge. Nothing like "Sorry for your loss" is true. Not one word of it. There is no 'sorrow', no 'you', no 'loss'.

I share Kahlil Gibran's chapter, *On Death* when need be. That works.

***

Amara

When I think of death, which isn't often, I realize that the one who thought there was such a thing died in the glimpse! It was like a baptism of sorts; a complete dissolution into the waters of the Absolute. Whatever it was that believed in the possibility of death, didn't make it back out.

That being said, death and birth happen every moment, relatively speaking. All that can die (appearance) passes away constantly. But I'm not that. This can all sound very philosophical, and conceptual … and safe. What of the body? I have no idea. When I'm faced with the passing of the body, it will be an experience appearing to me. I guess I'll get to see just how much residual identification there is at that point! In any case, What I Am is okay. "Being is, not being is not." So simple. I feel no need to 'survive' as a person, or even a soul. If that happens, that's okay too. There's simply this Knowing that Is, no matter what. No worries.

***

Richard

The major thing awakening did for me was change my perspective on death. In fact I'd go as far as to say it's not that awakening changed my perspective on death, but that awakening *was* a change of perspective on death.

I wrote in another chapter how my spontaneous awakening experience brought me into a sense of peace and an appreciation for the wonder and beauty of life. I also wrote that this came as the result of a deeper cause. This cause was largely the direct perception that life is eternal and this mortal realm is but one small part of what is. This sense of eternity took away all the stress of being compressed into time. At that time I perceived this from within my vaguely Christian world-view, of existing forever in time. Now I would look at it more in a non-dual context, of our essential, unborn nature existing outside of time.

That's not the full story however. Over time I have also become far more aware of the physical reality of death. Through meditation I have opened my imagination in a way that has allowed me to directly experience my own death and the death of loved ones, with the full horror that entails. I don't take the subject lightly. I believe that most people unconsciously insulate themselves from fully contemplating death; if they didn't do so they wouldn't be able to function. When I've met people (without spiritual insight) for whom that psychological insulation has fallen away, they are really tormented by everyone's impending doom. Worse, as everyone else *appears* to cope, they believe that this sense of torment indicates that there is something wrong with them.

The story of the Buddha is utterly true, in that an awareness of death is a major catalyst for spiritual awakening, although a painful one.

***

Erick

Death takes on much less meaning as the days go by. Perhaps it is my own aging … holding less to the dreams of the body and more to the light that shines through it all. Perhaps it is from seeing more friends and family members move on that I get a deeper insight into the passages that we all take. There are dimensions we traverse and places we go that are not unlike this life.

Chapter 24 – Death

When I think about my physical transition there is a little tingle of excitement – like a new adventure waiting to be discovered. The body's collective consciousness is not so delighted, but it goes along for the ride.

The most important message of death is for us to live totally alive right now, for there truly is nothing else. In that eternal moment death holds no mastery over us. We are partners with it and the dance goes on.

***

Ben

My life's defining moment was my father's death when I was a teenager. It made me question everything I had known. I also had several friends and other family members die in various circumstances over the next few years, so from a very young age mortality was on the top of my list of things to understand.

Until very recently I also hid from it emotionally and unfortunately this denial caused an awful lot of pain to many different people. Only from the peace I found, and with the support of my partner, was I able to truly deal with it. It was probably the very last pain to truly bring to the fore.

What happens when we die? Who knows? I suspect it's just a change in perspective for our consciousness.

And for the record, I would like my tombstone to read: "It's not really that tragic when you think about it."

***

Echinacea

Photos by Maureen

Chapter 25

Ego and suffering

Lisa

As I mentioned elsewhere, when the final knot of ego snapped, I finally saw it for what it was: a tangle of old trauma, memories, thoughts, concepts, emotions and dreams. If I could draw it, it would look like a person with an entangled ball of all this stuff held somewhere in the body and strands extending throughout the body and even sticking outside the body. (By using the word 'outside' here, I mean in an etheric or spiritual sense, not a physical one.)

When living from the ego, we're identified with all this stuff and think it's 'me'. The hardest knot in the middle is perceived as the center of 'me' and when the mind or consciousness follows one of the strands, it is felt as 'mine'. 'My' memory, what happened to 'me', 'my' thought, 'my' pain, 'my' joy. This also goes for 'my' will. 'I' want this, or 'I' don't want that, preferences of likes and dislikes and a bunch of other things too which people generally think is a 'normal' way of being. And maybe it is during a certain phase of human development, I'm not sure.

In any case, the difference between living from this perception of the ego-tangle and simply living, is the identification with the tangle and the strands. And this is where the suffering comes in. If there is pain in the present moment, for example, it starts to reverberate in the tangle with past experiences, memories, thoughts, emotions etc. which makes it multiply, and on top of that consciousness or mind identifies with it and calls it 'me' and 'mine'. So on top of the actual and echoed past pain, mind or consciousness goes: 'Oh no, this is happening to ME! It's happening to ME again! Why is this happening to ME? Am 'I' a bad person? 'I' don't want this to be happening! 'I' don't like it when this is happening, and so on. The same thing occurs when there is pleasure. "Wow, I like this! I want more of it. I deserve it, because I'm a good and worthy person. I'm better than others. I want this to happen again in the future."

This whole mess takes away the ability to actually experience what is happening in the present moment, whatever it is, and react in constructive ways if a reaction is warranted. When there is no tangle to identify with, there is pain. Or there is joy. There is something happening. It might be enjoyable or not. There is laughter. There is crying. There is beauty. There is ugliness. There are beginnings and endings. If there are emotions or thoughts, they are not perceived as 'my' emotions or thoughts, even if we call them that for convenience. It's not even 'my' body. It's a body. It's a consciousness. It's a mind. It's a thought. It's a feeling.

So when simply living, the drawing would look like the same person but without the tangle. Instead, there would be currents and flows of emotions, thoughts and perceptions flowing by and disappearing, as they occur in the present. They are not clung to or identified with, and no new tangles or knots are formed. So the emotions don't multiply; there is no additional head-banging against the wall with questions of 'why me?' or feelings of being 'worthy or unworthy'. Life is lived in the present and the next present moment isn't contaminated by what was there in the present moment before it.

***

Kiran

Initially, my knowledge of ego was shallow; I tried to not be egotistical. Later I came to realize that my entire way of living was from ego regardless of my efforts to not be egotistical. Before we recognize ourselves as *not* this ego self, ego is everything that we are.

I could see that all my suffering was because of this ego entity which was a mistaken identity developed within the body, mind and emotions. Mind identified with the body as a 'me', and so the body created a sense of mortality which required protection; things were labelled as 'harmful' (including emotions). Everything together created confusion and a constant need to fix and change, and want something more or different. I was perpetually dissatisfied with life. But the more I understood and realized the deep-seated mechanism of this ego, the more I came into my beingness and so suffered less. Still, I had not yet realized my trueness.

I started to see that the one who suffers, is not really me. It is a created phenomenon within, which has been mis-perceived as me. These misperceptions within mind and memory had consciously or unconsciously held my beliefs, habits and patterns, and directed or controlled life.

The whole structure of this ego entity came from outside and had no authenticity to it. Through meditation and simple contemplation I paid deeper and quieter attention to it. I kept uncovering its patterns, holdings and workings, and as a result no longer participated in them. I reached depths within myself using this ego entity and its experiences, past and present. From this perspective, ego was a great help.

It is through uncovering this ego entity that I came closer and closer to my beingness. This naturally prepared me for major awakening/the shift of consciousness.

The recognition of my trueness gave me increased awareness of the egotistical or psychological phenomena and its workings. As a result, ignorance and suffering reduced and was replaced with clarity and peace. I became open. I realized that there was room to include all that ego kept separate from formless silence. Silent presence has built-in wisdom and rather than using ego and its structure, it has the clarity to perceive happenings the way they are actually happening in reality, thus allowing them to happen in their original way.

Ego is based upon duality; it always divides and sorts every movement of life into good or bad. Ego and its divisive nature results in outcomes of either pleasure or suffering; true nature is non-dual and without any such self. Although the psyche and its differentiating capacity is still used by awareness for the functionality of life, it has now lost its other influences as there is no self or entity to be influenced. It does arise to play every now and then but the light of awareness very quickly shows it up, rendering it useless. As stated earlier, it brings a great opportunity to include or embody those unconscious or separated parts and so feel grace and fulfilment of the purpose.

***

Erick

I never fully knew what ego was until after awakening. Sense of individual self I perceived, but I never saw that as an obstacle to awakening. Perhaps it was my studies with my teacher who said that we should not try to obliterate ego, rather expand it to infinity that made me feel that way. That made a lot of sense to me. Why should I spend my precious energy trying to blot out what I am? If I succeeded, who would have been the victor?

As it worked out, my individual ego did not expand to infinity, rather it was replaced by Infinity while the individual operating in the world remained. From that perspective, ego was clear to see. It was also clear how the ego-centered habits of thought had dragged me into suffering. Resting in pure Existence, it was no longer possible for my heart to turn against my individual nature, for I could see that the core of suffering is the mind attacking its own individual sense of self. Infinity sees the individual as just another beautiful bit of creation, and, since its nature is love, it cannot attack the individual.

If I were to define ego from an awakened perspective I would call it the stickiness of a thought that makes it so real that it overtakes the primal perception of infinite Being. So it's not even the thought of oneself, but the tendency within any thought to be believed as absolutely true. Interestingly, it is the Absolute nature within the thought that lends it the stickiness to be believed. Separating the two natures of thought and then allowing them to merge into a conscious wholeness is the path of awakening, as I have seen it. This happens spontaneously, but balanced attention to one's practices is the catalyst.

**

Stacy

Let us all remember that we did not have an 'ego' until a cigar-smoking cocaine addict in Austria said we did. Before that maybe we called it 'the devil' or an 'evil spirit' or some other thing. But it is no more real than 'self'. It is completely made up. Somehow I never really latched on to the concept even before awakening.

As for suffering, Byron Katie says that when you argue with reality, you always suffer. There isn't much more to say about that unless you want to go into how to resolve it. I did the Work of Byron Katie for years before my fuller awakening and it helped a lot to make the cognitive leaps.

**

Chapter 25 – Ego and suffering

Timothy

Here's my description of 'ego' and how I've come to express what it is from contemplating my own journey:

When I was a kid I tried to get an idea of who I might be. I was always modifying this bundle of thoughts about who I am. My parents would tell me something new about how I could be a better person, which I would then attempt to place in my bundle. Even if a thought didn't quite feel right, I would still consider it because I wanted to know who I was.

It was an ongoing challenge to come up with the perfect idea of myself. I'd lie awake at night trying to figure out the ideal caricature. Tons of energy and time went into this endeavor. I never really got comfortable with my constantly changing results, and that gave me a lot of anxiety. If someone criticized me, I'd spend even more time trying to change myself so they'd be happy with me. When some kid on the playground called me a bad name they were essentially attacking who I thought I was. Again, I'd waste time trying to adjust. No matter how hard I tried, I just couldn't seem to get all the right pieces together. Consequently, I was miserable and wanted to die.

Then one day I had this weird realization and I told myself "Enough! I'm just going to be whoever I want to be and I'm never going to let anyone make me feel like that again." The struggle with who I am, what psychologists call the 'ego', took a back seat in my life and everything opened up for me. I was suddenly free from the conflict and the criticism. I no longer wasted time judging myself. All I had to do was wait ten more years, get through school, and stay out of trouble. Then I could live on my own, only do what I wanted to do, and just be myself. This simple awareness forever freed me from the shackles of ego.

***

Marianne

As I sit here trying to find words, it is as though I am wading through mud …

The sense inside is that it is all so very simple. But years ago when I was suffering greatly and had yet to awaken, those words would have been taken as arrogance, as a denial of how great suffering can be, and as a dismissal of the utter sincerity and commitment with which I pursued the journey to find Truth. And yet … sitting here and looking from the perspective of awakening, it really *is* all so simple. In this Being-ness no words are necessary, it just *is*, and it has always been that way.

But still, for a book I need to find some words ...

If anything ego or self-sense could be described as a verbing that divides reality into 'me' and 'not me'. It identifies ('identification' being a narrowing of consciousness) with the 'me' and then pits this 'me' against the 'not me'. This 'me' includes thoughts/thinking, feelings, behaviours, beliefs, conditioning, memories, assumptions, body-mind, impressions, unconscious impulses, blind spots, defences etc. But this ego as an entity, as a separate self, is a fabrication. It doesn't exist. It can't be found. We aren't a 'thing' surrounded by other 'things'. We are one indivisibility. We are already whole and complete. This is our birthright.

In retrospect, looking back over my life, I did vaguely seem to know this. I was always trying to fit in and 'be someone' even though that seemed like such a strange thing to do. On some level I sensed that ego and its attributes (such as self-esteem and self-worth) were actually arbitrary nonsense. However, at that time I assumed I was perhaps a little 'slow' in this regard; everyone else seemed to know what to do. I wonder now, how many people suspect the flimsiness of the 'ego'/self-sense construct and suffer as a result.

And yet, solid functioning is needed in this world, not as an 'ego' as such, but as an individual organism. We need to be able to erect boundaries, understand what is in the best interests of *this* organism over any other organism, sense danger, plan a future, 'have' relationships, earn money, buy food. We are not born in a monastery or on cotton wool. We need to be able to function; good-enough functioning is necessary. But beyond that, the relentless pursuit by 'ego' to build itself up, to come out on top, to complete itself through 'other' is entirely misdirected. If we are identified with 'ego' we will *always* feel its inadequacy on some level; we will never feel at home, never feel complete, never be truly happy. We are trying to maintain a fortress that doesn't exist ... this is why 'ego' suffers. And additionally, if one's past is filled with trauma and as a result we have not developed a 'good-enough' individual functioning capacity there is further suffering by virtue of our inability to operate and relate in the accepted or 'normal' ways.

With awakening, one's true nature (natural state) is known and we actually *see* what 'ego' is for the first time. We see that the tightening/identification around a small-self sense is a conditioned response that is not necessary; 'egoic' verbing is not necessary. What we *are* is *already* everything we have ever wanted. We don't have to 'try' or 'compete' our way anywhere. Nor do we have to fight reality. Reality is what we *are*, and it is already infinitely wise and intelligent and clear and whole.

But awakening is just the beginning. After awakening, layer upon layer of identifications are still there to be seen and then shed. This process frees 'us' further and further allowing our realisation to deepen … into Life, Oneness, Mystery …

***

Ben

The word Ego has so many definitions and interpretations that all I will try to do is explain what I understand it to mean, and why this relates to so-called suffering.

For a start I no longer see Ego as false, dirty or undesirable. I no longer even see it as something one can 'have'. Instead I now understand there to be two basic stages of Consciousness in humans: Ego and Awakened. The night I found myself in Awakened, I perceived Ego very differently to the way I had imagined it up until that point. I had imagined they were opposites. Or as least separate from each other. They aren't. They are different stages of exactly the same thing, which is Consciousness itself. It is only when seeing things through Ego that the idea that Ego and Awakened are separate comes in.

There is also not really 'my' ego, or 'your' ego, no 'big' egos or 'small' ones, any more than there is 'my' awakening or 'yours'. That's why I'm capitalizing Ego and Awakened as the way I am talking about them differs from that traditional usage. I am talking about them as eternal, universal states of Consciousness. Ego manifests in so many different behaviours that Ego, whose favourite behaviour is to divide in order to label and categorize, wants to make each expression of itself seem like a different, important, independent entity. They aren't. It is a case of myriad expressions, one thing. Ego is "10,000 things, one suchness". Just like the whole of Consciousness itself.

Awakened recognizes Ego is absolutely as impersonal, permanent and universal in all of us as Awakened is. It must be the case; they are after all the same Consciousness at two different points in Its lifecycle. That is why the behaviour it generates is so predictable in everyone and why when we look closely we can see the expression of Ego changes in individuals only by life circumstance, not fundamentally. In terms of analogy Ego is a child, Awakened is an adult, and Consciousness is the human. We are no less fundamentally us now than we were at ten years old, we just have a fuller understanding of the world as an adult. I find thinking similarly on Ego and Awakening is useful.

My perception of Ego changed dramatically when I moved to Awakened because until then I was only seeing Ego through Ego, thus my perception of it up until that point was limited. Not wrong, that would be the word Ego would put to it, Awakened would just acknowledge it was limited. Simply put, a child cannot have the same understanding of the world that an adult does. And this point is crucial really. Ego gets a hard time. But only from itself. Ego believes itself inferior to Awakened because it lacks the same maturity, but Awakened recognizes Ego as an equal and to be honoured for the role it plays. Just as a child cannot understand what it is like to be an adult because it's never experienced it, but an adult can understand what it is like to be a child, likewise it is that Ego cannot know what it is like to be Awakened, but Awakened can know Ego.

This is the natural development of Consciousness and the reason why spiritual lessons constantly say that Ego is something we must move beyond. To move beyond is not to destroy, it is to move beyond; to encompass, not deny or reject. How can Oneness possibly be achieved if we are rejecting things, casting them out, along the way? When Ego gets hold of this message though, it doesn't understand. How can it? Ego is the first stage of self-awareness, it has not evolved into what we might loosely call spirituality yet, and its nature cannot be changed. Importantly, neither should we want it to change. Without Ego there would be no Awakened. Moving from animal instinct (let's call it Stage 0) to recognizing self-awareness via Ego (Stage 1) is a necessary prerequisite to the deepening of Consciousness and self-awareness experienced in Awakened (Stage 2).

In truth then, Ego is essential and should be cherished for the role it plays in both our material and our spiritual development. The issue is that Ego doesn't recognize the spiritual contribution it makes because its primary function is to focus on the material world. On the material side of things, Ego can be seen as survival instinct made conscious. For example, the desire for a bigger house can be seen in a roundabout way as about the gathering of resources for survival. The fast car, like a peacock's feathers, for attracting a mate. Very basic stuff, and slightly amusing/strange to look at it that way in the modern world. But historically, moving from Stage 0 to Stage 1, and being able to order our survival instincts rather than just react to them (build farms, plan pregnancy,

Chapter 25 – Ego and suffering

fashion hunting weapons, stockpile for the winter, store harvest for famine) proved incredibly useful and effective at turning a slow, weak animal with no claws, no sharp teeth and no fur into the dominant species on the planet. It also had another consequence. It moved our experience from being unwittingly always in the present moment in Stage 0 to having a conscious acknowledgement of time in Stage 1. In the spiritual sense being lost in the mind, the past and the future, certainly has limitations, but as an aid to survival, the ability to imagine ahead and learn from the past is one of Ego's most invaluable assets.

So, Ego by its very design is limited to first stage self-awareness which is focussed on the physical world. Without it we wouldn't survive long enough in these bodies to be able to start developing spiritually and move towards Awakened. Awakened is not limited to the spiritual though. It is able to know the physical world thanks to its experience as Ego as it develops and the spiritual world due to its own nature and primary function. This is as it should be but it does mean that at a core level it is an actual impossibility for Ego to ever understand its worth in the spiritual sense, because it isn't the spiritual state of Consciousness. And it never will be. This truth has to be acknowledged before we can understand why suffering goes hand in hand with the Ego stage of Consciousness.

The illusion of suffering is triggered by the illusion of separation. Ego feels constantly separated because it thinks it has somewhere to go but hasn't got there yet. So at one level Ego is constantly suffering. Suffering stops at Awakening because Ego is absorbed into Awakened. Ego is no longer seeing itself as 'cast out' or alone, it is integrated. It finally sees that it is part of the One, the all-ness and always has been. Ego is not a trap. It is not hiding our true nature. As a stage of the evolution of Consciousness, it is actually a significant part of our true nature. A young part. The stories it makes up about itself – 'my' ego and 'yours', the trials and tribulations of our dramatic lives, the author of our own soap operas – that is where the false and illusory come in, but Ego itself is neither false nor illusory. It is part of us as the Consciousness we are. And as such, as yet another form of Love, it needs love. I felt that so clearly when I Awakened. With all its pain and neuroses and fear, and all the acting out in harmful and self-destructive ways that come with it, ultimately Ego was just terribly lonely and begging to be loved unconditionally. That was it. In that moment, this thing I had considered an enemy (really Ego considering itself an enemy within me) stopped and love for it poured in. And in that moment compassion for others was also born. Because it isn't a case of starting to love 'your' ego, because the idea there is a 'your' ego is part of the illusion, it doesn't exist. I started loving Ego as what it is truly is, this misunderstood stage of Consciousness which is part of everyone, and which is torturously under-acknowledged, or grossly misunderstood when it is acknowledged.

What people call their true nature, which they say they discovered underneath 'their' Ego is in fact their first glimpse at their evolving nature as they start to reduce the amount of Ego-stage Consciousness and increase the amount of Awakened-stage Consciousness being translated through them. This is also why many Awakened people talk about a deepening, or a cleaning out of old Ego wounds which can take years and years to finally be free of; you Awaken and come to know yourself as Awakened before you are translating 100% Awakened Consciousness. I know this from personal experience. I live more through Awakened than I did, but still live enough through Ego to understand Awakening is not going from zero to hundred per cent in an instant ... at least not in this individual, on this timeline. The rate of movement is different for everyone. Some people make a few giant leaps and others take a thousand small steps. But in each individual there is a point when Awakened Consciousness becomes the dominant Consciousness being translated through them even if Ego still exists in part.

Finally, an aspect of separation, confusion also causes suffering. Consider a spiritual seeker. This is someone committed to moving from Ego to Awakened and who therefore must still be in the Ego stage of Consciousness. This means that every spiritual lesson they hear to start with, by default, will be mis-understood because only Awakened Consciousness can understand the spiritual message. Consequently Ego converts the spiritual language into language it can understand: the language of the material, the language of conquest. Soon, rather than hearing the Awakened message (you are One, love all, incorporate everything into your understanding) the seeker hears the Ego's translation of that spiritual message:

"To gain this treasure you must conquer the villain, you must 'destroy' the evil Ego. Plot twist. It was you all along. You must destroy yourself. Ego is bad ... you are bad, ego is unworthy, you are unworthy."

This isn't true. This is one of Ego's famous illusions. This is the mindset of anyone in Ego, spiritual seeker or not. When you consider the level of self-loathing, judgement, hierarchical thinking, doubt and fear that Ego has to live with, and which is completely unaddressed on a societal level, it goes a long way to explaining the state of the world, the lack of compassion in human behaviour when it comes to sharing

Chapter 25 – Ego and suffering

resources and the pain in both individuals and society at large. When you look at the world through this idea of Ego and Awakened, it is clear that Ego rules the world. Awakened is what will turn the world into a better place. Fighting racism, sexism and so on is worthy, but when it come from Ego it is counter-productive however good the intention. This is why we've been fighting these things for decades or even centuries and very little has changed. In a very simplistic way, Ego is the consciousness that should be dealing with providing plenty, and Awakened is the Consciousness that should be distributing it. But since Awakened incorporates Ego, we could all just focus on becoming Awakened and everything would be taken care of.

Evolve yourself first if you want to help the world. To be Awakened you simply need to know yourself. Don't reject yourself, whatever stage you find yourself in. Absolute inclusion is part of Awakened Consciousness, so be aware to be actively more inclusive of things you had previously been excluding. When you can do this in yourself you will be able to do it in the world too. Being angry about anger will make it stronger. Hating hate, being sad about sadness, or frustrated about frustration will perpetuate the emotion, whether in you or society as a whole. Love the things you thought you had to conquer and cast out, include them without indulging them, forgive them and yourself and you will have converted one tiny bit of personal and global Ego to Awakened. Know yourself. Don't be confused about where you are any longer, or feel guilty about it. Wherever you are in the journey, marvel at it. You can't possibly get further without having been here first. Focus on your now, not your future. Focus on the reality of what you are now, not the version of yourself you hope to be so you can feel good about yourself. You can only affect reality here and now. Be fully here now, in Ego if that's where you are, observing Ego and its playful conjurings. By forgetting the ideas of triumphing and succeeding, the change you want will take place without you having to worry about it. And as you get closer, don't be scared of the unknown. You won't be somehow lost when you Awaken, your personality won't disappear, you won't lose your emotional capacity, that's not what moving beyond Ego means. If it was, who would want it? What it means is that beyond Ego you will finally know, not just have to trust, that nothing can ever be lost and Everything truly is One.

***

Pilgrimage site in New Mexico

Photo by Kathy

An annex of a church called Sanctuary de Chimayo which is known for its healing properties in the dirt.

Chapter 26

How to awaken

Michaela

You realize your false identification with the thinking mind and drop all beliefs. It should not take any time, as who you are is timeless.

Yet on the linear level of the ever-unfolding life, it seems we need to go through a purifying, learning period, in order to get there (where we always have been) consciously. Such a wonderful even though painful process – to fight your way through that scary jungle into the purity of your heart and discover the source of love that you are.

To be true is crucial in this journey of rediscovery. There is no place you can hide from yourself, even most subtle self-lie or self-excuse will hinder you from seeing truth. Any feeling of pride, superiority, or the opposite, any form of victimhood, has to go. Mind has to understand itself in order to be ready to deliver its content as explored and understood. Then, the game can stop. And start again on a conscious level.

***

Kiran

According to me, to be in the present moment without any previous holdings and perspectives is awakened living. How we come to this point differs from individual to individual and depends on inner readiness, honesty, courage, commitment and sincerity.

So although the answer to this question is very simple and the same for all, it lands differently depending upon the state of the inner ground; how identified/attached the questioner is with their thoughts and feelings as 'me'.

I would guide the person to be more attentive to the deeper reality of every moment instead of only trusting the surface thoughts or feelings. If one pays attention, one will recognize that the surface scenario is not the way our mental and emotional bodies take it to be. This can slowly open the person up to see that they are suffering because of the perspectives, beliefs and personal agenda that come from conditioning. The conditioned mind jumps ahead to label occurrences from a very narrow individual perspective and automatically responds without a clear or deeper investigation. Slowly one can come to recognize that the conditioned mind is not necessarily true.

In the beginning, one needs to be dedicated to deeply seeing one's personality and how, to a great extent, it is supported by beliefs, perceptions, judgments, resistances, patterns, values, and the whole psychic, personal and social construction. This may take different kinds of effort for different people such as meditation or the presence of a teacher established in Self. Then one arrives at the recognition of formless Self or no-Self as our true nature, rather than the egoic entity that we mistakenly thought of ourselves as.

This can also become very clear to some through the awakening experience and subsequently learning to live that awakening (embodiment). In that recognition, it becomes clear that mind is just presenting a perspective at any given moment and 'I' am not really the changeable egoic entity that is seen by mind. I like to use the example of being a baby in the mother's womb; one is the body, mind and soul but not yet the story of self that is held in the mind. Without yet being separated as an 'I thought', consciousness is still there with all its sensitivities to manifestation at both individuated and collective levels. 'Me' and 'mine' is only an expansion of a thought which then gets identified with this body as 'me' and assumes that this body's duration is 'my' duration. This can be experienced by bringing attention meditatively to the innermost silence which is always there and never not there. It is the Eternal Self that came into this physical body while in the mother's womb.

So as a teacher I feel I can help someone see this with clarity, learn to stay with it and learn more and more how to live in this world of form as pure awareness or formlessness, unaffected by it but still experiencing every facet of it in its very simple true nature without adding or deleting anything. I would like to add here that this does require a lot of courage, honesty, sincerity and dedication.

This may all seem to be such a doable thing, but it is this very doing that keeps us landed in that 'me thought' which is doing it. It is by differentiating what I am as pure awareness and what is becoming

Chapter 26 – How to awaken

conscious in me this moment where attention is focused, that one realizes It. I feel sharing and meditating regularly with someone established in that, can really help the seeker until he/she gets deeply connected with his/her own inner Guru. This way, a mentor can help the seeker in moving through states which can be easily perceived as real awakening but are not yet the real awakened state.

With awakening and its eventual embodiment we realize that we are life itself which is manifesting spontaneously in each moment.

***

Jennifer

I have no idea. I do know that I decided it was possible for me to awaken about a year before my experience. Prior to that I did not think it was: Who was I to awaken? That is only for really special people! I couldn't possibly be that far along! I have a sense that not only deciding it was possible, but actually wanting it, had something to do with it.

I remember meditating in a candlelit cave in Northern India on The Ganges just north of Rishikesh where countless people had allegedly awoken or attained enlightenment over the years. I made the silent prayer/request, I want to fully awaken but only if I can do it with ease and grace. I heard back, "Then you don't really want it".

Years later after my first profoundly shifting experience, I prayed, asked, declared: I am willing to do whatever it takes to fully awaken however difficult it may be. I really don't recommend doing this. To say life has been challenging since then is definitely an understatement.

***

Ben

I'd ask why they wanted it. Their answer would inevitably include some form of perceived increase in happiness/peace. I'd try to explain that just as materialism has them striving for a car/house/promotion, only to eventually get it and still feel unfulfilled, chasing awakening is a form of spiritual 'materialism'. In both cases they are looking for happiness in something other than themselves and at a time other than now.

I would then tell them that because they started the search from an unawakened place, a place that always looks for happiness anywhere but here and now, the 'search' itself is the very opposite of the truth they are trying to find. This means that for as long as they are 'searching' for it, they'll never find it, because it implies that the present moment isn't good enough. So stop searching because it's already found. I'd tell them that they already have what they want, there is in fact no other way of being (because in truth we are always here and now) and to focus on appreciating the present.

And they'd probably look at me like I was nuts ...

***

Richard

I would discourage them. In fact that is universally what I have done whenever I've encountered a person who says they 'very much' wish to awaken, as it implies a person who feels a fundamental lack of satisfaction with life, which they believe an awakening experience will correct. I recognize this as I've both been there myself and seen it in others.

I encourage people to see that we are immersed in this immense mystery right now; that our mundane existence is actually more mystical than any drugs trip could ever be. Our familiarity with existence has bred a contempt for it. Life is amazing, as it is, without the need for any sort of awakening experience.

Of course, paradoxically, seeing this is a kind of awakening experience, but not the sort that needs to be striven for.

Now, if a person is fundamentally happy with life and really interested to explore consciousness, that's a different story. Then I'm full of helpful suggestions

***

Sarah

Each person is completely unique and so I point to and support changes intuitively, depending on where they are at. We start with the closest proximity to truth there is. And so it begins with relative level truth.

If being awake is a total openness to what is, without the medium or filter of a conditioned 'self' and an inclusion of the great totality of life (the emptiness AND fullness, the nothingness that we are as well as the everything-ness that we are), then it starts with being able to open to sensations, emotions, and to what feels true in their body.

So a relationship with the present moment, as dualistic as it sounds, is more than fine to begin with. In fact it's vital. And so we start with basic stuff: sounds, sensations, the feel of the body, the breath.

I emphasize a meditation practice, as this helps the nervous system and readies the person for clear seeing.

With the transcendence of the first glimpses or awakenings, we become very sure there's no one here, both ultimately and relatively. But as awakening into unity and beyond matures, it seems that the body is required for the fullness of truth to live! And so we are back again in the body – the descent that is thankfully talked about more these days in non-duality teachings. Full circle living. Embodiment. There is no one here … and yet here we are!

So we start with the body, with acceptance of what is here right now. Bringing people to the awareness of their body no matter where they're at on the path - whether pre-awakening, or deep into awakening – has proven to be helpful. And often reality, or truth, will take them by surprise.

As they become stabilized in being able to be the container for experience, we begin to explore sensing into who they are without their habits, without their stories, without their desires. Can they sit in the expanse of no answer, of no clarity, of no immediate habitual reaction? Who are you when you don't 'do' the character of you? This becomes a practice in their day to day life, with the relationships they have as their greatest teachers, and as emptiness begins to come to the forefront.

The doer begins to fall away and a familiarity with this spaciousness deepens.

I find many people have unattended trauma in their system which makes a total surrender into the no-thingness of self alternately terrifying and glorious. It might be transcendent and lovely at times, or jolt their bodies into dissociation due to past trauma. And for the realization to live in their being in a day-to-day way where they are free, often somatic healing work with a trained psychotherapist who specializes in trauma release is needed. I often send people out for that. The students will return, more at home in their bodies, with their nervous systems more regulated, and they find their body is now a more capable vessel through which to live the truths they are discovering and realizing.

And often just resting in presence with someone melts their armor. Transmission is a real thing, I've found. Just sitting in presence, in silence, in stillness, is often a powerful medicine that reveals exactly that for which the seeker is ready, no matter what their prior insights or realizations.

***

Lisa

How does one awaken? ... My experience is that each and every one of us have our own individual path to awakening and realization, and that this is best guided by our own intuition. This may or may not include outer help and teachers on the road, or simply mirroring from the outside which can help us see where we stand in the moment. Sometimes our path goes through spiritual practice, sometimes through suffering, sometimes through something completely different. Our path might include powerful transcendent and spiritual experiences of different kinds, or not. So if someone would ask me how to awaken, I'd say there is no one-fits-all answer. I'd ask the person about their life – what they feel, what they long for, what they need at the moment, and about their past.

Sometimes you need to dive into the past and work through it to be able to let go of it and come into the present. Basically, it's about untangling and releasing the knots of what we are *not* (the identifications that occupy our system) in order to be able to know what we *are*. This is what most spiritual teachers mean when they say that we are all already awake and that enlightenment is always here now. But in my experience, this can be difficult to grasp before you're actually there, and it might also lead to spiritual and psychological bypassing, which only makes it more difficult to awaken.

What's real to us is where we actually stand at the moment, and that is where it's meaningful to start. This can be done for instance with the help of therapy or self-inquiry. If we feel like shit, if we believe we are unworthy, if we hate everyone and everything, that is our reality right there, and the first step is to acknowledge that reality, accept it and embrace it instead of denying and resisting it and running away from it as we so often do. It is necessary to inquire into it, maybe release old feelings and experiences connected to it and finally let it go. In doing this, it's important not to add "this isn't real" or "this isn't truth anyway" into the mix of our suffering.

So, my personal basic 'teaching' would be something like this: first, find out what you actually, *really* feel, think or need in the moment. Then, accept it and embrace it without judgement, resistance or indulgence. Just stay with it. If feelings come up, let them flow through you until they dissipate by themselves. Next, inquire into the parts of it that make you suffer. Why? From where? When? Really? How so? The answers are all within yourself, not on the outside. And then, when you're ready, let it go. Find outside help, support and inspiration when you need it, but check and run everything past your own inner authority, your inner guru, your intuition. You are That. Always.

***

Amy

Depending on who they are and the sense I get from them, my answer might be to look them in the eyes and say, "I'm sorry but you can't awaken." That's my mischievous answer!

Or if they have a squirrel-like mind that wants to keep asking or giving 'buts', I might just tell them to stop. Just stop. Close your eyes. And stop. (Which I've had to do with a few people).

For me, I don't have a teaching or help anyone 'wake up'. I'm extremely unqualified for that job. But what I *can* do is help them find this moment: the one we're in together. And maybe it gives them silence even if just for that moment.

Because as we know this person asking how, is already awake, they are just caught in a deception that they are separate from everything. But again, I'm not a teacher. So I don't wake anyone up.

***

Maureen

I don't know how to awaken. I don't know why I did, or why others do not. It's a mystery. There are some things I have learned that may be useful to others.

I was a long time meditator, practicing Dzogchen Tibetan Buddhism. I wouldn't recommend that path. Very few people in that program awakened, and there was no support for those of us who did. But maybe I awakened because of the practices; I have no idea.

I do recommend meditation. A tightly focused meditation is useful training to calm the mind and a good place to start. But I would recommend, as a next step, a spacious meditation. Let the mind be wide and still. In my brain, focused meditation feels like when I'm stargazing and staring at one star. Spacious meditation feels like looking for meteors, with a soft focus to include the whole sky. Meditate like that, at least some of the time.

I've never had a one-on-one relationship with a teacher. I did find it helpful to read and listen to teachings, to marinate in an awakened teacher's presence (yes, that works through books, audio and video).

To my great surprise, boundaries became important. I don't do dysfunction any more, with family or friends. That ended some relationships, or left them more distant. It is much healthier for me. Many spiritual teachings focus on compassion, and neglect discussing setting strong boundaries. Some teachers are starting to include this understanding that compassion does not involve allowing anyone to abuse us. The most compassionate thing we can do is set firm boundaries. No, that is not okay and if you continue, I'm walking away. The most spiritual people I know have the firmest boundaries, and it's a critically important lesson to learn.

After awakening, old trauma comes up to be felt and released. I'd advise working on that beforehand. Start the psychological work along with the spiritual, or first if there's deep trauma that needs support. Ken Wilber coined the phrase Wake Up, Grow Up, Clean Up; I think that's a great combination. If we do the spiritual work and not the psychological, we risk spiritual bypassing, which is a cul-de-sac of no value.

Exhaustion happens. Accept it, relax into it. We need flat time. Lie down and sleep, read, watch a show, listen to a teaching. Rest allows our bodies the time they need to adjust to whatever is happening to us.

Finally, the single most important lesson, the absolute hardest and most vital, is surrender. Allow this to happen. Let go. Say yes. Bring it on. Dive in, fall off the cliff, float in the river and allow it to carry you. Surrender is the magic key. This includes being okay with not knowing. Relax into not knowing, and let go of control.

I was chatting with an old friend who was interested in my experiences. I told him the most important thing, the essential thing, was letting go. I knew this would be the hardest for him, and so did he, as he laughed and laughed. It was a beautiful moment of understanding.

***

Chapter 26 – How to awaken

Stacy

How to awaken? The first thing to know is that if anyone tells you they can tell you how to awaken, they're lying. Run the other way if they do not admit that, really, we have no idea.

Still, there are pointers, meditations and ways to create conditions in which some people *are* likely to wake up. They aren't for everybody. There are several decent methods that seem to work for a lot of people: Liberation Unleashed is one. I heard that they tried to see how many of the people who were guided there actually woke up. It was about half. That's pretty good for something as unpredictable as waking up.

Fear and expectations, past and future keep us from awakening. Awakening only happens *now.*

The basic instruction is to look. Question everything you think and that you think you see or understand. You don't. There is a layer of false thinking that we all learned and most of the world believes. That has to go. This can be upsetting to some. That's why it is good to do your psychological work first. Me, I did The Work of Byron Katie and questioned all kinds of things from my blame of others to "there is a problem" (laughed for 3 days after that one) to "there is a me".

Relaxation is key. You are unlikely to wake up if you're tense and anxious.

For most, it's probably good to have a guide. It seems to help us let go of fear. It's nice to communicate with someone who can already see that there is no self, no story, no world.

Trust your gut about guides and teachers. If your gut is clenching and tight and something feels 'off', it probably is! But if you relax and open and feel safe – well, you might be with a helpful guide.

Reading about other people's enlightenment experiences can be helpful as long as you don't build an expectation that it will be exactly like that for you. It won't.

I can't even say "keep trying" or "don't give up", because sometimes people wake up when they finally get exhausted and give up. There is no one way to do this. Your way to awaken will be your own.

***

Marianne

Firstly, it's so important for people to work out what their motivation is: Why do you wish to awaken? What is it that you really want? It's really good if they spend some time asking themselves those questions. Delve deeply. Occasionally people will indicate that their motivation stems from a desire or belief that awakening will provide them with some sort of acquisition, power, or betterment. But mostly people fall into two categories: they want their suffering to come to an end or they want to know the Truth. Sometimes these two come together. Generally, I have found that if there is not an underlying, very powerful and often lifelong quest to know Truth, nothing much can happen. You have to *want* it and be prepared to question everything, give up everything, see through everything, leave no stone unturned. You have to be utterly sincere. Utterly honest. You have to have worn out any desire for game-playing, artifice or subterfuge. If you don't have that fire in your belly, yes, you may still awaken, but more than likely, you won't. This quest for Truth is like fuel for the engine. Rocket fuel.

Secondly, it's imperative that anyone who is *not* awakened is open to the idea that they have absolutely no clue what awakening actually *is*. It isn't anything you think it will be. There has to be a complete openness to the fact that you are a novice and don't know anything. Even if you can recite every sutra ever written, even if you have read all of Buddha's teachings, even if you can parrot neo-Advaita *par excellence*, you still won't know anything about awakening. I have met people who tried to pretend an awakening with a few carefully chosen words. You can't. Sometimes, with the written word alone it can be harder to ascertain if someone is awakened, but in person it is not. If you think that you already know what it is, then that will be a very major hurdle. Humility and not-knowing are vital.

Thirdly, deep inquiry is essential, even *after* awakening. It is necessary to learn how to inquire, to look at the world without the mind and inquire into what is actually *here* before labels, before definitions and before our thoughts ... to look and sense deeper and deeper into this *Now*. What is here? What is this thing we call a 'person'? It can all be known. Nothing is missing. We just need to learn how to look. People are very used to being *told* and not so used to inquiring for themselves. It is also about learning to 'hold' a question over time. Deep questioning.

Fourthly, it's necessary to understand that there are no guarantees. There is no how-to manual on awakening. You can't make it happen. A teacher can't make it happen. But you can certainly till the soil.

A big part of tilling the soil for me was therapy. The premise of therapy is undoubtedly to become a well-functioning, adjusted and happy 'person'. But for me, therapy did not do that. With each therapy, as I let go of more

Chapter 26 – How to awaken

and more angst, pain, trauma and outmoded behaviours, as I saw through more and more of my conditioning and where it had come from, I actually became emptier and emptier. This emptying out is necessary. If you don't do it before awakening, you may still need to do it afterwards. The stuff that is unconscious will come to the fore somehow. It is a lens through which the world is seen and is mistaken for reality. It isn't reality.

Additionally, I found my therapists were far better 'teachers' than the spiritual teachers I met. Teachers can be helpful and some are quite clear, but it was person-to-person interaction with therapists that always brought me back to *Here* - and this was done with great love, gentleness and expertise.

Meditation can also be a preparation for some. I personally never found meditation helpful. I found inquiry far more valuable. Meditation can all too easily become a destination in itself.

Fifthly, awakening entails a shift in perspective. The perspective of awakening is beyond what is considered normal everyday or egoic functioning/thinking/emoting, and so cannot be 'produced' from within it. But there *are* ways in which our perspective can be 'shifted'.

The first way is to move one's awareness to the body rather than the mind. The body is much 'truer' than the mind, in that it can never not 'be here'. The body is here. Most people are quite removed from the body. This entails not only learning to be aware of the body (its holdings, pains, sensations) but to learn to move awareness *within* the body and eventually also *outside* the body. The body, in essence, becomes a semi-permeable membrane. As a starter one can focus one's awareness in the *hara* centre just below the navel. This is considered by some cultures to be the spiritual centre of gravity in the body. The *hara* has its own innate wisdom. With practice the movement of awareness can become more and more fluid … it can expand, contract, embrace … infinite potential. The mind's boundaries of what we believe we are, can slowly be loosened. This is not awakening, but it is very helpful.

Secondly, a shift in perspective can come through a sudden shock, the bottoming-out of desperate suffering/turmoil, or the sense of utter failure and a complete giving up: "I can't do this anymore. I've tried everything! I give up!" These can't be *done* as such, but in knowing that this is quite a valid (and well-documented) 'path' in autobiographies, there is an invitation to not disregard suffering and dark places. Certainly, the wearing out of 'myself' and the belief that I could 'do' it, was pivotal. I had nowhere to go. The only place was a plea to God … which God answered. It's not an 'easy' way in any sense, but many are in this terrain anyway.

***

Timothy

First, I'd ask those who wish to awaken what they think enlightenment means, and what, in their understanding, it entails. I would try to determine if they're generally happy, or unhappy. Then I would attempt to find out why they want to find enlightenment. From the answers to these questions, based on my experience and knowledge I can make suggestions about what they could try first. I'd let them know that they will probably have better luck if they find the process interesting, and keep a positive attitude; when a negative memory or thought arises, think of three positive ones to cancel it out. This sets the atmosphere for enlightenment to happen. It won't happen if your negative thoughts hog the airwaves. Feeling grateful and appreciative helps too.

I'd let seekers know that no one can make it happen and that it's really more of an accident. It's also better to avoid looking forward to it, and to stay in the moment because that's when it could happen. If we're busy imagining a future experience we're not present enough for it to happen. We can make ourselves more prone for this accident to occur but it's not something we can purposely add to our repertoire. That's why it's better if it's an enjoyable experience.

Another important aspect is to stop holding on to what you think about spirituality. Definitely don't hold on to who you think you are. Examine your beliefs and accept only what you know to be truth. It's quite alright not to know any truth. We can survive quite well without it and people do it every moment of every day, but it's beneficial to be open to what rings true for you.

If you want to avoid enlightenment continue to learn everything about it before you look for it. All that is needed is to know that the ability to rewire the way we are experiencing life, and the world around us, is already inside of us. Also, be cautious. If seeking becomes overwhelmingly intense it's okay to take a break and get some counselling if needed.

Investigate what is your true inborn personality so that you can stop holding on to the caricature that has been added by society; this includes what others have told you about yourself or what you 'should' be. Realize that everything that worries you is a question of survival that probably isn't looming, and isn't really the case in the moment. This approach leaves you in a general mood of openness to experiences that are very likely far from anything you ever thought you knew.

Chapter 26 – How to awaken

There are many techniques, or tricks, that can be experimented with to begin the journey to enlightenment, and for proceeding beyond. It's the start of an expanded journey of heightened exploration. Enlightenment isn't the culmination of achievement and may even feel very ordinary even though you know it's not.

***

Erick

I recall the clearest sense of there being no way to determine a reason or any mechanism surrounding the experience of awakening. From the perspective of the awakened awareness, there is no reality to the non-awakened state. There is no cause and effect that can relate to this because the non-awakened perspective bears no relation to the awakened. It's not like comparing apples to oranges – it's like comparing apples to steam engines – they are two completely different things. The truth of time and causation in the relative world has no meaning in the dimensionless Existence.

Over the years the integration of the inner vastness with the relative experience has led me to see that there are factors that can influence the onset of awakening. As with anyone, I resonate most with the factors that led up to my own awakening.

- Live honestly – be true to yourself.
- Inquire into the nature of your experience.
- Practice meditation – it should bring you easily beyond thought to the inner silence. Be regular in your practice.
- Listen to the Teacher – integrate those aspects of the Teaching that resonate with you – don't worry about the other things.
- Trust your heart.
- Develop your mind.
- Live in a healthy manner.
- Love by default. If so moved, practice devotion.
- There is not one true teacher – every moment is the Guru if you are deeply listening.
- In this awakening you will have to let go of even the most cherished teachings. In that unattached openness you can find the Truth from which the Teacher speaks.

***

Tori Gate and Stupa

Photo by Jennifer

Chapter 27

Recommended reading

Lisa

Spiritual Emergency: When Personal Transformation Becomes a Crisis, by Stanislav Grof M. D. and Christina Grof. An anthology with authors like Ram Dass, Jack Kornfield, R. D. Laing and others, that can help navigate the sometimes rough seas of awakening.

The Stormy Search for the Self: Understanding and Living with Spiritual Emergency, by Stanislav Grof M. D. and Christina Grof. Experience and knowledge from decades of consciousness research, very valuable when the going gets tough with cleansing of the psyche and/or psychospiritual experiences on the road.

The Cosmic Game: Explorations of the Frontiers of Human Consciousness, by Stanislav Grof. Useful maps of the pre- and post-awakening terrain drawn from a lot of experience.

Lessons from the Light: What We Can Learn from the Near-Death Experience, by Kenneth Ring. Near-death related, which has been one of my paths to awakening.

Enlightenment Blues: My Years with an American Guru, by Andre van der Braak. A sad but very revealing story about the guru-disciple relationship. Good for remembering that the true guru is always yourself.

Out of the Darkness: Awakenings and spiritual growth through suffering, by Steve Taylor. The spiritual path is no bed of roses.

***

Maureen

The End of Your World: Uncensored Straight Talk on the Nature of Enlightenment, by Adyashanti, was my lifeline for the first year after awakening. I have found nothing else that is so clear, so practical, and so focused on what happens after awakening.

***

Erick

Be Here Now, by Ram Dass.
Commentary on the Bhagavad Gita, Chapters 1-6, by Maharishi Mahesh Yogi.
Journey to Ixtlan, by Carlos Castenada. I would also include his other books including *Tales of Power*.
My Secret is Silence: Poetry and Sayings of Adyashanti, by Adyashanti
Buddha at the Gas Pump. Not a book but a webcast series; www.batgap.com . Nothing helped me navigate the post-awakening landscape more than this resource and community. I found the early interviews most helpful, though all are good.

***

Amy

The Big Book of Alcoholics Anonymous. While I was participating in AA, although the words on the pages were brilliant, I had no personal experience with them. It discussed things like "the 4th dimension of existence" and being "inwardly rearranged". It wasn't until after awakening that I understood and felt a personal connection to the book. Quotes from the book, which I hadn't read in over 5 years, suddenly came to mind, but now with a lived experience: "Common sense would thus become uncommon sense" for example. I haven't been in AA for many years now, after I realized that I was not actually an alcoholic, but the book stays with me and I recommend picking it up, even if out of curiosity.

Chapter 27 – Recommended reading

After The Ecstasy The Laundry: How the Heart Grows Wise on the Spiritual Path, by Jack Kornfield. This was the first book I read after awakening and it helped guide me and keep me calm. It explained the things that I wasn't able to put into words while they were happening. As I read, it was like the next chapter was exactly where I was; I felt like a canoe floating on the river of his words. It carried me through so much. Before the awakening I had little to no experience with these things, so to find this book was like finding a warm comforter on a cold night.

***

Richard

Meditations, by René Descartes, was the most influential book I read prior to any awakening experience. Descartes asks the fundamental questions about the very nature of the self that would come to dominate my life.

The Power of Now: A Guide to Spiritual Enlightenment, by Eckhart Tolle. I was very influenced by *The Power of Now*, however I'm never sure whether to include it when asked questions like this as the influence was for good *and* ill. On the good, encountering Tolle's description of his awakening was the first time I really felt that sense of "Yes! This is what happened to me!" On the bad I'm not sure his recommendations of recapturing that experience were very helpful, although I wouldn't be surprised if my youthful interpretation is more to blame.

As It Is: The Open Secret of Spiritual Awakening, by Tony Parsons, was the first book that unambiguously helped me. It helped me shed a lot of the concepts I'd built up around enlightenment. It was a turning point for me into becoming really quite happy.

I've been very influenced by the author Tim Freke, both for his revisions of spirituality and insights into consciousness and meditation. I spent a lot of time in Tim's groups over the years so I can't exactly point to one of his books, but if I had to I'd say *Jesus and the Lost Goddess: The Secret Teachings of the Original Christians*.

The Journey: How to Heal Your Life and Set Yourself Free, by Brandon Bays, is the best book I've encountered on the link between consciousness and healing. Out of all the books of our era, this is the one I'd bet people will still be talking about a hundred years from now.

I would like to give honourable mention to Richard Gordon's *Quantum Touch: The Power to Heal*. Although really a book on energy healing, it showed me how to employ spirituality to fix my rather nasty back problem, for which I will be eternally grateful.

Also the collective works of Paul Feyerabend. Feyerabend was a writer on philosophy not spirituality, but his ideas so changed the way I thought about spirituality (and everything else) it would be remiss not to.

***

Marianne

No Boundary: Eastern and Western Approaches to Personal Growth and *One Taste: Daily Reflections on Integral Spirituality*, by Ken Wilber. Prior to awakening I read a tremendous amount. In retrospect I see that I understood very little of it; this terrain can't be understood from separation. In trying to write for this chapter and reflecting on which books *did* have an impact, it surprises me that it is these two earlier books of Ken Wilber. They pointed in a way that I felt changed within.

A Path with Heart: A Guide Through the Perils and Promises of Spiritual Life, by Jack Kornfield affected me deeply pre-awakening. I underlined almost every word. I was hungry to understand.

Spiritual autobiographies were also important; I saw my own questing and journeying reflected in them. I was particularly touched by the life of Alexandra David-Neel.

Post-awakening I read a lot for a couple of years, but since then my reading dwindled. Currently I read almost nothing. There are, however, a few books that are standouts for me and which I would wholeheartedly recommend:

Emptiness Dancing, by Adyashanti. My all-time favorite book. Layers of depth that allowed me to find words for what was being experienced and also deepen immeasurably at the same time. I could probably still read that book and get something out of it. I also read a lot of Adyashanti's online material and listened to his talks. His clarity and ability to communicate is, I feel, unparalleled.

Beyond the 'I': Notes on Waking Up to Oneness, by Dhyan Dewyea. This book is little-known and I can't remember how I stumbled upon it. Although I didn't align with everything she wrote, it allowed me to put my 'journey' through suffering, therapy/psychological work and then awakening, into perspective. It is a very independent work and has some profound reflections. I contacted her at the time and we had some interesting interactions. Eventually she stopped all contact with her readership and I don't know what became of her. I imagine she is just 'living' Life. She wasn't really interested in teaching and frequently mentioned to me that most were not interested in Truth.

The Inner Journey Home: The Soul's Realization of the Unity of Reality and *The Point of Existence: Transformations of Narcissism in Self-Realization*, by AH Almaas. It was extraordinary that for a time these two books provided a map of my journey *in retrospect*. Each time I opened their pages I was surprised to find I was a little further along and Almaas was writing of the terrain I was currently living.

Cutting Through Spiritual Materialism, by Chogyam Trungpa was very important in my living of this terrain. I saw so many around me using spirituality as a marker of attainment or importance, and this never felt right to me. This book addressed the multiple ways we can deceive ourselves. Any time I felt myself grasping or claiming ownership in any way I recalled this book. Ownership is not 'it'.

***

Timothy

The Finders, by Dr Jeffery A. Martin. The information in this publication put the big picture of enlightenment into perspective for me, on a personal and global level. Dr Martin calls enlightenment, Fundamental Wellbeing. He interviewed over a thousand people around the world, during the 12 years he did this scientific research, in order to delve deeply into the whole experience of enlightenment.

How Enlightenment Changes Your Brain: The New Science of Transformation, by Andrew Newberg, Mark Robert Waldman and Fred Stella. Here I found the science behind the physical changes that a person goes through upon enlightenment. It separated many of the myths I'd heard from the factual reality.

The Book of Secrets: 112 Meditation to Discover the Mystery Within, by Osho. This is the book in which I found the meditation technique that triggered enlightenment. There are 112 choices.

***

Michaela

The Power of Now, by Eckhart Tolle.
A Course in Miracles.
To Have or to Be? By Erich Fromm.
Awareness, by Anthony de Mello.
Who am I? by Sri Ramana Maharshi.
The Philosopher's Stone, by Johannes Anker Larsen. Also many other books by this Danish author.
Various books written by mystics from my country of origin, Czechoslovakia:
Frantisek Drtikol, Míla Tomášová and Eduard Tomáš.
I also loved to read Papaji.

***

Kiran

Two books that motivated me to turn towards this side other than just reading and understanding Sikh scriptures, *A New Earth: Awakening to Your Life's Purpose*, by Eckhart Tolle's and *An Autobiography of a Yogi*, by Paramahansa Yogananda.

Two books that really helped me after awakening and I enjoyed reading, were *Consciousness and the Absolute: The Final Talks of Sri Nisargadatta Maharaj*, by Sri Nisargadatta Maharaj and *The End of Your World: Uncensored Straight Talk on the Nature of Enlightenment*, by Adyashanti. They both helped me in different ways. Since I am not a big reader, a book like *I Am That*, by Sri Nisargadatta Maharaj, which someone had gifted me, was too threatening because of its size. I did invest in the reading and understanding of Sikh scriptures, as I was raised in that environment from childhood. These books and Sikh scriptures guided me through embodiment of awakening, helping me to stand firmly in this new way of living always connected to deepest wisdom. Other than reading some books, listening to or watching videos of different teachers has been useful too.

***

Chapter 27 – Recommended reading

Ben

The Power of Now: A Guide to Spiritual Enlightenment, by Eckhart Tolle sticks out in my mind as it made me realize I wasn't alone in this experience.

In general though, I prefer the 'art' versions of wisdom, rather than the more practical writing:

The Book of Love: Poems of Ecstasy and Longing, by Rumi, is mind-blowingly exquisite. *The Marriage of Heaven and Hell*, by William Blake is also full of wisdom and clarity, and beautifully expressed. *Hamlet*, by William Shakespeare is pretty good for the existential stuff. Oh, I enjoyed *By The River Piedra I Sat Down and Wept: A Novel of Forgiveness* by Paulo Coelho and also his *The Manual of The Warrior of Light*.

***

Jennifer

The End of Your World: Uncensored Straight Talk on the Nature of Enlightenment, by Adyashanti, after awakening. I don't know what I would have done without it. It was all such uncharted territory; some part of me desperately needed some guidance. I love *My Secret is Silence: Poetry and Sayings of Adyashanti*, especially the poem called *Meet Me Here*.

***

Stacy

The Book: On the Taboo Against Knowing Who You Are, by Alan Watts. I listened to radio broadcasts of Alan Watts in my early teens before going off to sing in the church choir, followed by Sunday School, which for me, included comparative religion taught by a youth minister from California I later learned was gay. I had a rather liberal upbringing in a very open-minded church. All books by Alan Watts are recommended.

Spiritual Awakening: The Damnedest Thing, by Jed McKenna (not his other books, so much). The author's name is a pseudonym no one has ever figured out, at least not that I know of. This book is the 'tough love' of waking up.

Waking Up: A Guide to Spirituality without Religion, by Sam Harris. I read this after waking up – more accurately, after my most impactful and more recent waking up. (I had experiences like this for years without calling it that).

A Course in Miracles. In spite of all the God and Jesus belief and terminology, the 365 days of meditations in the Workbook *are* waking up meditations and can certainly lead to waking up, but there will be a clean-up of concepts needed later.

Loving What Is: Four Questions That Can Change Your Life, by Byron Katie. Here is where I began to unravel what is true and what isn't. I had many, many awakenings through Katie's Work, and by this I mean mind-blowing shifts in my perception of reality that left me feeling a bit wonky while things rearranged and settled down. Don't believe anyone who tells you that you can't wake up through words and questions. You absolutely can. In fact, having done so much questioning of stressful thinking, I had far less to unlearn when awakening took a more … hmmm, words don't work so much here … but a kind of more permanent turn.

I Need Your Love: Is That True? by Byron Katie. This one is The Work applied to relationships. It clears up all kinds of need, want and obligation patterns we go through, in terms of reality and real love, which is simply who we are.

Vivation: The Science of Enjoying All of Your Life, by Jim Leonard and Phil Laut. This is a clearer BreathWork process than some others I've seen, done and read about. There are five simple elements, engaged concurrently: 1. Circular Breathing, 2. Complete Relaxation, 3. Awareness in Detail, 4. Integration into Ecstasy, 5. Do Whatever You Do. Willingness is Enough. This was my first love in awakening, which I began in 1985.

On Being Certain: Believing You're Right Even When You're Wrong, by Robert A. Burton. A clear explanation of logic as related to what is true and what isn't. It includes the famous experiment that shows we can see a decision happen in the brain up to two seconds (a very long time) before a person knows a decision has been made. We make decisions? I don't think so! This is science that proves it.

The Mind's Past, by Michael Gazzaniga. Similar to Burton, this book explains clearly how we have no idea how we think or decide anything.

By Any Other Name, by Spider Robinson. There is a short story in this anthology about what would happen if we all told the truth, all of the time. It's called, "Satan's Children". Just read it.

Hitchhiker's Guide to the Galaxy, by Douglas Adams. You thought these were all going to be serious spiritual or scientific books? No way. This is a fun poke at humanity and all our foibles and weird beliefs.

The books that follow I read more recently and are more directly concerned with Awakening.

Gateless Gatecrashers, by Ilona Cuinite and Elena Nezhinsky. Actual guided conversations in which the client wakes up. You can actually read where the shift takes place.

Liberation Unleashed, by Ilona Cuinite and Elena Nezhinsky. More guided conversations in which the client wakes up.

On Having No Head, by Douglas Harding. I confess I have not read the book, but I have used his method, The Headless Way. It works.

The Direct Path: A User Guide, by Greg Goode. Contains direct pointing exercises for waking up.

After Awareness: The End of the Path, by Greg Goode. Just what it says. Good stuff about what it's like post-awakening.

Waking from Sleep: Why Awakening Experiences Occur and How to Make them Permanent, by Steve Taylor. Discusses aspects of awakening with labels like spontaneous awakening and permanent awakening.

A Mind at Home with Itself, by Byron Katie. Finally, Katie puts more about awakening into a book.

The Surrender Experiment: My Journey into Life's Perfection, by Michael A. Singer. What it is like to surrender - about everything.

The Untethered Soul: The Journey Beyond Yourself, by Michael A. Singer.

Siddharta, by Herman Hesse. Published in the 70s this is a modern telling of the story of Siddharta Gautama Buddha. Yes *the* Buddha. I was lucky to read this in my teens.

***

Glossary

A Course in Miracles (ACIM) – Written in 1976 by Helen Schucman, it is a set of three books, a Text, a Workbook and a Manual for Teachers. The purpose of these is to "remove the blocks to the awareness of love's presence." A miracle is defined as a shift in perception from fear to love.

Advaita (neo-Advaita) – See Non-duality

Adyashanti – US spiritual teacher born in 1962 as Steven Gray. His prolific teachings are available through his non-profit organization Open Gate Sangha (with wife Mukti) and include many formats: books, online courses, podcasts, CDs, DVDs and in-person satsangs. He is renowned for the sincerity and clarity of his teachings.

Awakening – Defined more fully in the first chapter. With awakening there is a movement from the small-self separate egoic identity into the ineffable reality of what we are. Awakening also describes the process of deepening and opening evermore into our essential infinite nature.

Byron Katie – US author and speaker born as Byron Kathleen Mitchell in 1942. She is founder of The Work, a way of questioning and working with stressful thoughts. Its basis is four questions and a turnaround. The four questions are:
1. Is it true?
2. Can you absolutely know that it's true?
3. How do you react, what happens, when you believe that thought?
4. Who would you be without the thought?

The turnaround is a way of experiencing the opposite of the believed thought.

Darshan – An opportunity to see or view a guru, 'holy' person, deity or sacred object. Originally from Hindu tradition.

Direct experience - The capacity to directly know one's immediate experience, without the mind's categorizations, attitudes, beliefs and thoughts in the way.

Enlightenment – There has been much misunderstanding and disagreement about this word, and as such many avoid its use. Although some may use it to indicate 'awakening', in a very general way this word indicates the awakened state when conditioning no longer holds sway, and there is liberation.

Inquiry – One of the fundamental practices of spirituality. It is a felt-questioning (as opposed to a mind-questioning) into one's direct experience; what is actually *here*.

Kundalini – Essentially the energy or life force of the human being. Kundalini may be naturally active or lie dormant at the base of the spine. The activation of that energy, either spontaneously or through practices may cause disruption to people's lives if the vessel (human body) carries blockages such as trauma or hasn't been fully prepared. Activation of Kundalini is sometimes referred to as 'awakening'. Although Kundalini 'awakening' may be part of a person's spiritual process, on its own it does not necessarily lead to awakening as it is described in this book, that is, awakening to one's true nature (Self-realization).

Liberation Unleashed (LU) – A free online forum where participants are guided to see that there is no separate self. There is a qualifying questionnaire at the beginning and the end.

Near-death experience (NDE) – A profound experience associated with death, impending death, or a situation of physical or emotional crisis. Positive NDEs can include separation from the body, serenity, unconditional love and mystical light. Negative NDEs may include anguish and distress. NDEs can orient people more towards the spiritual dimension and values such as altruism and unconditional love.

Non-duality – A translation of the Sanskrit word Advaita. This literally means 'not two'. It is not a belief system, religion or prescription. It is a description of the fundamental oneness which is all there is. It is beyond duality and separation, but is not opposed to them. It is a wholeness that is already here and requires no addition process. Neo-advaita - a relatively recent phenomenon that takes non-duality merely as a catch-phrase the reality of which can be repeated and basically forced on people, with no preparation, teaching, inquiry, understanding or practices.

Prana – Basically 'breath', 'life force' or 'vital principle'. The word can have many layers of meaning.

Ramana Maharshi (1879-1950) – Hindu sage recognized worldwide as an enlightened being. He lived most of his life at the holy site of Arunachula in India. His most important teaching was done in silence.

Sadhana – A spiritual practice or discipline used as a means of achieving something eg. *samadhi* or absorption.

Samadhi – A state of union with the divine. Absorption into the divine. It is cultivated in some practices.

Satsang – A spiritual or sacred gathering of people.

Sat Chit Anand – Truth Consciousness Bliss – a description of the unchanging reality that we are.

Shaktipat – The transmission of spiritual energy by one person upon another.

Siddhis – Supernormal powers, abilities, gift or states that can be associated with spiritual endeavor, practices, deepening, Kundalini awakening or occur naturally. These can include clairaudience, clairvoyance, spontaneous body movements and spiritual postures (mudras).

The Ten Fetters – In Buddhism, the mental bonds or shackles which tie one to the wheel of samsara (the cycle of continual rebirth, mundane existence and death). They include Self-illusion, Doubt, Attachment to Rule and Ritual, Lust, Ill-will, Cravings, Conceit, Restlessness and Ignorance.

Tolle, Eckhart – Spiritual teacher and author born in Germany in 1948 as Ulrich Leonard Tölle, and now living in Canada. His best-selling books include *The Power of Now* and *A New Earth*.

***

Biographies

(Alphabetical by first name.)

Amara Palmer

Amara spent much of her childhood entranced by floating dust particles in sunlight, rolling rain drops on windows and studying the intricate activity around the large fire ant mounds outside her tense suburban home in the southern US.

Later, during an entry level college philosophy course, the professor led her to the understanding that nothing that is experienced can be proved to exist as an independent object. This teaching landed hard, creating a crack in a foundation built on fallacious assumptions and beliefs. What instantly sprang from this seeing was the declaration: "There is a Whole Truth, and I'm going to find it!" So began three-and-a-half decades of seeking and a love of truth that would grow to overtake all else.

Seeking took the form of psychic development, channelling, and all things metaphysical; a working of the 12-steps through Al-Anon; study of *A Course in Miracles*; being 'undone' by The Work of Byron Katie; and a very sweet and active seven-year devotional relationship with Mata Amritanandamayi Devi (Amma, the 'Hugging Saint'). Paralleling all of this was a full-blown spontaneous Kundalini awakening that began in 1992 and ran its course over the next 15 years. With all that the Kundalini brought – profound insights and a re-worked nervous system to hold them – it remained clear that there was still a deep yearning to know what is True.

Early in the morning of July 2nd, 2014, after a full year of intensive, yet effortless pre-dawn practices including chanting, meditation, prayer, contemplation and sungazing, a spontaneous and sincere inquiry arose that led to a shattering and dissolution of all that had been thought to be real. All that remained was Aware Stillness. It was undeniably seen that This Aware Stillness is all there Truly Is.

The years following have brought more glimpses of Truth and a transformation of 'inner' and 'outer,' with the two collapsing into One more often than not, and continues without thought of end.

Amara happily resides at Splinter-Haven Hermitage, her tiny round off-grid homestead in the Mojave Wilds near Joshua Tree National Park in Southern California. She delights in visits from the families of California Quail, a variety of snakes, bobcats, hawks and other local critters that come to call around her watering dishes.

Amara holds space for herself and others to come to know and live the Peace, Happiness and Freedom We Are at FreedomThroughInquiry.com.

***

Amy Dedis
Amy was born to a single mother who had mental health and addiction issues.

She was able to maintain a longing deep inside for what is True. This was despite many traumas and life experiences which included drug and alcohol abuse, severe depression, suicide attempts, sobriety, and her own dramatics and self-loathing.

She is currently a psychology major, a wife and mother of two young children. She is the founder of *Trailer Park Zen*.

She was not seeking this but has been stumbling her way around with the very generous help, guidance and love of many others.

***

Andrew Eastman

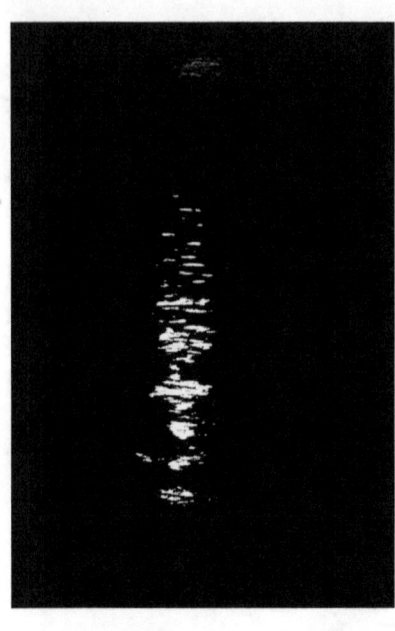

Andrew is a shy introvert and learned very early that a good way to avoid talking to people was to get them to talk about themselves. He would keep asking them questions about themselves. This led to a deep interest in people and how they worked and why they did what they did. It's funny that by avoiding people he was drawn to them.

That's his photo. He could easily spend 15 minutes describing the levels of understanding of that one photo and the implications on our lives, but he'd rather just ask you what it means to you. If he sees a spark he'll ask more. He loves to find out how things work, and pull them apart (even if only in his mind) and try to make them better. He is an engineer by training and by nature. The entire universe can be described in terms of systems and processes, and patterns are fascinating to discover and unravel. He's always looking for the alternative.

It's no wonder he has tried to unravel himself and how he works. If it doesn't make logical sense then it doesn't get another look, but he understands that logic is limited and is only a tool. He spent the vast majority of his life trying to be normal and to fit in to society, that is, until he realized that normal is just another word for ordinary. He will question everything, including himself and what he believes and why. He no longer believes in beliefs.

Finally the ideas swirling around in his head were so vast and far reaching he had to get them on paper so he could understand what he was thinking. This led to a book on how people work and why they do what they do.

They say awakening takes less than a second but it can take a lifetime for you to be ready for that to happen. This is probably true for Andrew, and his biography needs to be either a detailed explanation of all that happened to reach that moment, including the ups and downs, as you need both, or a disjointed summary of bits and pieces for a brief insight. Thankfully he gave the latter.

He thinks he is fascinating when he reads what he says about him, but he doesn't always believe what he reads. Otherwise he is pretty ordinary and you wouldn't look twice if you walked past him in the street. That's just how he likes it.

***

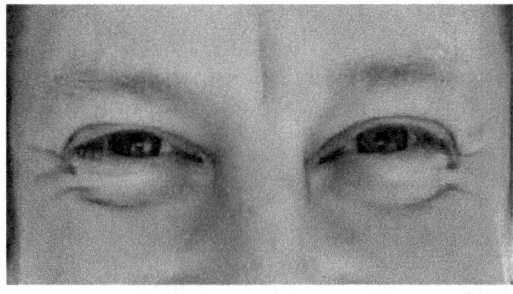

Ben Forsythe
Factful Bio: Ben was born in Reading, UK, in 1983. His parents moved to the USA when he was three. He went to Kindergarten there, but returned to UK a couple of years later, schooling around Oxford until the age of 18.

When he was 15, Ben's father died and this had a significant impact on the way he would approach the rest of his life. Not wanting to simply live, work and die, after leaving Manchester University he travelled extensively, living in Japan and Mexico for a couple of years in his 20s and working as a teacher.

Returning to the UK in his late 20s to try and live the standard life, he worked for three years as a subtitle producer on Sky Sports/News. Throughout this time, despite some significant spiritual moments which never lasted, he battled depression, which repeatedly led him to thoughts of suicide. He sought help and went through a year of therapy which was the best decision he ever made. It was the first time he became truly mindful of his thoughts and it began the process of being able to separate from them.

After therapy he packed up his life and moved to Vietnam, initially for nine months. He ended up staying for three and half years moving from teaching to being a full-time musician, a life change that felt absolutely right. The depression never returned. But it still wasn't inner peace. On returning from Vietnam, he applied to the Abbey Road Institute and was accepted to train as a music producer and sound engineer.

He now works as a songwriter, recently signing his first publishing contract in Nashville. He would like to use the reach of music and lyrics to help guide people towards more self-acceptance and understanding. The lasting awakening experience began in October 2018.

Biographies

Truthful Bio: Throughout his 37-year life, Ben has consistently displayed a mixture of insecure, arrogant, defensive, offensive, irresponsible, belligerent, violent, wounded, smug, selfish, apathetic, narcissistic, mean, immature, greedy, angry, ashamed, self-pitying, and generally unpleasant and pointless egotistical behaviour. Secretly all he really wanted was to love and accept himself but he didn't realize this for a long time so rather foolishly he sought validation everywhere except from within himself and consequently, frequently acted like a bit of a self-destructive asshat. The wider consciousness that now sees this roguish imp loves him anyway, and we are working together to bring an end to his ridiculous shenanigans so that from now on he only brings love and compassion into his life and the life of those around him.

***

Elizabeth Seifried

Elizabeth spent most of her life in the Deep South, USA. She grew up an only child exploring her backyard woods in Alabama. Her childhood was largely shaped by her mother, a pianist and English literature teacher, and her father, a freelance nature/commercial photographer. They inspired her lifelong love of the arts, adventure, and extensive travel.

Elizabeth has Bachelor Degrees in both Art and English literature with a Masters in Art Education. She has had multiple writings published and her artwork has been exhibited in a number of art shows, galleries, and museums. She taught art in the public education system for 17 years and continues to teach art to small groups at the local art museum.

A life of exploration and travel led Elizabeth to a meditation retreat where she met her husband. At the current time, she delights in the little things in daily life - playing piano, dancing, singing, gardening, writing, bird watching, creating art - and feels especially grateful to be sharing it all with her five-year-old daughter.

From the very beginning, mystical experiences played a major role in her life. Nature, animals and the ethers were her teachers.

More traditionally, after college graduation, she met several influential spiritual teachers who guided her with meditations, yoga (*kriyas, pranayamas, asanas*), and brought a deeper spiritual direction. One of the highlights of her deepening took her to residence in an ashram in India where she taught for a while. After the ashram experience, she returned home to enjoy being near her family and to resume teaching locally.

Awakening is always present with Elizabeth though it occasionally plays hide-and-seek with her consciousness.

Elizabeth has discovered that having a sense of humor even in the darkest of times and holding things lightly are two keys to a happier, more balanced life.

***

Erick Feucht

Erick grew up in suburban New York with an interest in nature, science and the arts. Learned TM (Transcendental Meditation of Maharishi Mahesh Yogi) at the age of 18 and has practiced regularly for over 45 years. Studied at Maharishi International University for four years graduating with highest honors. Studied to become a teacher of TM travelling to the Philippines and Switzerland. Taught TM in New York and New England for many years. Settled into business with his wife, Kim, and has been doing that full-time since the late 1980s.

Erick is also a passionate musician with a lively 'jamgrass' band called The Wool Hats String Band. (Erick's photo is courtesy of Alissa Silber of *The Newtown Bee*.)

"My words in the chapters of this book are simply descriptions, cross sections of my perspective when they were written. They are not prescriptions and they are not the only way to describe awakening. Awakening is indescribable, unquantifiable and ever an enigma, yet it is more real than anything in this world, even more real than my own self.

I hope that these words can resonate with the awakening that is within everyone, that it might add a little more power to the glow within you until, like a star being born from a ball of cosmic dust, you burst into self-radiant effulgence. May you ever radiate Love, Light and Truth, and, above all, be your own natural Self."

***

Georgette Star
Georgette's intentional spiritual search began around age 12. Both of Georgette's parents were metaphysically-oriented healers who supported her quest to visit all type of churches, monasteries, and ashrams around the San Francisco Bay Area where she grew up. Her first powerful spiritual awakening came with the strike of peacock feather on the forehead by an Indian guru when she was 13. She was given a mantra and would often meditate in her bunk bed in the evening before sleep, dissolving into bliss.

As a young girl, Georgette often sat in the kitchen of her home listening to her Mom and her friend, Jane, who was also her Godmother, discuss perennial Life questions such as "Who am I?", "Why am I here?" and "What am I to do"? She found those talks mesmerizing and fuel for her search to find the "God who is Love" that she learned about in Sunday school.

Through these kitchen table conversations, Georgette discovered that every person has a specific "Soul Code", comprised of "Number Archetypes" pointing to the unique configuration of each person's operating system, the instrument through which Consciousness awakens in human form along nine distinct pathways of development. Georgette's Mom called them the "9 Pathways of the Soul". This body of knowledge formed the foundation for all aspects of her life's work through its various forms of expression over the years and for understanding the adventures on her own Awakening Journey.

In private practice as a Soul Stream Coach and Mentor for over 30 years, Georgette holds an MA from the Naropa Institute, a Doctorate of Ministry from the University of Creation Spirituality and is Founder of the Life Blessing Institute www.lifeblessing.com.

Holistic Practitioners and Coaches who are in her courses and programs receive training in the SOUL STREAM CLIENT BREAKTHROUGH METHOD, a signature system designed to take clients through a powerful and effective Awakening Process protocol for Self-Discovery, Healing and Integration.

Georgette dwells in the fairyland of her Pacific Northwest forest home in Oregon near Mount Hood. She enjoys sharing the journey of 'Awakening' with others who resonate most of all.

***

Jennifer A. Smith

There was a mysterious aliveness and depth which Jennifer hungered for with every ounce of her being since she was very young. She had no idea what she was looking for but she built her life around the freedom to explore these things.

For two decades, she immersed herself in a deep passion for the arts, spirituality, healing and transpersonal psychology. This love affair took her around the world on solo adventures to places like Bali, Thailand, Peru, India, Greece and Spain where she studied with dancers, healers and spiritual teachers.

In her early 20s she discovered an unusual university where she began to meditate and study in a Tibetan Buddhist tradition which taught her (among many life-changing things) how to be kinder to herself and others. She also started practicing yoga, dance and contemplative writing. Jennifer eventually graduated from Naropa University with a Bachelor's degree in Contemplative Psychology and concentrations in Traditional Eastern and Healing Arts and Improvisational Dance. She then moved to The San Francisco Bay Area to study dance with world-renowned temple and tribal fusion belly dancers and received her Master's Degree in Psychology from The Institute of Transpersonal Psychology with specializations in Teaching, Education & Research and Creative Expression.

Because these things made her feel so alive and awake, she wanted to share them with others in the hope that they would do the same for them.

In 2003, Jennifer began an intuitive healing practice in which she offers spiritual and intuitive guidance, energy healing, past life regressions and transpersonal counseling to groups and individuals. She also founded The School of Awakened Living schoolofawakenedliving.com which offers nine-month professional intuitive healing certification programs for women around the world. One of her greatest loves is teaching.

Jennifer teaches mindfulness and meditation in Naropa University's Graduate Transpersonal and Contemplative Psychology Counseling Programs. She is also researching 'The Passionately Engaged Experience' for her Doctorate in East West Psychology at The California Institute of Integral Studies.

Jennifer enjoys teaching and performing contemplative world dance, painting goddesses, and writing poetry. She lives in the United States in Boulder, Colorado with her feisty, affectionate cat Sundari.

Every day she practices gratitude and aspires to accept reality as it is.

***

Kathy Adams

Ever since she can remember, Kathy was fascinated with spirituality. As a child she was interested in religion and voraciously read anything she could. Before the age of eleven she had read the Children's Bible, as well as works by Richard Bach, Elisabeth Kübler-Ross, Raymond Moody, and some books on reincarnation and astrology. One of the most impactful books she read was *The Prophet* by Kahlil Gibran which was given to her by her great grandfather.

At age 11 her childhood was abruptly derailed when her parents divorced. Faced with a series of traumatic situations as well as shuffling from mother to father and finally to her grandmother, spirituality took a back seat. It wasn't until an automobile accident in her twenties which resulted in extremely debilitating pain that spirituality returned to her life. Much of her identity had been taken away due to the fallout from the accident and it was while flat on her back and very alone that she experienced significant glimpses of awakening.

Several years later, Kathy left New England for a job opportunity in Arizona. It was here that she found a nondual teacher and self-inquiry. On her days off she would often head out to the desert and ponder on the teachings. A few years later, Kathy had an opportunity to move to Costa Rica and quickly responded. It was this move that led her to a path of service. In her spare time started working with street children and at-risk youth. Eventually, she formed a formal non-profit called Empowerment International (www.empowermentinternational.org) and started working with Nicaraguan children as well. As the non-profit took a life of its own, it became clear she had to make a choice, and decided to focus full time on the non-profit.

While still in Nicaragua, Kathy had a series of profound spiritual shifts and insights, precipitated by a deep look into her core childhood wound. If she were to ever write a book about her awakening journey, she is sure the title would be *The Only Way Out is In*.

After 20 years, Kathy has returned to the USA and lives in New Mexico where she works virtually with her team of 12 in Nicaragua and has also taken on some virtual tech work. When not working she can be found enjoying the magic of the mountains, desert and the great wide-open spaces, either on her mountain bike or hiking with her dog Ginger.

***

Kiran Mitra
Born and raised in Punjab, India, Kiran was the middle child in a very religious Sikh family. She was introverted and introspective even as a child and the introspection only got stronger with age.

Although academically strong, she was married through arrangement at the age of 17 as was the custom in India at that time. After marriage she lived with her husband and two children in New Delhi for 13 years.

The 1984 riots in India brought about a major change and her family decided to move to Canada. Life kept evolving for Kiran and after a few years in Canada there was a breakdown in the marriage which resulted in divorce. She then had the sole responsibility of raising her two children and no marketable skills to earn an income. She worked at many different jobs during this time and went to school part-time in order to upgrade her skills to be better able to provide for her children. She was successful in obtaining a professional accounting designation. In 1991 she married again.

Through all the trials and tribulations, ups and downs, the one constant that remained was her inner journey. The spiritual path she followed was the culmination of all that she had been through in life and within herself. Eventually Kiran became deeply connected with innermost stillness bringing equanimity and peace to herself and others around her.

***

Lisa Meyler

Lisa Meyler was born 1969 in a Jewish family, in the then communist Soviet Union.

As a 5-year-old she had a Near-Death experience which affected her deeply, and set the stage for the human and spiritual path she would follow. When she was 8, her family emigrated to Sweden, where she has been living ever since.

She studied nursing, counselling, psychiatry and social care, and worked with the elderly and the disabled.

During a period of about 15 years, she went through a psycho-spiritual emergence process, which was at times turbulent. She went on to study transpersonal psychology, and work as a transpersonal-centered therapist.

She has recently written a book about her journey and Near-Death Experience, which also includes the stories of other NDE-ers: *Born to*

Love: The Near-Death Experience and the Meaning of Life (for now only in Swedish, Parthenon Publishing 2019).

She is currently working as a custodian for the elderly and lives in Stockholm with her partner Dan, 11-year old daughter Fannie, and their four-legged family members Baltazar, a Burmese cat and Casper, a mix breed puppy.

***

Marianne Broug

Marianne was born in Sydney, Australia. Even as a child she had a longing to understand life and to know what was true. This introspection, seriousness and questioning was at odds with the people around her, and also with society as a whole.

From her early 20s she began to experience depression and anxiety, and sought out healing, wholeness and Truth. She underwent two lengthy therapies and pursued intensive spiritual practices, meditation, dialectic and inquiry.

Early in 2008 Marianne awakened to her True Nature (described fully in the preface). Much deepening and clearing was still to take place, but rather than the suffered turmoil and suicidality of the past, there was now the sense that all was deeply well.

Marianne was a professional musician and music teacher and has performed extensively throughout Australia, in all arenas of music including opera, chamber music and symphony orchestra.

She has also worked as a concert organizer, an artist, a mental health advocate and a care worker for people living with both a 'mental illness' and a terminal illness.

In 2003 her music book for children, *Flute with a Twist* was published by Bushfire Press bushfirepress.com.au/onli.../flute-with-a-twist/. In 2008 her book *Seventeen Voices: Life and Wisdom from inside 'mental illness* was published by Wakefield Press wakefieldpress.com.au/product.php?productid=689&cat=0&page=1. In 2017 she published a book with reflections from her spiritual journey entitled *Suffering, Spirituality and the Inner Journey Home: Walking the Path from Desperation and Fear to the Peace of Lived Awakening* mariannebroug.com/suffering-spirituality-journey-home. Her websites are mariannebroug.com and meaningofdepression.com.

Late in 2017 she started the Facebook group *A group of 'baby Buddhas'*, after being unable to find an online community for those negotiating the post-awakening terrain that was not only authentic, real and honest, but was also not centred around a particular teacher or teaching. This book has grown from the members of that group.

She currently lives in the beautiful Adelaide Hills, with her partner and two dogs. She enjoys bushwalking, photography and gardening. She is also a passionate conservationist of the fauna and flora native to the region in which she lives.

***

Marieke Trompert

Marieke was born and raised in the Netherlands. As a child she often felt misunderstood and as though she did not belong. She sensed truth deep inside but did not see it reflected in the world around her. At a young age she began to suffer from depression and anxiety.

After a classical education at a higher-level high school, she went on to study Medicine. She found being a doctor incredibly beautiful, but the internships in combination with depression and (especially social) fear, were too demanding. She suffered a severe burnout. Her identity, which had been completely tied up with being smart and studying, was now lost.

In the meantime she kept looking for truth. For many years she pursued all kinds of therapies and devoured psychology books. In addition to volunteering, she started studying Psychology, which she recently completed.

When she was 29 a psychologist gave her a book by Eckhart Tolle, *The Power of Now*. She did not understand it but it touched something very deep inside. At the same time she was advised to do mindfulness meditation. This brought a turnaround in her experience of the fear and depression; she learned to recognize and feel her feelings, and realized that she was not her thoughts! The healing journey had begun. This led to the awakening of the Kundalini and the realization of her true nature.

The process of dissolving conditioning and energetic blockages continues to this day. It has been hard but immensely beautiful! There has been much healing and underneath it she always knows that she is already One, not separate.

She is now a mail carrier and is building her healing business.

***

Maureen Bush

Maureen has a BA in History, and a Master's degree in Environmental Design (Environmental Science), trained as a mediator, and no longer does any of these things. She has five novels published for children, and an essay on aging and spirituality in an anthology on women and aging.

She began meditating when her mother dragged her to a Transcendental Meditation class when she was a teenager, and stopped immediately after. This did, however, set the seed for a later interest in Tibetan Buddhism, which she practiced for 15 years.

Following a transformative moment of awakening, she found the Buddhist group she belonged to offered no support. She has been exploring on her own ever since. Adyashanti's teachings and books became a lifeline during the first year, especially *The End of Your World*. After a six month honeymoon period, the real work began as the suppression lid came off childhood issues. She worked through numerous courses with counsellors and healers, and is now, perhaps, in a more settled place. She lives in Canada.

***

Biographies

Michaela Marie

Although usually very creative in nature, Michaela never felt as totally uninspired as when she was handling the impossible task of writing her own biography for this book.

To cut her life story short, here are the basic facts:

She was born in Czechoslovakia into a family of musicologists. Like many other intellectuals, her parents were persecuted under the communist regime and as a consequence their children were not allowed to study. The only possibility for Michaela was music education. She played piano from the age of five. At 13 she picked up a cello and to her surprise won a music competition only two years later. With the help of many kind people she eventually studied music at the academies in Prague, then Copenhagen and later in London, with cello as her main instrument.

She received numerous prizes and awards in some of the top international music competitions and this led to an active career as a solo cellist. During her concert tours, she spent years in hotels all over the world, performing with the world's leading orchestras and conductors. She has recorded numerous CDs (including winning Grammy awards) and has been invited to share her musical knowledge and experiences in masterclasses worldwide.

After the eye-opening shift in 2007, in an attempt to capture and share the amazing beauty that was suddenly everywhere, Michaela also became a passionate photographer. Her photos have been warmly recognized, exhibited and used as illustrations for magazines and books.

Recently she started to explore the art of painting; she loves to discover and learn this new field of creativity and hopes for good results to come.

Michaela speaks six languages, Czech being her mother tongue. She has now settled in Denmark, where she lives in beautiful peaceful surroundings in the countryside, and enjoys family life with her Swiss husband and their two sons.

***

Richard Cox

Richard Cox resides upon the same small island on which he was born and will one day no doubt perish. A spontaneous alcohol induced mystical experience at the age of 16 set the direction of his life, leading him to study non-dual self-inquiry as a way to understand and recapture the state he had slipped into.

Richard runs The Deep State Consciousness podcast, deepstateconsciousness.podbean.com which provides him with an excuse to speak to interesting people. He also writes articles and reasonably acceptable poetry on diverse topics such as spirituality, consciousness, philosophy and anarchy – all with an underpinning theme of questioning our perception.

***

Sarah Taylor

Sarah is a Los Angeles based stand-up comedian and actor and has been a spiritual mentor and energy healing practitioner (Reiki Master and more) for over a decade.

Initially an atheistic insomniac, she simply wanted to ease her decades-long anxiety, and began studying Buddhism and practising meditation. She quickly began undergoing a series of profound, radical, and abiding inner shifts. Awakening to her true nature, and finding nothing and everything simultaneously, has been a journey of clearing, integration, and wondrous deepening. There is now a core of peace, wellbeing, and seamless, unified presence that is the foundation of her lived experience. Not bad for someone who just wanted to sleep better at night!

Sarah has been seen on NBC, CBS, ABC and at all the top comedy clubs like The Laugh Factory and The Comedy Store, and has produced regular shows at The Hollywood Improv. She tours with her unique creation, The Divine Mess Show, bringing comedy, healing and meditation to audiences all over.

Sarah lives with her husband, two cats and an opinionated little dog.

She has done a TEDx talk www.youtube.com/watch?v=FvRB31cRriA, an interview on Buddha At The Gas Pump https://batgap.com/sarah-taylor/ and has a website www.LightOfYourBeing.org.

***

Silvia Lucia

Silvia was born into an average European working-class family and had a rather happy childhood. However, her entrance into this world was very difficult: she experienced significant prenatal and birth trauma. Although she has generally been a calm and adventurous person, this birth trauma resulted in episodes of profound anxiety and panic attacks.

From childhood she had an ongoing interest in people. Although her real longing was anthropology, she worked as a school teacher for many years. She raised two children on her own, was a very dedicated mother and managed to travel around the world, both with and without her children

Silvia's interest in 'God' was there from early childhood and her spiritual search started deeply around the age of 11 or 12. In her travels she tried to learn how other cultures related to God and the metaphysical, and afterwards her own search continued in earnest, mainly through looking within and inquiring on her own.

In 2016, during a time of intense suffering she had a radical spontaneous awakening while cleaning the house. At the time she had been trying to do an experiment of her own invention, consistently pulling her attention back from manifestation into its source. (This episode is more fully described in Chapter 2).

She recognized Source and all things as being ONE and the same 'substance'. This came through as a 'seeing' which deepened over a period of nine days, during which there was only bliss and total absence of thought.

The photo of a baobab tree is entitled *Between Heaven and Earth* and was taken by Silvia in Senegal, Africa.

***

Stacy Clark
Stacy Clark, or the story of a 'Stacy Clark', was born in 1959 in Fort Worth, Texas. This put her just at the tail end of the Baby Boomers years. Her mother was born in 1939, just at the beginning. It was inevitable that both of them would be hippies to some degree.

She counts herself lucky, as it was her mother who introduced her to mysticism (direct experience of something that transcends the human experience, beyond emotions and intellectualizations). In the early 70s she spent Sunday mornings listening to Alan Watts just before she went off to sing in the church choir. It was quite a liberal church where she studied comparative religion with a young youth minister from California.

For the next 40 years, she collected 'things that work', including sex, staring at moving water under a bridge, the wind in the trees, particularly those with leaves that have a different color on each side, BreathWork, The Sedona Method, meditations of many kinds, particularly Instant Advanced Meditation (you won't find it - there was only one class, but it was recorded), The Work of Byron Katie, Direct Pointing and Deep Looking, among others.

Stacy has incest in her history - a phrase she finally settled upon after realizing the whole thing was in the past and no one was perpetuating that story any longer, so there was no problem. Not that there was in the first place, but that is hard for most people to follow. This went along with her passionate interest in sex, which was one of the ways in which she first saw clearly that there was no separation, no individualized 'self' separate from others or the world. In the early 90s, attempting to bring clarity and understanding to others, she trained as a sexual surrogate while completing her master's in psychology and co-authored *The Complete Idiot's Guide to Being a Sex Goddess*. However, it was soon clear that most clients were not involved in sex as a vehicle for transcendence, so she gave that up and returned to working in offices.

She attempted self-employment with each new 'tool' but that never really amounted to anything, so she continues working in offices, which is comfortable and works well enough so that she can volunteer to guide others in their awakening, mostly at Liberation Unleashed.

For over 25 years, Stacy was a student of *A Course in Miracles* (ACIM), completing the Workbook five times. (Yes, it says no more lessons are necessary, but she's an eternal student.) In 1998, she encountered 'The Work of Byron Katie' and immediately dropped ACIM, realizing that The Work is ACIM in four questions and Turn Arounds, unencumbered by concepts of a god or Jesus. ACIM focuses on forgiveness. She came to understand that the key to all human relationships is forgiveness, which she calls, 'No blame'.

Her first 'longer' (there is no time), 'deeper' (whatever that is) awakening happened in April 2007 in the context of the recorded Instant Advanced Meditations (IAM) mentioned earlier. She spent months relaxed, often blissful, clear and alert in a way she had only glimpsed before. However, there were still unturned stones.

What is the best way to find out where you aren't clear? For Stacy, and many others, it's getting into a romantic relationship. Soon, all that clarity felt like mud and the only thing that was clear was that there was more work to do.

Years later, in 2016, a friend introduced her to Liberation Unleashed, where she was guided into clarity once again. She is now a volunteer guide on that site.

This time there was more cognitive awareness provided by a specific group of exercises called 'pointers'. Groovy. The same friend pointed her to the Baby Buddha group, where, for the first time, she had companions who saw what she sees. (Or at least it seems that way. We can never really know.)

So, what happened next? Ha. She got into a relationship again and found even more unturned stones to work with! Of course! That was April of 2019. This is a work in progress as she practices 'finding the gap' via someone guiding folks in the Buddhist 'Ten Fetters' and doing even more Work of Byron Katie. While there is no need to 'seek' or 'search', some corners are being dusted off, sometimes with a shovel.

Truth is the most important thing of all to Stacy, so she continues to question even (especially!) her most cherished beliefs to surrender more and more to 'what is'.

***

Timothy A. Wilkerson
As a child, Timothy wasn't very coordinated. In an attempt to remedy that, he found a book about yoga, specifically written for young people. It contained a number of easy poses that he practiced for several years. It was a hobby that slowly improved his physical abilities. In the back of the book was a single meditation, which helped him in stressful situations. He described it as his 'ace in the hole' and growing up used it fairly often.

As a teenager, Timothy read a handbook about higher consciousness, which is when he began focusing more on the search for enlightenment. At 25 years of age he came across a book that provided 112 varied meditations with which to experiment. By the time he was 26, in 1983, one of those meditations worked and enlightenment happened.

During more than three decades of living as an ordinary enlightened person, Timothy has met a few people who asked him how he stays so kind and peaceful. He would usually offer some advice or point to what he deduced would be a good resource for them. Eventually, some close friends suggested that he write a book about how to find enlightenment, which he completed on March 14th, 2019: *Awakening to Enlightenment*, by Timothy A. Wilkerson. Websites are http://awakeningtoenlightenment.com/ and lulu.com/spotlight/kcwilkerson

Biographies

Presently, Timothy speaks professionally on the subject of enlightenment, but has no notion of becoming a 'famous teacher'. It is his belief enlightenment is available to everyone, that there are over a million people just like him, and feels that a good percentage of them are much better instructors than he could ever be. In his heart he's grateful to connect with others who have also had a similar experience, and he still occasionally provides pointers to those who are asking for clues. In reality though, he's "just a Midwestern guy living an ordinary life", and he's very happy with that.

***

www.ingramcontent.com/pod-product-compliance
Lightning Source LLC
Chambersburg PA
CBHW050852160426
43194CB00011B/2123